FAMILY REDEEMED

MeOtzar HoRav Series
Selected Writings of Rabbi Joseph B. Soloveitchik

The *MeOtzar HoRav* series
has been made possible
by a generous grant from
Ruth and Irwin Shapiro.

The publication of *Family Redeemed*

has been enabled by a grant from

Leonard and Beatrice Diener Foundation
Mordecai D. and Dr. Monique C. Katz
Dr. Samuel and Paula Rosenblum
Joseph and Gwendolyn Straus Foundation

FAMILY REDEEMED

Essays on
Family Relationships

by

Rabbi Joseph B. Soloveitchik

Edited by
David Shatz and Joel B. Wolowelsky

Published for
TORAS HORAV FOUNDATION
by KTAV Publishing House

FAMILY REDEEMED

ESSAYS ON FAMILY RELATIONSHIPS

Rabbi Joseph B. Soloveitchik

Edited by David Shatz and Joel B. Wolowelsky

Library of Congress Cataloging-in-Publication Data

Soloveitchik, Joseph Dov.
  Family redeemed: essays on family relationships / by Rabbi Joseph B.
Soloveitchik; edited by David Shatz and Joel B. Wolowelsky.
    p. cm. – (Meotzar horav; v. 1)
Includes bibliographical references and index.
  ISBN 0-88125-795-8
1. Jewish families – Religious life. 2. Marriage – Religious
aspects – Judaism. 3. Parent and child – Religious aspects – Judaism. I.
Shatz, David. II. Wolowelsky, Joel B. III. Title.

  BM723 .S657 2002
  296.7'4—dc21

                              2002069464

Printing year: 2021

ISBN 978-0-88125-795-3

Published for
THE TORAS HORAV FOUNDATION by

KTAV PUBLISHING HOUSE
527 Empire Blvd.
Brooklyn, NY 11225

Website: www.ktav.com
Email: orders@ktav.com
ph: (718)972-5449 / Fax: (718)972-6307
Price $29.95

• Table of Contents •

• Preface •

Rabbi Joseph B. Soloveitchik *zt"l* (1903-1993) was not only one of the outstanding Talmudists of the 20th century, but also one of its most creative and seminal Jewish thinkers. Drawing from a vast reservoir of Jewish and general knowledge, "the Rav," as he is widely known, brought Jewish thought and law to bear on the interpretation and assessment of the modern experience. On the one hand, he built bridges between Judaism and the modern world; yet at the same time he vigorously upheld the integrity and autonomy of the Jew's faith commitment, and in particular the commitment to a life governed by Halakhah, Jewish law.

For over four decades, Rabbi Soloveitchik commuted from his home in Brookline, Massachusetts to New York City, where, several times weekly, he gave the senior *shiur* (class in Talmud) at Yeshiva University's affiliated Rabbi Isaac Elchanan Theological Seminary (RIETS) and, for many years, also taught Jewish philosophy at the University's Bernard Revel Graduate School. Generations of rabbinical students were taught and inspired by him — among them many of the future leaders of the Orthodox and broader Jewish community. By his extensive personal teaching and influence, as well as by serving locally as the chief rabbinic figure in Boston, where he founded the Maimonides School, and nationally and internationally as the halakhic authority and spiritual leader of the Rabbinical Council of America, he contributed vitally to the dynamic resurgence of Orthodox Judaism in America. The thousands of people who regularly flocked to his public lectures on halakhic, philosophical and Biblical topics were consistently enthralled and inspired. Rabbi Soloveitchik stands, indeed, as one of the great religious leaders of our time. Even now, after his passing, his teachings — "the Rav's Torah" — are always eagerly sought, and his words continue to ring with relevance and authority.

Although many of Rabbi Soloveitchik's writings and discourses have been published over the years, much additional material, rich and evocative, remains in handwritten manuscripts. THE TORAS HORAV FOUNDATION was established by family members and former students to disseminate these and other works, with the aims of enhancing both our grasp of Rabbi Soloveitchik's philosophy and our understanding of the diverse topics he addressed. Alas, it is impossible to read the Rav's powerful and challenging essays without undergoing a profound sense of the loss we have all incurred with the passing of this giant. But the reader who experiences them, who absorbs and appreciates their rare blend of intellectual sweep and energizing passion, will find the essays to be an invaluable, integral part of his or her own spiritual quest.

● ● ●

We express our profound appreciation to THE TORAS HORAV FOUNDATION for affording us the opportunity to prepare these manuscripts so that a long-waiting public can gain further understanding and appreciation of the Rav's Torah.

The first stage in preparing the book consisted of deciphering, organizing and ultimately transcribing the Rav's handwritten manuscripts. This arduous task was coordinated and supervised with great skill and attention to detail by Rabbi Reuven Ziegler of Yeshivat Har Etzion, Director of the *MeOtzar HoRav* Archives, who organized and supervised an able and devoted staff, reviewed all the material, and also provided valuable editorial comments and suggestions. Most of the material was also closely reviewed by Rabbi Yair Kahn.

To produce this volume, the editors selected materials from the manuscripts and arranged them into integrated chapters. The Rav had not readied these manuscripts for publication, and editing was required. The editors also provided section headings, in some cases titles for the chapters, and finally the title *Family Redeemed* for the collection as a whole. When necessary, they inserted references, furnished transliterations and translations of Hebrew and other foreign-language terms and sources, and, to aid readers' comprehension without interrupting the flow of the material, added synonyms for some technical philosophical terms (generally set off by brackets), and explained others as footnotes.

The manuscripts, all undated, were used by the Rav in presenting his public lectures, and in some cases tapes of these presentations are available. Some of the essays presented here include material added by the Rav in the oral presentation.

> "Adam and Eve" was presented as a lecture at Stern College for Women, Yeshiva University, on December 22, 1971. The chapter here also includes material on natural man taken from a short manuscript titled, *"Pesukei Bereshit:* Man as a Natural Being Within the Universe and as a Unique Being Opposed to the Universe." The section on the respective sins of Adam and Eve was taken from another manuscript concerning marriage.

> "Marriage" is taken from an essay on marriage and from what are apparently subsequent redrafts of some of its sections. The Rav lectured on this subject in 1959.

"The Redemption of Sexual Life" is taken from a longer piece that also discussed the redemption of the act of eating. That self-contained section, which was originally a separate essay, will be published *be-ezrat Hashem* in a subsequent volume of *MeOtzar HoRav*. "The Redemption of Sexual Life" manuscript ends abruptly, and the concluding paragraph of the essay in this volume is from another manuscript on marriage. The Rav lectured on "The Redemption of Sexual Life" in 1959.

"Parenthood: Natural and Redeemed" is primarily a manuscript titled "Motherhood" and includes material on fatherhood taken from another manuscript. The different roles of mother and father in educating their child is also discussed in a shorter manuscript, "Avraham and Sarah: On the Equality of the Sexes," a section of which, dealing with the distinction between clan and nation, is included here.

"*Kibbud u-Mora:* Honor and Fear of Parents" was originally composed as two consecutive lectures. Overlapping summaries were eliminated and the section on the search for one's ontic roots was added from another manuscript. The Rav lectured on this subject in 1959.

"Torah and *Shekhinah*" was presented as a lecture on the first yahrzeit of the Rav's wife, 11 Adar 5728/ March 10, 1968.

Several rabbis, educators, and laypersons were generous in sharing their expertise with us by responding to various queries. It is a pleasure to extend thanks to them here: Joshua Bacon, David Berger, Michael S. Berger, Pearl Berger, Alan Brill, Shalom Carmy, Yaakov Elman, Joseph J. Feit, Louis Feldman, Daniel Frank, Mark E. Gottlieb, Warren Zev Harvey, William Kolbrener, Abraham Kurtz, Thomas Pitoniak, Gila Rosen, Josef Stern, Avner Taler, and Bella Hass Weinberg. Atara Segal collaborated with us on the indices, and we thank her for her valuable contributions. Finally, we are deeply grateful to

Rabbi Aharon and Tovah Lichtenstein for their guidance during the editing process, and for reviewing our work at various stages, including the final manuscript.

The essays in this book focus on family relationships and end with the first *yahrzeit shiur* given by the Rav in memory of his wife. It therefore seems fitting to recall here the dedication that Rabbi Soloveitchik composed for *The Lonely Man of Faith*:

To Tonya

A woman of great courage, sublime dignity,
total commitment and uncompromising truthfulness.

David Shatz
Joel B. Wolowelsky

❧ Introduction

The six essays in *Family Redeemed*, the first volume of the series we have called *MeOtzar HoRav (From the Treasure Trove of the Rav)*, focus on family relationships. These relationships — between husbands and wives, parents and children — must be understood, the Rav shows, in terms of a theory of the human personality. An important feature of Rabbi Soloveitchik's analyses is his method for arriving at them, for they emerge from his reading of the Bible, the Talmud and Midrash, and the wider corpus of Halakhah and Aggadah. For instance, in the first essay, "Adam and Eve," the author defines his aim as follows:

> *The purpose of this paper is to gain an insight into the nature and destiny of the woman and man whom God created in a specific way, and to begin to formulate on the basis of these insights a philosophy of man. Yet, the frame of reference we will employ will be a scriptural one. We will avail ourselves of Biblical hermeneutics or interpretation and try to detect the spiritual message contained in both what has been unequivocally stated in the text and*

*what has been omitted and concealed. What I want to
achieve is an understanding on our part that the Bible is
not just a book of the past. It is far more than that; it is the
book of the present and future. In all times, in all periods,
in crisis as well as in success, man may find his problems
and anxieties defined in this Book of Books.*

Anyone who follows the argument of these essays will
appreciate how deeply the method of scriptural interpretation
runs through them, as does an unyielding faith in the Bible's
enduring relevance. But, as we said, the Bible is hardly Rabbi
Soloveitchik's only source for his theory of personality. Time and
again in the volume, he also mines the Talmud and the
Rambam's (Maimonides') legal code for insights into the human
being, illustrating his abiding conviction that halakhic norms
reflect deep truths concerning the human personality. As the
Rav spells out this image of humanity — as he unveils the complexity, conflict and paradox that mark the human psyche —
the reader cannot help being struck by his penetrating ability
to discern delicate shifts of language in the texts at hand and
relate them to the subtleties of interpersonal relationships.
Whether he is describing spousal ties, parental feelings, or filial
duties, an authentic, profound Jewish vision of man comes
through eloquently.

Rabbi Soloveitchik draws not only from his encompassing
fluency with classical Jewish texts, but also from his wide-rang-
ing familiarity with classical and contemporary philosophy and
literature. Thus, in the third essay of this volume, "The
Redemption of Sexual Life," he contrasts the Jewish view of
sex with that presented by St. Methodius of Olympus in his
Symposium. He also describes levels of sexual life that include
the "pandemic," which here means vulgar and carnal, and the
higher "Uranian Aphrodite Eros." These terms derive from
Plato's *Symposium* and are used in, for example, the prose of
the Romantic poet Percy Bysshe Shelley. He cites as well the

20th century Protestant theologian Emil Brunner, who also discussed sexuality and marriage in religious terms. He uses these sources to articulate and elucidate aspects of those Jewish concepts and texts on which he focuses.

The Rav identifies human growth with what he terms "redemption" and spiritual heroism. These central concepts may be elucidated by means of a single sentence in the first essay. "Man," the Rav writes, "experiences both oneness with and otherness from nature." This statement is critical to the volume as a whole, for several of the essays focus upon the transition that a human being must make from biological being to person, from "man-*natura*" to "man-*persona*." To make this transition is to "redeem" oneself. And redemption requires heroism. Thus the Rav writes in "Parenthood: Natural and Redeemed":

> *A physiological reaction changes into meaningful hallowed action at any time the individual displays courage and the ability to answer the violent, orgiastic, hypnotic call of nature in the negative, thus incurring pain and suffering because of his refusal to cooperate with biological pressures that have not found their total release.*

The key point is that Halakhah summons man to meet this challenge — and provides him with the means, the discipline, to accomplish that goal. The Divine command is what makes the emergence of spiritual personality possible. Thus, ultimately it is the encounter with God's will and His norm that ennobles Adam and Eve; that confrontation, and only that confrontation, infuses human life with direction, structure, purpose and meaning. To act heroically, however, is not to deny physical and passional drives; the human being is after all, if only in part, a biological creature. Rather, to act heroically is to sanctify urges by allowing their expression only within a framework of norms. Holiness, consisting as it does of disciplined submission and channeling, "is not given as a grant but is created by man."

The duality of biological being and spiritual personality is mirrored by the Rav's discussion in "Parenthood: Natural and Redeeemed" of two dimensions of parenthood, the one biological, the other educational and covenantal. As the Rav examines further the responsibilities of children and parents to each other, his dominant theme is that these relationships may and must be integrated into one's relationship to Torah and to God.

> *The relationship of God to us and our relationship to Him lend themselves to description and interpretation in finite human categories. The Jew has learned to confess his faith in and impassioned love of God by telling the story of people whom he loves and with whom he seeks to identify himself. Judaic faith and theology are linked with finite experiences and meaningful human relations.*

Thus, writes the Rav in *"Kibbud* and *Mora,"* when a child finds his finite-conditioned origin in his father or his mother, the latter also "discovers his infinite and ultimate origin in God." The feeling of rootedness arises in the finite world, but it results in consciousness of "the One and Only root." Likewise, in extending *mora* — fear, respect and reverence — to parents, one opens oneself to the transcendent, and thus ultimately "adores and worships God." In short, "by developing proper human relations structures, the Jew learns how to love, revere and serve God."

In the closing pages of the volume, the denouement of "Torah and *Shekhinah,"* the Rav beautifully locates the experience of one's father and mother in the study of Torah — an activity whose importance to his own life and thought can never be overstated. Not only are we commanded to love God and serve Him, but, the Rav affirms, there is a separate commandment of *"u-bikkashtem misham et Hashem Elokekha"* (Deut. 4:29) — "to search for God, to quest, yearn and crave for Him, to continue searching until one finds Him."

In my opinion, the Torah, in recommending to us the search for God, was concerned with total religious experience, with religious reason or, if I may say, religious sensibility or sensory experience. We are called upon not only to believe in Him, to have faith in Him, to comply with His law, but to find Him with our five senses, to perceive Him the way one perceives light, to feel His presence in our midst, to cleanse the doors of perception, as a mystic [William Blake] said once, in order to apprehend Him right here and now.

In consonance with this understanding, Talmud Torah, the study of Torah, is not for the Rav an intellectual act alone, but "a total performance claiming the whole of the personality." The Rav shows how this dual experience of Torah, cognitive and experiential, grows out of proper ties to parents. Already in prior essays in the book, he showed that in Jewish tradition, parents not only must impart formal knowledge to their children, but must form with them an existential union and provide them with a total experience that integrates them into the covenantal community. Hence the various links Halakhah forges between parents and children are also, for both parties, links to Torah and to God.

Many of Rabbi Soloveitchik's characteristic themes and methods resonate in these essays. As in his *Ish ha-Halakhah (Halakhic Man)* and *The Lonely Man of Faith*, we are presented in *Family Redeemed* with striking typologies — that is, abstract, idealized, and contrasting personality types — as well as vivid, evocative images. Thus, human existence, we are told, may be either "Natural" or "Redeemed"; Parenthood may be that of Mother or that of Father; God may be experienced as either King or *Shekhinah*. Here, as elsewhere, we hear of "dialectic," "polarity," "antitheses" or "antinomies" — the contradictions that we experience within reality. The central ideas that human beings must redeem their inner selves rather than expect God to do so for them, and that such redemption requires submission to divine norms, are likewise well established motifs of the Rav's philosophy.

We also encounter in *Family Redeemed* a distinction crucial to much of the Rav's thought: between, on the one hand, a friendship, community, or marriage founded on pragmatic needs or biological urges, and, on the other hand, a relationship that is founded on an existential union of personalities. In addition: the relationship between outer deed and inner experience, a theme that is crucial to the Rav's analyses elsewhere of prayer, repentance, mourning and festival rejoicing (all of which commandments have both a behavioral and an experiential component) here enters as well into the elucidation of the honor and fear due to parents, duties that require both act and emotion.

Just as in his Talmudic learning, the Rav excelled at defining broad concepts and distinctions that would explain a remarkable range of halakhic data, so too in his philosophical thought, the reader is continually amazed at the power of his central categories, methods, and distinctions to capture the gamut of intimate and poignant experiences.

● ● ●

Before turning to the six individual essays in greater detail, we should note that the reader unfamiliar with philosophical terms may be somewhat unnecessarily intimidated by some of the technical language that appears in the text of this volume. The Rav treated hashkafic discussions with the same rigor and exactness of language that he used in halakhic ones. In general, difficult terms in this book are subsequently explained, and therefore the reader who meets up with a hard term should not, in frustration, overlook these clarifications. But most fundamentally, it must be said that the Rav — not only in Halakhah but also in philosophy — expected effort from his audience. The difficulty of the essays is a function of the high level of the discussion; edification, learning from genius, comes with — to invoke a theme of the Rav's writing — labor and struggle. At the same time, those who meet Rabbi Soloveitchik's expectations are invariably rewarded. Master teacher that he was, the Rav goes on to explain his core concepts in a manner that is clear and accessible even to readers who are not familiar with every word of the presentation.

The summaries that follow are, of course, no substitute for *experiencing* the essays themselves. At the end of "Torah and *Shekhinah*," the Rav establishes that Torah study has not only an intellectual dimension but an experiential one as well. Rabbi Soloveitchik's profound, passionate, textured exposition must be experienced firsthand, so that one can fully appreciate his remarkable ability to plumb a point to its very depths, to tap textual subtleties, and to construct a world view from a linguistic nuance.

"Adam and Eve"

Much has been written about the contrast between the account of creation in chapter one of Genesis and the account in chapter two. Readers of Rabbi Soloveitchik's classic *Lonely Man of Faith* will recall that that essay is framed as an interpretation of some of these contrasts. The essay "Adam and Eve" focuses on the same Biblical chapters while developing the contrast in a distinct, albeit related, way.

Man, as we said earlier, is both part of nature and yet something apart from it. Man-*natura* — "man as part of nature" — is described in chapter one, while man-*persona* — "man as personality" — is portrayed in chapter two. Man-*persona* has imagination; he longs for vastness and boundlessness. Indeed, God's planting the garden arouses in man two urges: to live and to know. Man is haunted by the prospect of ignorance and the possibility of death. More significant than this "birth of fantasy" is man's confrontation in Eden with God's will — conveyed by the verb *"va-yetzav*, and He commanded" — which results in man's moral awareness (Gen. 2:16-17). Alien to man-*natura*, the experience of norms is essential to the life of man-*persona*. "The transition from *natura* to *persona* occurs at the instant man agrees to take defeat at the hand of God."

Man-*persona* experiences something else as well: loneliness. Man-*natura* may be "alone" but he is never "lonely." Aloneness is a physical fact or perhaps a psychological experience that some people actually prefer. Loneliness is — to use a word that appears throughout the volume — an *ontological* experience, that is, one that relates to the essence of one's being. Loneliness is a "spiritual human situation" of "ontological insecurity," that is, a sense of the incompleteness of one's being. Only a being who meditates and experiences estrangement from nature can be lonely. "It is not good that the man be alone" (Gen. 2:18). Man needs help ontologically, that is, he needs someone to complete his existence and endow it with meaning and directedness.

What helps man to escape his loneliness is encountering another *person*, the woman, as opposed to mute, two-dimensional nature. This is the import of the verses that describe how no other creature brought before Adam could prove a satisfactory companion (Gen. 2:19-23). Adam can only name the other creatures, observe them, classify them. But observation and classification yield only so much. To understand himself, man must confide in another. Only woman, who is an independent person with her own I-awareness, can liberate the man from loneliness.

The essay also includes a brief reference to God as *Shekhinah*, the Divine Presence, a theme that is elaborated in the next essay and again in the final essay of the volume. God is both *Shekhinah*, signifying finitude, and the transcendent, infinite Being.

"Marriage"

The essay begins by outlining two theories about the institution of marriage, one "transeunt," that is, outer-directed, the other "immanent," inner-directed. The first locates the value of marriage in group survival, which is an aspect of the natural scheme of things. The second finds the value of marriage in the personal experience it creates between the partners. In its first two chapters, the Book of Genesis refers to both aspects: "Be fruitful and multiply" (1:28); yet also, "It is not good that the man be alone; I shall make him a helpmate opposite him" (2:18), which implies that man yearns to share experience with someone unknown. Both aspects have a foothold in Judaism. When spiritual man emerges in chapter two of Genesis, charged with norms, and takes the place of natural man, the biological and the "teleological" accounts of marriage merge. For the procreative act itself is transformed from a biological push to a norm or command, and the desire for children on the part of Adam and Eve represents now "a human metaphysical cry of lonely man and lonely woman for fatherhood and motherhood." Procreation comes to reflect the norm of *Imitatio Dei*, walking in God's ways. Such creation involves sacrificial action, as the Jewish mystics emphasized when they said that God must constrict Himself, must retreat, if there is to be space for the world.

The core part of "Marriage" outlines six characteristics of marriage in Jewish law and thought. Marriage is a covenantal obligation, similar in some ways to ordinary contractual agreements, but different in crucial respects as well. Whereas ordinary contractual agreements involve placing one's goods at another's disposal, Jewish marriage requires also a sharing of personality. Furthermore, unlike an ordinary contractual agreement, a covenantal agreement is permanent and constant, abiding throughout the fluctuations of history, and thus exemplifies steadfastness and loyalty. The community of Israel, bound by covenant, remains thus forever faithful to God. So too, a Jewish marriage is a covenantal commitment; indeed, like Israel's faith in God, the abiding loyalty of the couple bound in matrimony at times defies rationalization.

Of course, this emphasis on steadfastness and loyalty in marriage, and the comparison to Israel's everlasting relationship with God, forces Rabbi Soloveitchik to confront a stark fact: Judaism permits divorce. He addresses this challenge by means of a theological justification of divorce in terms of the philosophy of the personality and the concept of the sacred.

What else does a covenantal marriage community entail? One element is sacrifice, as reflected in the prohibition of adultery and the laws of separation. Covenantal marriage is also *hedonic*, that is, pleasure-oriented, as reflected in the Halakhah's insistence on conjugal rights. Halakhic marriage is natural and procreative, reflected in the law that a husband may not force his wife to use techniques for birth control; and a marriage community is also a cooperative community, as reflected in economic obligations of the parties. A marriage community displays affection, appreciation and friendship; but it is also an educational community, as reflected in the law that parents must educate their children, and as such even the infertile couple, lacking natural children, can participate in the full covenantal experience through adoption.

In closing, Rabbi Soloveitchik explores the importance of "existential polarity" — differences between typological man and woman. Axiologically, that is, in terms of values, the sexes are equal and in particular equally worthy of communing with God. But on the metaphysical plane, typological man and woman are different *personae*, with singular qualities and distinct missions. Invoking Kabbalah's stress on the duality of male and female within the cosmos, Rabbi Soloveitchik argues that this mystical world view suggests that such duality is a fundamental feature of existence itself. Marriage, then, is a reflection of the cosmos itself.

"The Redemption of Sexual Life"

This third essay begins with an analysis of the ideal of *kedushah*, holiness. As in other writings, such as *Ish ha-Halakhah (Halakhic Man)*, the Rav maintains that holiness is created by man rather than bestowed by God as a gift. "Holiness is released from the primitive in man through redemptive action," specifically the restraint of physical urges. Even prayer and ceremony are sacrificial only symbolically; they do not involve discipline as greatly as does harnessing the body, organizing its drives, and relating these to a higher frame of reference. Through the anguish of withdrawal, man renews and rehabilitates his world, giving him understanding "of what is worthwhile in human existence, how to take advantage of it and how to elevate it to great heights." Thus, in Judaism, marriage is blessed with dignity and sacredness — as is manifest in the blessings recited at the Jewish wedding ceremony, which affirm the dignity and Divine image of man.

Rabbi Soloveitchik focuses next on the Hebrew term *"bushah,"* used to describe the feelings of Adam and Eve after their sin. The word can connote both shame and shyness. Unlike shyness, which results merely from being viewed by others, shame entails moral self-criticism and self-condemnation — guilt, culpability. Such feelings arise from perceiving a gap between what one should be and what one is, between one's ideal self as a being created in God's image and one's real self. A person's conscience condemns him "because of an unfulfilled wish, an unrealized ideal, an aspiration which did not come true, or a wrong of which one is guilty." Whether as a result of social conventions, religious inhibitions, or human nature, sexuality evokes an element of guilt in the person experiencing the desire. Hence the term *"bushah"* in the context of Adam and Eve.

The Rav describes three forms of sexual life. First is the "natural-paradisiacal," which is but a biological function and lacks "personal moment" — it creates neither memory nor anticipation. Second is the aphrodite-hedonic, in which the love becomes more selective and assumes a personal character bent on *hedone*. This is "pandemic" love, vulgar and carnal, and is characterized by the quest for self-gratification, by insatiability, and by ruthlessness. Finally there is the highest stage — redeemed "Uranian-Aphrodite" sexual activity. Here the "unique, lonely individual" seeks "to flee his solitude, to share his personal existence with others," and "finds fulfillment in a carnal medium." Erotic love leads an I to a Thou whose personal existence is cognized — hence the Hebrew term *leida*, to know, connotes sexual activity.

All three accounts are found in Genesis, and in particular the blessings given to the animals and to man convey a crucial motif. The Rav points out that when the Bible (Gen. 1:28) describes God's blessing to humanity of "Be fruitful and multiply, replenish the earth and subdue it," it introduces the blessing with the phrase, "God blessed them and God said to them," while in the blessings given to animals (Gen. 1:22) we read only, "God blessed them, saying, 'Be fruitful and multiply.' " The addition of "and God said to them" implies the workings of personality and I-awareness. An imperative emerges. The clear implication is that it is the norm, God's command and law, that plays a role in the very making of the human personality.

"Parenthood: Natural and Redeemed"

Extending yet again the difference between natural man and spiritual man, this essay develops a contrast between biological parenthood and educational-spiritual parenthood. Whereas Eve is called "the *mother* of all living beings," it is Abraham, not Adam, who is called "the *father* of many nations." This is because while Adam was the father of a "natural, unredeemed community," Abraham elevated Adam's role and sired a community that is "redeemed, covenantal, ethical …"

In the natural community, motherhood is central because of the mother's powerful biological ties to the child she carried and nurtured. Lacking the vivid, intense bonds created by this natural reality, the father remains a distant figure, and is destined to occupy a peripheral place. But in the covenantal community, the situation changes: the father freely accepts the role of educator and transmitter of the tradition. At the same time, the mother's role is transformed too, from she who bears and nurses the child to she who joins in the great task of promoting the child's intellectual and spiritual growth. With this transformation, marked by the addition of the Hebrew letter *hei* to their names, Abraham and Sarah (formerly Abram and Sarai) accept responsibility for "the multitude of nations." They do not merely raise biological progeny — they lead a "universal" community open to all who would join. They raise not a "clan," but a "nation." Thus are motherhood and fatherhood "redeemed," and infused with meaning and purposiveness.

The teaching and training of the child involves a double task, intellectual and experiential. The typological father bears responsibility for the former, the mother for the latter. Both ingredients are indispensable in introducing the child to a redeemed existence. In the course of the essay, Rabbi Soloveitchik comments as well on the tragic role of the Biblical woman, who manifests leadership when crisis looms, but who, after the crisis is resolved, retreats quietly to her tent and lives inconspicuously.

"Kibbud u-Mora: Honor and Fear of Parents"

This essay focuses on the relationship between outer deed and inner experience with respect to the two Biblically commanded filial duties referred to in the essay's title. As the Rav notes, outer deed and inner experience do not always match. Thus one person might act properly toward his or her parents on an external, behavioral level while remaining emotionally cold or indifferent to them on the inside; another individual may experience love and respect, but not act upon these feelings. The ideal realization of *kibbud u-mora*, honor and fear, is attained when not only does the person perform technically correct outer deeds, but these behaviors express his or her own proper inner attitudes. It is precisely these inner experiences and attitudes that the Rav tries to capture and define.

To do so, he outlines three aspects under which the norms of *kibbud u-mora* may be viewed. First there is the pragmatic: the child treats his parents with respect and kindness mindful that in his own adulthood — especially old age — he will want his children to do the same for him. This utilitarian approach grows out of a sense of human interdependence; and because our Sages stress the interdependence in creation in general and human society in particular, Rabbi Soloveitchik submits that Judaism "has never been embarrassed" by pragmatic reasoning when it fosters ethically proper action. Not only does the Bible appeal to "our good always" as a motive for doing the *mitzvot* (Deut. 6:25); but people, after all, need each other, and *hesed,* acts of kindness, can be based on this recognition of mutual dependence.

Yet, there is a second, higher level of motive for *kibbud u-mora*: the ethical. The reference here is to a feeling of gratitude to parents. Citing Bahya ibn Pakuda, the Rav places gratitude at the core of religious and moral thinking and feeling. Gratitude creates a sense of "ontic (or existential) solidarity," a solidarity of being. We must feel ourselves as belonging to others. "There are three partners in a person, the Holy One, Blessed Be He, the father, and the mother ..." (Kiddushin 30b).

This brings us to a third aspect of filial obligation, the *ontic,* that is, relating to real and ultimate existence. The child's very awareness of self must include father and mother; he must sense "that he is irrevocably bound to his parents and that this unity is an indestructible fact from which he cannot break away." *Kibbud u-mora* is distinctive among *mitzvot* in imposing this demand, for with regard to "love thy neighbor as thyself," the Halakhah, argues the Rav, does *not* require ontic *union*, but only ontic *solidarity*.

In the powerful conclusion to *"Kibbud u-Mora,"* the Rav shows, as we discussed earlier, that "the encounter of man and God can only occur if man, in his quest for the great ultimate and eternal root, is also concerned with his little, conditioned and transient this-worldly roots." In showing how the search for finite roots and the search for God, the Infinite root, go hand in hand, Rabbi Soloveitchik calls our attention to an intriguing difference between *kibbud* and *mora*. Insofar as *kibbud* involves sharing with others and uniting with them in love — he often renders *"kibbud"* as "love" — it is readily found in the sphere of human inter-relations. But *mora* transcends anything we are expected to live up to in our other human relationships. Even if parents publicly revile and humiliate the child, the child, to quote Maimonides, must "remain silent, to fear and revere the King, King of Kings, who has this decreed ..." This feeling has no analogue in other interpersonal contacts, but rather is borrowed from religious life, where we finite beings encounter an Infinite Being for Whom we must be ever ready to sacrifice. Thus the norm of *mora* in particular "whisks us away" from the material universe into the realm of the transcendent. Though our parents are finite, our relatedness to them "hides in its essence man's longing and craving for God." In closing, the Rav shows that by relating to parents one comes as well to unite with the *masorah*, the tradition, and with the community of Israel that is its bearer.

"Torah and Shekhinah"

In this closing essay, the Rav paints poignant contrasts between the typological mother's and father's relationship to the child, using a distinction between two types of memory. The mother has a "timeless event memory," which fuses the past into the present. The father, however, has a "progressive event memory," which makes the past distant to him. As a result, with the passage of years the mother intensifies her emotional attachment and refuses to let go, whereas the father gradually moves away from the child, allowing the latter to exercise freedom. In addition, the father acts as a disciplinarian, the mother as a comforter. God, though, acts as both Father and Mother, as the One who disciplines His people and the "*Shekhinah*" who comforts them. The duality in the father-mother contrast reflects the duality of man himself, for man is both an adult, free and independent, and a child, weak and helpless. As we noted earlier, the essay comes to a beautiful climax as it speaks of the study of Torah and the search for God. The book thus ends on a note that leaves us with the indelible image of Rabbi Soloveitchik himself.

FAMILY
REDEEMED

❧ *Adam and Eve*

A Scriptural Philosophy of Man

The purpose of this paper is to gain an insight into the nature and destiny of the woman and man whom God created in a specific way, and to begin to formulate on the basis of these insights a philosophy of man. Yet, the frame of reference we will employ will be a scriptural one. We will avail ourselves of Biblical hermeneutics or interpretation and try to detect the spiritual message contained in both what has been unequivocally stated in the text and what has been omitted and concealed. What I want to achieve is an understanding on our part that the Bible is not just a book of the past. It is far more than that; it is the book of the present and future. In all times, in all periods, in crisis as well as in success, man may find his problems and anxieties defined in this Book of Books.

I am sorry to say that many Jews don't look to the Bible for guidance and that its spiritual message, so indispensable for man today, is completely ignored. Our approach to Biblical interpretation is too often homiletical; it is the pulpit and the synagogue approach. The Book of Books has become a compilation of sermonical inspirational texts, popular maxims and vulgar common sense. However, the most beautiful aspect of the Bible is its *Weltanschauung*, its world view, its spiritual outlook upon both the world and man.

The Bible is concerned and preoccupied with human tragedy and success, with human contradictions, with human smallness as well as greatness, with the destiny of the Jewish community, the hierarchy of its spiritual values, its victories and failures, its tortuous, twisting and winding road, its fall and rise, its hopes and despair. Yet all this does not attract our attention. We never try to understand the metaphysic and axiology of the Scripture [its theory of being and its system of values]. This essay is an experiment in a metaphysical and axiological interpretative approach to Scripture, an exercise in detecting my own self in the scriptural portraiture of man, of finding my own acute problems and questions, my own torturing anxieties and fears, my own inspiring hopes and aspirations in the story of Biblical heroes. The detection of one's own self in Biblical man is an exciting experience. It strengthens one's spirit and relieves him of his cares. It is a redemptive and enhancing awareness.

The Creation of Adam and Eve

Let us start our explanation of the text, raising a few questions concerning the sequence of events recorded in the second chapter of Genesis. The Torah tells us that the Almighty "created man of dust from the ground and breathed into his countenance the breath of life" (Gen. 2:7). It is self-evident that for the sake of continuity the Torah, after telling us about the creation of Adam, should have immediately related the story of creation of Eve. Verse 7 should have been followed by, "And God said:

'It is not good that the man be alone; I shall make him a help-mate opposite him'" (v. 18). Then, without diverting attention from the story of Eve, the Torah should have immediately told us how God made the helper Eve. In other words, verse 18 should have been followed by verse 21, which tells us how God created woman: "And God cast a deep sleep upon the man and he slept, and He took one of his ribs ... And the Lord God fashioned into a woman the rib He had taken from the man and He brought her to the man."

After concluding the story of the creation of man, of his being alone and of the emergence of Eve, the Bible could have told us about the planting of the Paradise in Eden (vs. 8-14), the placing of man there (v. 15), the command to eat from all the trees except the tree of knowledge (vs. 16-17) and the observation that "the two of them were naked yet they felt no shame" (v. 25). Thus we would have been presented with two complete continuous stories: first, the creation of Adam and Eve; second, the planting of the Garden, man's assignment to reside in, cultivate, and watch over it, and the command not to eat from the tree of knowledge. The Torah, however, did not narrate the two stories in the manner we suggested. The Torah apparently tells us one story, with both narratives merged into one.

After Adam's appearance, God was not concerned with his aloneness. Instead, the Torah tells us about something new, the Paradise. Then, suddenly, after it has reached the event of man being enjoined from eating from the tree of knowledge, it interrupts the continuous tale and picks up another thread, namely, man's loneliness and God's decision to provide him a helper. However, the Torah does not proceed directly to tell us about the creation of Eve. Instead, while departing from its recording of the events leading to the act of creation, the Torah reports another event, Adam's naming of the animals and birds. After having narrated this event, the Torah resumes the narration about the creation of Eve. Apparently, the story can be told only in this fashion. It is one story. The planting of Paradise, the command, and the naming of the animals are relevant events which cast a light upon and are relevant to the creation of Eve. The Torah had to tell us the story of the creation of woman in installments, advising us about other events that happened which are indispensable for understanding the drama of man.

Man-natura: Man as Part of Nature

In the first chapter of Genesis, the Torah tells us about the creation of male and female. Of course, the chapter is concerned mainly not with man but with the cosmos, organic as well as inorganic nature. The Torah mentions the creation of man since the latter is a part of the universe and the story of creation would have been imperfect if the Torah had omitted the fact that man was also created.

Man, as he emerges on that mysterious Friday at the end of the first chapter, is not an outsider to the cosmos, not alien to nature; he is not a foreigner and intruder. Man is a child of Mother Nature, as is the brute and the beast. God called into existence the living creatures in their various species, beasts of pasture, creeping things and land animals. The narratives about the creation of plant (Gen. 1:11-12), animal (1:20-26), and man (1:27) are almost identical; all three take account of the common origin of life, namely, the earth. Death is the common destiny of all three exponents of living matter that emerged out of Mother Earth, founded upon the affinity of the biological occurrences in man, animal and plant.

The Bible believes that Adam formed an integral part of nature on the day of his creation. The unity and continuity of organic life, considered an indispensable postulate in all biological sciences, was accepted by the Bible with regard to paradisiacal man. Indeed, the naturalistic formula of man — the conception of the human being as a part of nature — was a truism among *Hazal*. Christian theologians, beginning with St.

Augustine and ending with the Neo-Scholastics, rejected the philosophy of the naturalness of man as an attempt to secularize man and hence desecrate his dignity and sanctity. But the Talmudic and Midrashic tradition can be traced back to the Bible itself.

The Bible is cognizant of man as a natural being, placing him in the abode of animal and plant. The idea of the naturalness of man served as a motivating force in Jewish ethics and metaphysics. Instability, insecurity, life and death, the helplessness and vulnerability of man are popular themes in the prophets. Natural man is contrasted with God, the former's transient existence with the eternity and omnipotence of the Creator.

On the same day on which he was created, man — male and female — appears in his full naturalness. His existence is identical with the instinctive, organically uniform, and unbroken course of life functions. Man and beast share equally in the same biology, physiology, and pathology. Judaism never looked upon this relatedness of man to animal as something degrading, evil or corrupt. On the contrary, God's inscrutable scheme of creation embraced man and animal alike. Both belong to nature; both sprang forth from the soil.

Of course, there is a distinctive element in man, the *Imago Dei*, the *tzelem Elokim*, the image of God. Judaism considered the *imago* element to be not a gratuitous grant bestowed upon man but rather a challenge to be met by man; not as an endowment fashioned by God but rather as a mission to be implemented, as a *hyle*, formless matter to be molded by man. Perhaps the central norm in our ethical system is related to *Imago Dei*, to be like God, reflect His image, become a Divine being, live like a creature who bears resemblance to its Maker. It is up to man to either realize or shake off the *Imago Dei*.

Man and woman make their entry into the universe as natural cosmic beings. They are endowed with talent and exceptional ability. However, man and woman of whom chapter one speaks have not made as yet the momentous decision to turn a non-reflective, instinctive existence into a self-conscious one.

Man-persona: Man as Personality

The break with naturalness and functional, biological immediacy comes to full expression in the second chapter, which contains the story of man as a unique being in whom the potential called *Imago Dei* is involved in the process of realization, in whom the element of distinctiveness is about to become an actuality. In the second chapter, we find man in labor pains, about to give birth to himself as a *humanus,* to an I who secedes from his surrounding, meditates upon the things of his immediate environment, and sees the environment as something separate and foreign confronting him. In the first chapter he could not reflect upon the environment, as he was part and parcel of this environment. This being struggles hard to proclaim himself man-*humanus* instead of man-*natura*, to liberate himself from the anonymity of being just an individual man whose task it is to represent the species. He strives to attain the distinctiveness of an individual who represents not the species but himself, who bears a name identifying himself as an I who cannot be equated with the thou, who passes through this valley of tears only once in an eternity and who cannot be replaced or reproduced. The Bible in the second chapter tells us the story of a man who lived once upon a time and disappeared forever.

I wish to point out a certain variation in the second chapter which, in my opinion, corroborates the premise we have adopted, that while the first chapter is concerned with man-*natura*, the second tells the story of man-*persona*. We all know that while in the first account of creation *Elokim* is used as God's name, in the second chapter the Tetragrammaton *(Hashem)* is added; God is referred to as *Hashem Elokim. Elokim* conveys to us the idea of God as the Almighty, as the Creator, Maker,

Architect and Engineer of the world, as the source of the boundless cosmic dynamics, the supplier of indestructible matter and unlimited energy. *Elokim* has the semantic connotation of enormous power, unlimited might and vigor. The image of *Elokim* is found in the grandeur and might of the cosmic drama; the sanctuary of *Elokim* is nature. Man's relationship to God as *Elokim* borders on the impossible, for what is man within the vast and uncharted lanes of the cosmos — his significance equals zero. The Psalmist has already raised the question of what is man *vis-á-vis* the astral world: "When I see Thy heavens, Thy handiwork, the moon and stars that Thou hast established, what is man that Thou rememberest him, and what is the son of man that Thou thinkest of him" (Psalms 8:4-5).

The whole picture changes with the introduction of the name *Hashem*. The latter is symbolic of the special unique relationship between God and man. The name *Hashem* tells us that God communicates with man directly, not via the cosmos. Man relates to God not as a cosmic being but as an I, as an individual *persona* who has seceded from the unbroken union of cosmic phenomena, who has extricated himself from the uniformity of an instinctive anonymous existence consisting of stimulation and reaction. God befriends man-stranger; God likes man's companionship. That is why in the second chapter, where the whole story is concerned not with cosmic man but with man-*persona*, metaphysical man, man who rebelled against Mother Nature and attempted to gain an individual identity of his own, the name *Hashem* is used. The image of *Hashem* is reflected in human longing for the beautiful and noble, in love, in motherly tenderness and fatherly concern, in everything that is great, noble and fascinating in man.

The question that then arises is: Where is the critical boundary to be found, the line which separates cosmic man from *persona*, natural uniformity from existential complexity, a non-reflective life from a meditative existence? At what point did Adam make the leap into the new ontological dimension, this new dimension of being? I believe that the Biblical story has singled out two turning points. However, one is of primary significance while the other one is secondary. Let us begin with the latter.

Man's Aspirations

Man in chapter one leads a restricted existence in his state of naturalness and instinctive, unbroken, biological uniformity. A child of Mother Nature, he does not reach out for vastness and abundance. Mother Nature is ruled by a mathematical equation; everything in the universe is limited by boundary. So is natural man. Only by breaking out from his natural immediacy and instinctive uniformity, by discovering his unique identity, can man reject boundaries and long for vastness and boundlessness. Man-*persona* has an imagination, a fantasy which rebels against limitation and weaves a beautiful halo around him, crowning him with an enchanting vision of infinity. Man-*natura* is a realist, man-*persona* a dreamer — I might say, a bold dreamer, a visionary. He is an adventurer and a very daring one. He yearns for beauty and pleasure, for true happiness. He creates a civilization, a culture. Man-*persona* wants to accomplish more and more; man-*natura* is a happy with the little he achieves.

Judaism approves of fantasy-aroused man-*persona*. Indeed, God purposely planted the Paradise for man, who was called upon to cultivate and guard it. Man is encouraged to build, to plant, to beautify his life, to enjoy his life as much as he can. "And the Lord God planted a garden eastward, in Eden, and there He placed man whom He had formed; and the Lord God made grow out of the ground every tree delightful to the eye and good for food . . . " (Gen. 2:8-9). But two horrible fears haunt man steadily, trailing him like an everlasting shadow: the fear of nihility, of nonbeing — death — and the fear of ignorance. Man wants to live and to know. He is eager to lead an intelligent, enlightened, inextinguishable existence. His greatest aspiration, his most fascinating dream, is to defeat death and to grasp the *mysterium magnum,* the great mystery of creation. God did plant the garden with trees pleasant to look at and delightful as far as taste is concerned. And in the middle of the garden grew the two mysterious trees representing two basic aspirations of man: to live and to know. Yes, God planted the garden in Eden in order to place there the man whom He formed, for man is entitled to desire, to quest, to long for and be fascinated by something great and wonderful — immortality and omniscience.

By planting the garden, God aroused in man-*natura* these two basic urges. With that awakening, the *humanitas* began to dawn; man's uniqueness commenced budding and man started to sever the umbilical cord that attached him to Mother Earth. He was set on the road toward a creative daring life, his fantasy reaching out to the stars and his dreams about controlling Mother Nature burgeoning forth. In other words, the process of alienation is *ipso facto* a process of self-recognition and self-finding.

God's Command

The more significant turning point, however, is not the birth of human fantasy but the confrontation with God's moral will, which resulted in the birth of a moral awareness of man's own. After man had been placed in the Paradise in Eden, his fantasy began to aspire to an unlimited existence which knows only of forward marching, of surging towards the boundless, of victorious advance and conquest. Adam met suddenly with God's moral will, with the moral law which challenges man in numerous cases to do just the opposite, to refrain from advancing and to withdraw, to defy the very fantasy that made him man, to stop at times even if the fantasy tells him to move on, to give up when fantasy is about to grasp. This meeting between man and the infinite moral will of God brought about the metamorphosis that was initiated with the birth of the human fantasy that aspires to a paradisiacal existence. The final liberation of man from his environment, the transformation from natural into metaphysical man, occurred at his first confrontation with *Hashem,* at his first rendezvous with God Who tells him of a Divine imperative, reveals the concept of duty and burdens him with the moral load. Man turns into a metaphysical personality the very moment he realizes that to be human means to carry a load and that a human existence is not all *hedone,* not all pleasure. In a word, the critical boundary is to be detected in verses 16 and 17, in *"Va-yetzav Hashem Elokim al ha-adam,"* in God commanding man to refrain from eating from the tree of knowledge.

Previously, we read, *"Va-yomer lahem Elokim,* God said to them, *'Peru u-revu,* be fruitful and mul⁺iply, replenish the earth and subdue it ...' " (Gen. 1:28). Here, instead of *"va-yomer,* He said," the Torah uses the verb *"va-yetzav,* He commanded." *Va-yomer* signifies that God informed man and woman of a factual situation, of something which is. He advised them about the drive for procreation which is inherent in humans. Of course, when God discloses some information to man, it implies an imperative. However this imperative is commensurate with the biological natural push. The understanding of a fact turns into a normative experience. The perpetuation of mankind is an ethical law.

The same is true of the creative role which was assigned to man, "to fill the earth and conquer it." An inner aptitude of man — his curiosity and his questing for change, improvement and progress — was ethicized and elevated to the rank of an ideal to be sought and pursued. Yet this norm is felt in the heartbeat of man, pronounced in the tremor of his voice, in the passionate gleam of his eyes and in his warm handshake. Nothing extraneous has been foisted on natural man. He is creative, and the norm of creativity expresses an inner yearning of his soul.

When the verb *va-yetzav* is employed, however, a new area of existence is opened up — namely, that of a non-biological ethical existence. This norm is alien to biological man and does not fit into the scheme of his natural impulses. Hunger drives a man to certain actions without distinguishing between the forbidden fruit and the one which may be enjoyed. The mere fact that from among the satisfiers of a biological insistence one was set apart and placed beyond the legitimate reach of Adam indicates the unique character of the norm. Adam suddenly experienced an imperative which emerged out of an existential sphere unknown to natural man. The command not to eat from the tree of knowledge spells out the condemnation of man-satan who goes out after something which is beyond his ontic sphere, the sphere of his being, who overreaches by reaching out toward the nonself illegitimately, plundering and usurping something which is not his. In a word, the norm limits the existential area of man and bounds his rights therein. It declares surging forward toward existential sectors which lie outside of his God-willed existence to be the most dreadful crime. The urge for unlimited vastness and boundlessness must be overcome. The law of withdrawal was formulated in the first *mitzvah*.

Usually, the verb *va-yetzav* governs the objective case as a directly transitive verb. In such a case, our verse would have read, "*Va-yetzav Hashem Elokim et ha-adam*, God commanded Adam." Here, however, a distinctive grammatical form is used: the verb appears with the preposition *al* instead of *et*. We come across this strange form several times in the Bible. In Genesis we read, "*Va-yetzav alav Par'oh*, Pharaoh commanded his people concerning Abraham" (Gen. 12:20). Esther called Hatakh, one of the royal eunuchs who was appointed to serve her, "*va-tetzave-hu*, and she commanded him, *al* Mordechai, so as to learn ..." (Esther 4:5). In a word, whenever the verb "to command" is accompanied by the preposition *al* it has the connotation "about, concerning, with regard to." Direct grammatical transitiveness is missing.

In light of this analysis we will have to translate verse 16, *"Va-yetzav Hashem Elokim al ha-adam,"* as, "And the Lord God commanded (or instructed) Adam the man, as regards man." He told him something which is relevant to man, which is indispensable for a human who is bent on finding himself, his identity and personality.

What is the password which grants man admission into a new world of being, into an entirely new ontological dimension? It is the command: "From every tree of the garden you may eat, but from the tree of knowledge of good and evil you may not eat" (Gen. 2:16-17). It is the breakthrough of law, of the command, of the summons to retreat. Natural man turned into metaphysical man the very moment a heavy load was placed upon his frail shoulders and he was told to move on toward a moral destiny and pay the toll of the road along which he would travel. A man who cannot make the movement of recoil, who travels light without being burdened with commandments, who lives by his fantasy and not by his will, who refuses to pay the toll when using the highway, who eats from all trees of the paradise not omitting a single tree, whose existence is free from all commitments — such a person is only a man-*natura,* notwithstanding his bold thrust, daring enterprises, grandiose designs, and fabulous exploits. He may be good in mathematical computations, in physical theories and chemical experiments. Yet, all this does not suffice to open up to man the new ontological personalism of I-hood and thou-hood.

The transition from *natura* to *persona* occurs at the very instant man agrees to take defeat at the hand of God. Man defeated by God rises to the heights of a metaphysical existence. What does the Torah then require of man, if not the art of inviting defeat not at the hands of man but at the hands of God? The first law of limitation was given to Adam before the emergence of Eve, and referred to the world order. Abiding by this law in our contact with impersonal reality qualifies and trains the self to live in accord with this principle of limitation also in dealing with the other self. If the law of withdrawal is abandoned in the alien sphere of events and things, it cannot prevail in our personal relationships.

Aloneness and Loneliness

With his emergence, man-*persona* encounters another problem of the human situation. Now, after man has been burdened with the ethical, halakhic norm and has become a metaphysical being — only now *Hashem Elokim* decides to create Eve, the woman. Prior to being commanded, man-*natura* led a non-reflective, outer-directed, instinctive existence in union with his nature. Hence, he did not face the specific human problem by which *homo-persona* is troubled. Of course, we all know what the problem is; the Torah has revealed it. "It is not good that the man be *levaddo*" (Gen. 2:18). *Levaddo* has a twofold meaning: aloneness and loneliness. Man as a rule dislikes both; he does not want to be alone; he hates to be lonely. We understand very well that to be alone and to be lonely are two different problems. One may stand at Times Square where hundreds of people pass by every minute and yet feel very lonely. vice-versa, one may find oneself, in terms of distance, in seclusion, very remote from people, without feeling lonely.

To be alone is, first, a physical fact and, second, a psychological condition which is not at all universal. Some people are loners; they prefer to be with themselves without being intruded upon by others. Of course, at times this urge to be alone assumes abnormal proportions, as in the case of reclusion. However, to retreat from society and to spend time apart from people is a frequent and normal exercise. Many like being alone. Of course, usually man is (as Aristotle knew) a gregarious animal; the herd instinct is powerful. He does not like to shut off the world from his life and, if compelled to do so, he feels miserable. Man-*natura* as a rule hates aloneness.

However, loneliness is not a physical fact, nor is it a most painful psychological condition. It is far more than that. Loneliness is a spiritual human situation. If I may say, it is an existential awareness or a metaphysical state, not only of the mind but of the soul as well. Loneliness reflects both the greatness of man as a unique metaphysical being, as well as his ontological insecurity as an incomplete being who, like a trapped animal, searches for an exit from his labyrinthine existence. It is both an inspiring as well as destructive experience. Lonely man is both hero and coward, giant and dwarf. There is anxiety as well as joy in the loneliness situation. However, it is only man-*persona* — introspective, meditating, and experiencing estrangement from nature — who is lonely. Metaphysical man finds himself in the throes of loneliness. Man-*natura*, who leads a gregarious, complacent, ebullient non-metaphysical existence, is not acquainted with this situation.

Man-*natura* suffers from aloneness, never from loneliness. He is outer-oriented and success-minded, thinks scientifically, and is not conscious of another ontological order beside the natural one. In loneliness, humans long for bliss and beauty, for a higher and more meaningful order, purged of evil, redeemed from contradiction and absurdity.

Let us pick up the verse, "It is not good that the man be *levaddo*." We have asked, what did *Hashem Elokim* mean by this dictum, aloneness or loneliness, for *levaddo* lends itself to either interpretation. The answer to this question is, I believe, to be found in the laconic five-word original Hebrew sentence. The Torah could have said, *"lo tov la-adam lihyot levaddo."* However, it preferred the arrangement, *"lo tov heyot ha-adam levaddo."* What is the difference between these two formulations? The first would read, if translated into the vernacular, "It is not good for the man to be *levaddo*"; the second, "It is not good that the man be *levaddo*." The first, had it been used by the

Bible, would have expressed a utilitarian rule. A man alone cannot accomplish as much as two. He needs a helper from a utilitarian viewpoint. The second formulation, which the Scripture actually uses, has a different connotation: man's being *levaddo* is not good. This is an ontological postulate. A lonely human existence is not good; it lacks God's sanction and exposes an imperfect form of being. The helper whom God willed to make is indispensable not only for a pragmatic but for an ontological reason as well. Man needs help ontologically. Another homo-*persona* is necessary to complete man's existence, to endow it with existential meaning and directedness.

Marriage is not just a successful partnership, but an existential community. Adam and Eve met and a new metaphysical community, not just a successful partnership, was born. Had Adam needed a partner for practical reasons alone — to lighten his economic burden, to enable him to procreate, or to allow him a satisfactory sexual life — there would have been no necessity for the creation of Eve. We know from reading the first chapter that God created male and female. Both were endowed with great skill, talent, know-how and technical aptitude to control their environment. Male and female could have formed a dynamic, profitable partnership or company which would efficiently take care of all human needs, be they economic, physiological, or psychological. There was no need for natural man to meet Eve the woman, since he was already in company of the female who, for all practical purposes, would have made an excellent wife.

However, something had happened to man. The rendezvous with *Hashem* which resulted in man's encounter with the moral norm precipitated the birth of *homo-persona,* of a metaphysical man, of a singular spiritual personality. New man was burdened with a new awareness, one of inadequacy, illegitimacy and rootlessness; he was troubled by a great anxiety, by a sickness unto death — fright. In a word, he found himself lonely and forsaken. What he needed was not a practical partnership but an ontological community where his lonely existence could find completeness and legitimacy. The female of the first chapter did not qualify for that type of a community. A new woman had to be created, a woman who, like man, changed from a natural into metaphysical being, from female-*natura* into woman-*persona*, into a unique spiritual personality.

What is actually the difference between homo-*natura* and homo-*persona*? What is the main feature of the *persona* of metaphysical man? The Torah gives the answer in the story about naming the animals. The story appears to destroy completely the unity and continuity of the tale about the creation of Eve. However, the last sentence sheds light upon the link between this story and the emergence of Eve. "And the man gave names to all cattle and to the fowl of the air and to every beast of the field, but for Adam there was not found a helpmate for him" (Gen. 2:20). The story about Adam giving names to all cattle and fowl revealed to man the distinction between what he was prior to the command and what he became following it.

Man's Otherness from Nature

Adam named all the living creatures. What kind of a performance was it, and why did God encourage him to do this? It was a cognitive gesture. Sciences are divided into descriptive sciences (such as general botany, general zoology, geography and even astronomy) and explanatory sciences (such as physics). The job of the descriptive scientist is to introduce order into an allegedly chaotic world, to classify and generalize — their question is *what*. The explanatory scientists are concerned not with the *what* but with the *how*: Their question is, *how* do those objects function. Their prime instrument of cognition is the category of causality.

God wanted Adam to inquire into the what-ness of the world from a descriptive viewpoint. He encouraged Adam to classify and systematize a motley world which, at first glance, impresses us with its disorderliness and disarray. Primitive man saw no patterns in nature; he considered the latter replete with contradictions. Man started his progress by first introducing order into his environment, by classifying the fauna (and perhaps also the flora). This is the first scientific approach to nature: no magic, no spirit indwelling in every bush, no Golden Bough. Objective Adam approached his environment scientifically and tried to introduce orderliness.

At this point, there takes place man's breach with absolute, all-inclusive natural immediacy and his acquisition of a new capacity, that of turning around and facing the environment as something external and strange. Man, in order to become the ruler and developer of nature, must make an about face. Instead of marching naively with nature, he must suddenly stop moving along and encounter nature with the first question: what is it? When he begins to wonder what nature is and tries to understand it, he abandons the identity and unity of man and his environment and finds himself encountering it as a stranger and outsider.

At this point man discovers in himself an incommensurability with nature. He enters into a new phase in his emergence as a person: he views nature not from within but from without. While watching nature at a distance he gradually moves into a unique position of power and specific rights. The creative urge in man frees him from the state of all-out integration into one's environment.

Thus man experiences both oneness with and otherness from nature. He is an exponent of his kind, a representative of the group whose claim to existence is justified only at a generic level, and he is also an individual, a separate entity, who exists because he is himself, without being placed in a generic frame of reference. When man reaches the stage at which he is no longer a non-reflective being that forges ahead in unison with a mechanical-natural occurrence, but instead begins to single himself out in an act of confrontation with nature, he suddenly discovers in himself his own intelligence. He faces nature in a cognitive, critical, observant mood. The creative drive in him awakens in him curiosity and the desire for inquiry. The inquiry about the how, what and why, the quest for creativity comes to expression. Man begins to survey his environment and to uncover certain functional patterns of behavior.

When man breaks with immediacy and takes a look at nature from a distance, he encounters a reality which is not only outside of himself but also opposed to him. He is required to venture into an alien sphere. Aware of himself as an autonomous being capable of making decisions and charting a course of action, he also knows that the implementation of his decision depends upon something else, upon something outside of himself which can thwart the whole project he has conceived and organized. He must act, because God has implanted in him the urge to activate himself, and yet, at the same time, he cannot act, because he is removed from his exalted position as a subject and demoted to a mere object who bears consequences and is immobilized by the impact of events and things not of his making.

While Adam was busy describing, a great truth dawned on him. He realized that knowledge of the surrounding world by observation is gained by watching how the objects attracting our attention function. Objective observation is the source of knowledge of the world. However when it comes to man, observation alone will yield a very meager amount of knowledge. Man must confide in the person who is eager to understand him. Without confession there can hardly be an opportunity to learn why, who, and what a particular individual is. In order for man to be recognized, he must reveal himself; he must be interrogated and interviewed. The person whom I am eager to know must have confidence in the investigator, and be willing to state everything he knows about himself sincerely and truthfully. And even then the knowledge will not be complete, since many things are hidden from the eye of the person himself.

There is no depth to nature. Its existence is a flat two-dimensional one. The reality of nature exhausts itself in its functions. If you ask whether mute nature exists, I shall certainly answer "of course." However, if you continue to cross-examine me and ask me what I understand by existence, I will answer "activity." The existence of nature exhausts itself in its behavior, in its dynamics. There is nothing else to a mute existence. Hence, by watching the behavioral patterns I gain an insight into the substance. Nature does not lie.

However man has an inner world; he exists inwardly as well as externally. Man's ontological essence, that is, the essence of his being, is not to be equated with his conduct or routine activities. There is a *homo absconditus*, a "hidden man" whom no one knows. He hardly knows himself. Hence in spite of watching man's activity we gain little knowledge. The latter is a mystery which no one can unravel. "All men are liars," says the Psalmist (Psalms 116:11). Not because they want to tell the untruth. They are simply unable to tell the truth. I see my neighbor every morning leave his house at 6:30; I know to where he drives off. I am also familiar with his occupation. I know what he will do when he will arrive at his place of business. I willy-nilly watched his conduct; I am acquainted with his habits and responses to certain challenges. I overhear his conversation with the members of his household, I know his concerns and interests. Do I know *him*? No, he is a mystery to me. The uniqueness of man-*persona* expresses itself in the *mysterium magnum* which no one except God can penetrate.

In order to escape loneliness, man-*absconditus* had to meet woman-mystery. They have a lot in common; otherwise Eve could not be a helper. However, they are also different; their existential experiences are incommensurate. The I-awareness in Adam is totally incomprehensible to Eve, and vice-versa. Each of them has a secret which neither will ever betray. Man-*persona* and woman-*persona* resemble each other and at the same time do not understand each other. She is *ezer ke-negdo*, his helper and his opponent at the same time. For man and woman differ not only physiologically as male and female, of whom the first account of creation tells us, but also spiritually and personality-wise. This is the way in which the Creator has ordained human lonely destiny. Because the woman is not the shadow of man but an independent *persona*, because the woman projects a totally different existential image, her companionship helps man to liberate himself from his loneliness. In the interpersonalistic existential tension both man and woman find redemption.

Two Types of Defeat

Male and female are both defeated in their existential endeavor since both bear the print of the Divine curse. Both are engaged in a struggle for existence, but neither will ever attain the goal they so passionately pursue; they will never find complete self-realization and fulfillment. There is no fully successful life. Every human work, even the most "masterful," bears the imprint of incompleteness and insufficiency. Everyone must live through the experience of failure and distressing frustration. In other words, on some front, man loses the war life declared on him.

The two sex-personalities sin differently. Adam estranges himself from nature and tries to sever the bond between himself and creatureliness. He rebels against his conditioned, finite state of existence. He reaches out for the impossible, for vastness and boundlessness; his sin is that of self-absolutization and hypostatization [treating himself as a self-sufficient substance]. He ascribes to himself and to his works unlimited worth. He rebels against subjugation to the law, whether natural or moral; he likes to command, to chart his own course without accepting any transcendental counsel, to legislate an ethical code of his own, to unravel the cosmic mystery and thus usurp the omnipotence of God and become himself a creator. The phrase used by the serpent is typical of Adam the sinner: "For God knows that in the day you eat thereof, then your eyes shall be opened and you shall be as God knowing good and evil" (Gen. 3:5).

Eve's sin was not in attempting to gain unrestricted power and casting off her creaturely role, but in her commitment to *hedone*, to pleasure. She craved not for mastery but for enjoyment. She was the passive personality, the receptive mind, the indulging type. She wanted to redeem herself from her sacrificial destiny, from selfless involvement in motherhood; she thought that she could enjoy her status of a mother without employing passional action. She substituted *hedone*, which results in self-love, for commitment to an ideal of self-sacrifice. She wanted to take everything from nature without giving anything in return. She overstressed her receptive role and considered herself entitled to enjoy without working for this end since work entails withdrawal and self-discipline. The orgiastic experience was the fascinating mirage of Eve, while Adam was captivated by the vision of an over-active life dedicated to boundless conquest and domination.

Eve, when she encountered the tree, was attracted not by the promise of power but by the beauty and pleasantness of the fruit. "And when the woman saw that the tree was good for food, and that it was pleasant to the eyes, and that the tree was desirable to make one wise, she took of the fruit thereof and did eat; and gave also to her husband with her; and he did eat" (Gen. 3:6).

The serpent spoke in terms of Divine power (Gen. 3:5); the woman was attracted by the beauty and pleasantness. Even the intellectual motif is not bound up for her with power, with using human intelligence as a means of achieving mastery over the world, but with the pleasantness and aesthetic desirability of knowledge. The woman is driven by aesthetic motifs even when she engages in the intellectual gesture. Important is the process of questing for knowledge itself, as an aesthetic pleasure-providing movement. The aesthete enjoys the cognitive act, because there is self-gazing and self-loving involved in learning and searching for truths. Not the mechanical utility but the recreational aspect, the desire to assure herself of her own worth, beckons to Eve if and when she is ready to give herself to a theoretical life. She finds delight in knowing.

The fact that Eve gave of the fruit to the husband and made him eat bears witness to her aesthetic approach to the whole matter. If Eve had been driven by the satanic yearning for creating a world-self, if she had reached out for infinity and Divine absoluteness, she would never have shared the sinful fruit with Adam. The desire for power is a disjunctive or excluding emotion, limiting the thou from participating in the attainment of this objective, since this appetite is self-centered and brooks no interference or even sharing on the part of others. If Eve had been power-hungry, she would have wanted to subdue everything and everybody, including Adam. Inviting him to taste the forbidden fruit would have contradicted her very will for power. The Bible states explicitly that she "gave also to her husband with her" (Gen. 3:6). She wanted to share this experience with him, a wish which is only comprehensible within the aesthetic dimension. The enjoyment-experience is basically a conjunctive or inclusive emotion. The aesthetic personality resents isolation and loneliness; he wants to enjoy himself in company.

The two sex-personalities sin in various ways and are therefore differently defeated. In contrast to the defeat of the man, the woman fails in her attempt to enjoy life; she is never successful at a hedonic aesthetic level. She wants to unite in marriage with the man she loves and establish a home, raise a family and enjoy her children, and she finds herself in bondage to her companion and children. She realizes every wish of hers in sorrow. While enjoying, she restricts herself and her freedoms. Drinking from the cup of sexual pleasures is impregnated with pain and suffering. The woman succumbs to the Divine curse in her confrontation with her own self as a mother. She is defeated by her husband and children.

Man experiences defeat mainly in the realm of production, in his encounter with nature, with society, in his role as master, ruler and exploiter. The Bible describes the tragic role of man in unequivocal terms: "And to Adam He said, 'Because you have hearkened unto the voice of your wife, and have eaten of the tree of which I commanded you, saying, "You shall not eat of it," cursed is the ground for your sake; in toil shall you eat of it all the days of your life. Thorns and thistles shall it bring forth to you, and you shall eat the herb of the field. In the sweat of your face shall you eat bread, till you return unto the ground ...' " (Gen. 3:17-19).

Man will not be able to master nature the way he was destined in the original plan of creation. The returns on his investment in terms of toil and anguish will not be adequate with the effort. His drive for power, coupled with creativity and production, will not be fully realized. His boundless fantasy, his demonic will, will never be satisfied because a non-responsive, uncooperative nature will consistently resist his attempts to create and produce. In contrast with the woman who forfeits her freedom in order to experience motherhood and restricts herself for the sake of finding happiness, the man loses his freedom in wasting it, in overdoing his job, in over-reaching himself; in boundlessness and infinity and unlimited freedom. He roams and wanders around, he is free to commit himself or to remain uncommitted, he tolerates no intervention; fatherhood does not bind him to a homestead, and in his liberties and constant moving he forfeits everything. Freedom revenges itself on him in the dissatisfaction and frustration he experiences at being free.

In short, the woman-personality is nature-conscious and nature-involved. She pays the price of self-limitation and self-withdrawal from the vastness of spiritual personalism into the straits of naturalness. She exchanges her yearning for the vast and infinite, for a nature-encompassed and restricted life. She ends up as a mother attached to her children and husband. The woman yields to the dictates of nature and surrenders her dreams and vision of the infinite in order to be a natural mother.

Man was not denied the longing for boundlessness and greatness, the gesture of the "infinite" and self-transcendent. He refuses to trade the drive for the fantastic for a limited existence. He retains his freedom of action and movement; many a time he roams about the surface of nature, not striking roots in the very depths of nature. He tries to be selective, accepting from nature the pleasant and enjoyable but not the dutiful and restrictive. He tries to dominate and to master nature; he is the producer, the organizer, who rejects bonds and longs for power. He is engaged in combat with nature attempting to force her to yield her secrets and her wealth to him. He is the champion of a philosophy of limitless opportunities and vastness, of accomplishment. He struggles convulsively to free himself from the grip with which nature holds him fast, like Jacob who wrestled with his antagonist (Gen. 32:24-33). However, unlike Jacob, he does not emerge victorious from this encounter, and with daybreak he finds himself defeated; nature triumphs over him.

The division between the two sex-personalities has its origin in our dual religious experience. We feel the presence of God within creation as the *Shekhinah*, as Deity imprisoned in finitude, revealing Herself through the limited, determined and restricted, as the Princess in exile, the latter signifying finitude and the law-conditioned creation. Somehow, the *Shekhinah* descended from the great infinite beyond into the world, into a tangible, empirical existence, restricted and bounded in. Little wonder that we experience the immanence of God in the whole of the cosmos as the suffering, bearing, tending and nourishing Mother, with whom natural necessity interferes, and who is bound by indissoluble ties to an unalterable order of things and events.

We also are confronted with God beyond nature, far off, abiding in infinity and transcendence, overriding all natural laws and dispensing with all cosmic patterns, Whose existence cannot be limited and Whose power cannot be restricted; He is Who from far off controls, sustains and guides creation, not becoming Himself a part of it since infinity can never be involved in finitude. He is *Deus Absconditus* and *Revelatus*, the Hidden and Revealed God; yet the medium of His revelation is not the cosmic law but absolute freedom from this restrictive law. In this aspect of our experience, we feel Him in awe and amazement (rather than experience Him in lucid conceptual terms) as the master, creator of everything, as the active, masculine power, ruling, energizing and guiding the creation.

The Marital Community

What unites the man-*persona* who forms a community with the woman-*persona*? What keeps their metaphysical community alive? I believe that the answer was given by Maimonides in his theory of friendship, which was of Aristotelian origin *(Nicomachean Ethics,* book 8). After discussing utilitarian friendship, which is indeed only a business partnership, he goes on to analyze two other kinds of friendship (Commentary to *Avot* [Ethics of the Fathers] 1:6). Let us examine these two forms of friendship.

A person needs a *haver li-de'agah,* a person in whom one can confide both in times of crisis, when distress strikes, and in times of glory, when one feels happy and content. In both instances, the need to share despair as well as joy is overwhelming. By confiding in somebody and sharing with a thou one's grief and woe, one may lighten his load and alleviate his misery. The mere fact that somebody is listening to one's tale of woe has a redemptive impact upon the unfortunate sufferer. *"De'agah be-lev ish yashhenah,* anxiety in the heart makes it stoop," says Proverbs (12:25); but the alternate homiletical reading of the last word as *yesihenah*, suggests, "let him talk of his anxieties with others" (Yoma 75a).

On the other hand, the ability to share good news with somebody enhances the joy and happiness of the person upon whom God bestowed His grace. Somehow, misery and joy cannot remain isolated, immovable experiences. If they do remain imprisoned, then the suffering is magnified and the happiness is curtailed. Both the passional as well as the eudaemonic experience [the experience of happiness] push on, expand and urge man to release them to others and make them communal experiences. I know now how powerful this urge of communicating joy or suffering to others is. Woe to the person who cries or dances in seclusion. "She weeps bitterly in the night" (Lamentations [Eikhah] 1:2).

Not in everybody does one confide; not with everybody may we share our grief or excitement. For this purpose alone, one must have a *haver le-de'ah*, a friend in whom he or she has absolute trust and faith, a person about whom one has no fear that he is an insincere and false friend who will derive malicious delight from this misery and become green with envy when told about success. Marriage as a metaphysical community provides two lonely individuals with the friendship necessary for sharing one's experiences.

The union between Adam and Eve is an experiential one. They established a community of destiny, of feelings, of emotional vibrations — a union of two lonely hearts which beat with the same rhythm.

The second form of friendship, the highest and most noble, is achieved by individuals who have a common commitment, a dedication to common goals, who dream, hope, pray for the realization of a common great idea. The most exalted friendship finds its fulfillment in a comradeship sharing not only emotions but ideas as well. The relationship between *rav* and *talmid*, between Torah teacher and student, is characteristic of the beautiful friendship which is nurtured by common commitment and common sacrificial action. Of course, marriage, if it is to last, is fundamentally a community of commitments, a moral normative community, dedicated to a great vision and a noble idea.

The Torah has defined the central commitment of the marital community in an unequivocal manner. "Therefore shall a man leave his father and his mother and shall cleave unto his wife and they shall be one flesh" (Gen. 2:24). There is an equation here. The marital community replaces the parental community. Until one's marriage, the young man or woman belonged to a parental community consisting of three *personae*: the husband, wife, and child. On the day of their marriage they leave the community into which they were cast by the Almighty and substitute for it a marital community which they enter voluntarily, by free choice.

Apparently, the marital community has something in common with the parental. Moreover, the former is an extension of the latter. It is a change of name but not of substance. The marital community, notwithstanding the fact that only two people join it at the outset, is also a threefold affair. Who is the mysterious member of that community? Of course, it is the child who is unborn as yet, as verse 24 suggests. The child is anticipated at the very outset. Two join in order to expect a third member to enter the same community. Why is the child so important? Because in order that the marital union be a community of moral commitments and sacrificial dedication, the presence of the child is indispensable. What is the common commitment of the parents? What is the common vision that unites the parental community? The Torah has stated about Abraham, "For I have known him, that he shall command his children and his household after him that they shall keep the way of the Lord, to do righteousness and justice ..." (Gen. 18:19).

The parental household is a part of the great, endless community of the *masorah*, our tradition, whose task it is to pass on the covenant from generation to generation, from century to century, from millennium to millennium. Each parental household is dedicated to the same ideal, to participate in the march of the generations toward that final day on which every being will be redeemed and communion between man and God will be established, never to be lost.

The parental and marital communities are metaphysical ones in terms of substance and goals. Father, mother and child form an ontological unity dedicated to the realization of the will of God. Their existences are intertwined, their destinies interwoven, as they merge existentially into one being.

❧ *Marriage*

Two Theories of Marriage

There are two basic theories about the institution of marriage. One theory developed a *transeunt** axiology, that is, a value system that finds the meaning of matrimony *outside* of the matrimonial union. The other theory developed an *immanent* matrimonial value system, discovering meaning *within*.

According to proponents of the transeunt value system, marriage is committed to promoting the welfare of the group. The latter's survival is the main goal pursued by the two individuals united in marriage. It is irrelevant whether the term "group" is understood in a liberal fashion at the level of human universality and equality, that is, as the human race as such, or is rather interpreted in a restrictive manner, referring to a particular community. What is significant in the transeunt theory

---

Transeunt is outer-directed, while *immanent* is inner-directed. *Axiology* means value system—eds.

is the idea that the collective is sovereign over the individual and that marriage actually places the two individuals at the service of society.

Basically, this is not only a collectivist doctrine, but a positivist-naturalistic one as well. It denies the unique and specific in the marital union of two humans; it sees the union within the natural scheme of things, comparing it to the process of pollination in the vegetative world or seasonal mating in the zoological kingdom, where, indeed, the existence of the individual plant or animal makes sense only within the context of the species.

The theory of immanent axiology shifts the center of gravity from without to within the matrimonial union. Accordingly, the main value of marriage is to be found not in its collective utility, but in its creating a personal experience that enriches and enhances the lives of two individuals who were drawn to each other. Humans, this immanent theory of meaning argues, thirst for love and fellowship. They crave life in community, personalistic union, sharing destiny with somebody of the opposite sex. In marriage they find fulfillment. Procreation, according to this philosophy, is not the central theme of marriage. A childless marriage is just as sacred as one blessed with offspring, since the meaningfulness of the matrimonial union is to be found in the self-fulfillment of the wedded partners themselves rather than in the benefits which accrue to society. Thus, matrimonial individualism substitutes for matrimonial collectivism, and romanticism for utilitarianism.

The Biblical Perspective

When we examine this controversy in light of the Biblical story of creation, we discover that the Bible operates with both motifs, the objective-transeunt and the subjective-immanent. In the first account of the creation of man, the sexual union of male and female, *zakhar u-nekevah*, serves only one task: procreation. Man and woman are told to "Be fruitful and multiply"

(Gen. 1:28). The propagation of the race is the overriding — if
not the sole — motif of the sexual union. However, in the second
account of the creation, we encounter a completely different
etiology [description of causes]. The meeting of Adam and Eve,
of man and woman, is precipitated by the feeling of loneliness
and by the basic need for comradeship. "And the Lord God said,
'It is not good that the man be alone; I shall make him a help-
mate opposite him' " (Gen. 2:18).

The cause of marriage is the exasperating and desolate feeling of loneliness; the goal of marriage is the redeeming experience of life in fellowship. While the first account (Gen. 1:27) deals
exclusively with the physiological sexual differentiation of "male
and female" and their joint capacity for procreation, the second
account (Gen. 2:18) completely omitted this aspect of the
male-female relationship. Neither the physiological fact of sexual differentiation nor the biological moment of reproduction is
mentioned in the second account. The blessing — or the summons — of "Be fruitful and multiply" was imparted to an anonymous male and unknown female, but not to the two *personae*
Adam and Eve. In contrast to the sexual polarity of male and
female, *zakhar u-nekevah*, the Bible switches to *ish* and *ishah*,
man and woman, and "a helpmate opposite him, *ezer ke-negdo*."
Apparently, according to the second account, God was concerned
not with the couple's biological motives and goals, with the
meeting of male and female for the express purpose of procreation, but with the spiritual incompleteness of lonely man and
his need for ontological oneness with another individual. In a
word, the focal point in the second story of the emergence of man
is not the biological urge, but the tragic urge of man who as the
only conscious being in creation is well aware of his greatness
and the vast opportunities which lie before him, and at the same
time, of his inner contradictions, imperfections and final defeat.

In the first account, the Bible mentions this procreative
urge in the context of natural man who is immersed in a
non-purged and non-redeemed existence. At the level of natu-

ralness and immediacy, the sexual meeting, as is the case with animals, represents the *élan vitale,* the vital force, the biological push which is focused on the race or the species rather than on the individual. Within the natural scheme of things, the individual finds himself in bondage to the species. In this context, the individual, instead of acting spontaneously, reacts compulsively to the mechanical pressures of its own insensate nature. The individual is able neither to master nor to sublimate the biological urge. Hence, the natural drives of the individual — in particular the sex drive — aim at the survival of the collective. At the plane of naturalness, the Bible agrees with the positivists that the sex union pursues an extraneous goal and does not serve the individual, since natural man is a stranger to himself and lacks the very existential experience of himself as an "I." This is, in essence, the first story of the creation of man.

With the emergence, in the second chapter of Genesis, of spiritual man, the transeunt, outer-directed, naturalistic meaningfulness had to be replaced by another set of inner-individualistic semantics or meanings. The greatness and dignity of spiritual man consists exactly in his complete liberation from servitude to the class or species, in his substituting inward centeredness for outward surface existence.

Within such a context, marriage had to assume a different meaning, expressing not only the need of the race but also (and perhaps mainly) the desire of the human individual. Within the frame of reference of the human personality, even the reproductive urge is no longer to be interpreted in terms of biological mechanics blindly serving an extraneous group, but is nurtured by teleological-axiological motifs [motives of purpose and value]. In fact, Halakhah interprets the Divine blessing of "Be fruitful and multiply" in normative terms. Procreation is not only a biological capacity with which God provided man, but also a halakhic commitment with which God charged man. The mechanical motivation and biological push have been sublimated and raised to a level of ethical meaningfulness and intentionality. We no longer deal with mechanical motives, but with spiritual purposiveness. "Man and woman" replace "male and female," and their meeting presses for a more exalted togetherness experience, one whose aim is not only the survival of the race but also the formation and extension of a small, modest community.

The equation of the matrimonial relationship with the parental one and the substitution of the former for the latter holds the key to the teleology of marriage of spiritual man and woman. The marital community which supersedes the parent-child community must in turn become a parental community. Spiritual man, in his search for an existential partner, destroys the child-parent community and founds upon its ruins his own marital community, but his triumph is of transitory nature. His goal will not be achieved unless the matrimonial twofold community is elevated to a parental threefold one which, in turn, will be disrupted again by the spiritual man of the succeeding generation. Through experiencing this dramatic flow of events of destroying in order to build and building in order to be destroyed, man realizes his quest for the origin or source and gradually moves closer and closer to God.

Biological Motives and Teleological Commitments Converge

Halakhah merged both accounts of creation of man into one texture in which biological motives and teleological commitments are interwoven. Seen from the halakhic viewpoint, matrimonial community is not realized without embracing three personae. At this level, marriage redeems the productive urge from its animal species orientation and turns it into a spiritual tragic longing of man for his origin or source. The instinctive roar of the animal driven by biological pressure and pushed mechanically to the female in order to reproduce becomes a human metaphysical cry of lonely man and lonely woman for fatherhood and motherhood.

The collectivist theory is workable in the world of natural man but has no validity when extended to spiritual man, since the dignity of the latter is lost in such a philosophy of marriage. If natural biological procreation is the sole purpose of marriage, why not do away with the whole institution? Let man and woman lead a promiscuous life and the cause of reproduction will then be well served. As a matter of fact, totalitarian governments toyed with this idea. Nazi Germany tried to practice that. Of course, the proponents of the collectivist theory will meet this argument with the explanation that procreation includes not only biological conception and birth, but also the intellectual and moral upbringing of the child. Promiscuity, the collectivists say, would hinder the moral and cultural development of the child. Therefore, they argue, it is worthwhile to maintain and protect the institution of marriage. However, we may ask, why not entrust the state with the task of educating the child in both realms — the technico-scientific and the spiritual-moral? Who laid down the law, we may ask the positivist, that only father and mother united in matrimony are fit to perform this mission?

On the other hand, to base marriage on subjective love and the happiness experienced by two individual partners united in matrimony — as the romanticists, with their theory of immanent semantics, tried to do — is a very risky undertaking. Who knows what genuine love is? And who can guarantee that this sentiment will not exhaust itself with the passage of time and with the experience of boredom and fatigue engendered by monotony? In fact, the trouble with modern marriages stems from the overemphasis placed on the element of subjectivity in marriage. In general, to exclude the child from the marriage semantics and teleology is a result of selfishness and short-sightedness. The Halakhah says marriage fulfills a basic need of the human personality, namely, the need for existence in community. However, this community can be attained only through the quorum required by God in his original scheme of creation. The quorum consists of three people, and one of the three is a child. In the threefold community, the two original partners find their happiness and self-fulfillment.

Moreover, a person craves not only love to be bestowed upon him, but also love to be given by him to others. Loving is perhaps a more exalted experience than that of being loved. The urge to love is directed not only at people who do already exist, but at someone as yet unborn.

The lonely person yearns on the one hand to join another real person, to fill his life with the essence of another real life which has been summoned by God into his service, and, on the other hand, to create a new life to whose growth and development the lonely individual commits himself *a priori* fully and unreservedly.

The two lonely individuals with their urge to love commit themselves to creativity in order to love someone who will emerge in the course of time as a new member of the small community they founded together. This someone, as yet hidden in the recesses of the anonymity of non-being, gives purpose and meaning to the community and helps father and mother to find themselves and their exact position in creation. To repeat, the need for loving finds fulfillment in the act of creation. The "I" summons the "thou" into existence (to use an existentialist term) in order to shower love and affection upon the other. Loving means ecstatic gazing at a thou who belongs to and is rooted in the I.

In this context, we may say that sexual love is the expression of the powerful will to create in order to love, to give of oneself not only to others who do exist but also to those who do not exist as yet and who will at some point in time demand the love, care and devotion of the creator. Two lonely individuals meet and vow faith in each other; they form a community. They are driven by a natural sexual instinct, impanted by the Creator, in order to fulfill an ethico-metaphysical norm of "the world will be built with *hesed"* (Psalms 89:3) — to create in order to bestow *hesed* upon one's handiwork. In marriage they are summoned to cast their glance not only outside of themselves, namely at their respective partners, but at the other side of creation — at a child whose name is not as yet to be found in the register of creation.

Imitatio Dei

Fundamentally, man imitates his Creator. God created the world because He wanted to give of Himself to something outside of Himself. Yet, the act of creation of the world contains an awesome dichotomy of which our mystics were well aware. God is Infinity — all-inclusive and all-exclusive. There is no thou, there is no I, there is only He.

The ontology of the Book of Exodus, its theory of being, has taught us that God is Existence par excellence. The exalted name of "I am what I am" (Ex. 3:14) was interpreted by Philo (Quod Deterius Potiori Insidiari Soleat [That the Worse Is Wont to Attack the Better] 44.160; De Mutatione Nominum [On the Change of Names] 2.11; De Somniis [On Dreams] 39.230-40.231) and Maimonides (*Guide to the Perplexed* I:63) as expressing the equation of Divinity and Existence. Whatever exists, exists in Him, by Him, and through Him. The ontological autonomy of creation [its independent existence] is a contradiction in terms. Consequently, to say that there is a separate world which confronts God as an entity *per se* would be sheer absurdity.

Nevertheless, we Jews believe in the act of creation and we speak of the triple relationship of God, man, and world. We have always rejected the crude pantheism* of the mystics. How could the world be created outside of God if there is no outside? How could He impart an infinitesimal spark of His Being to some-

---

* Pantheism is the theory that God and the world are identical.—eds.

thing or somebody outside of Him? Does not finitude plus Infinity equal infinity? This antinomy [contradiction] will, of course, never be resolved. It will remain a mystery, a *mysterium tremendum*. However, the Jewish mystics who many a time substituted symbol for concept, sensuous metaphor for abstract thought, equated creation with a movement of recoil on the part of God. The Almighty, they said, sacrificed His all-inclusiveness, His all-consuming infinity, and withdrew from a here-and-now coordinate system and retreated into transcendence in order to let a world emerge outside of Him. He created a world in order to care, to sustain, and to love. Creation, according to the mystics, is sacrificial Divine action. God retreated and left a void for the universe to fill. Similarly, the two lonely human beings who are driven to creativity by their yearning for giving and bestowing love engage in sacrificial action and offer everything they cherish for the sake of the new member; they engage in *Imitatio Dei* by withdrawing from self-centered romanticism into a *hesed*-oriented community which binds man to a life yet unborn.

At this level, sexual activity is redeemed by infusing it with a metaphysical mystery theme — namely, man's desire to give love. One must love not only the real, but the unreal as well, in order to make it real. When Eve gave birth to Seth, the Bible relates, "And Adam lived for 130 years and begot a son in his own likeness and his image" (Gen. 5:3). Adam imitates God — he creates in his own image. The central Judaic ethical norm to walk in God's footsteps and to imitate Him obligates man to become a creator.

Objectivity and Subjectivity

At this juncture, however, let us digress and examine the problem of objectivity and subjectivity in Judaism. This examination will provide us with the proper background against which to view the institution of marriage.

We know very well that Judaism has always demanded that

the religious gesture, though steeped in the deepest strata of the human personality, must be objectified and crystallized in concrete physical deeds. There are two aspects to the religious gesture in Judaism: strict objective discipline and exalted subjective romance. Both are indispensable. For instance, the commandment of *Shema* requires, on the one hand, an inner act of surrender to the will of the Almighty. On the other hand, this subjective experience of submission must be translated into a physical act of reciting the *Shema*. The same is true of prayer. It consists of both experiencing the complete helplessness of man, his absolute dependence upon God, and the performance of the ritual of prayer, of reciting fixed texts. The Bible spoke of the commandment to love one's neighbor (Lev. 19:18). However, in Talmudic literature, emphasis was placed not only upon sentiment, but upon action, which is motivated by sentiment. The *Hoshen Mishpat*, the Jewish code of civil law, analyzes not human emotions but actual human relations. The problem of the *Hoshen Mishpat* is not what one feels toward the other, but how he acts toward him.

Judaism has always believed that wherever actions are fair and relations are just, whenever man is able to discipline himself and develop dignified behavioral patterns, the latter are always accompanied by corresponding worthy emotions. Feelings not manifesting themselves in deeds are volatile and transient; deeds not linked with inner experience are soulless and ritualistic. Both the subjective as well as the objective component are indispensable for the self-realization of the religious personality. Yet Halakhah lays emphasis upon actions rather than upon experiences, for it is confident that, while actions are capable of stirring the soul, exciting the imagination and firing the heart, feelings — no matter how noble and dignified, no matter how strong and violent — may exhaust themselves in an inner tempest without breaking through to the surface at all. Man, Halakhah has been teaching us, must first of all respond to the call of duty and act in accordance with Divine discipline.

Only then may he relive these acts of discipline as fascinating ideals and great experiences. The central dimension of Judaism is the *voluntas*, the will; God summons man to affirm the binding authority of the Divine norm. Only then does an inner relationship between God and man begin to bud and blossom. Judaism is first a discipline and second a romance.

In light of this thesis, we may say that the marital union is both an objective institution and a subjective experience. Of course, the motivating force driving man to unite with another self, wholly and forever, is the distressing feeling of an incomplete lonely existence which can be redeemed only through love. The latter constitutes a very important element in the formation and sustenance of the marriage community. The Bible often mentions love in conjunction with the act of entering into matrimony. Yet, to confine the essence of marriage to love would be tantamount to building a magnificent edifice upon quicksand. First, as we mentioned before, it is impossible to determine the genuineness and the depth of the love feeling. Many times the latter expresses merely a surface transient emotion which is due to physical attraction. Second, no one can predict how long love will endure. The permanency of emotion, no matter how sincere and truthful, is always doubtful. Third, love can be given to many. It is not necessarily limited to one person. That is why Halakhah used as its base of operation not the subjective feeling of marital love, but the objective awareness of marital commitment. The latter expresses itself in the reaching of a covenantal arrangement between two individuals who, desirous of forming a community, commit themselves to each other.

The Bible equated the great historical covenant binding the charismatic community to God with the limited private covenant that unites two individuals in matrimony. On the one hand, the great covenant has been compared by the prophets time and again to the betrothal of Israel to God; on the other hand, the ordinary betrothal of woman to man has been raised to the level of covenantal commitment. Marriage as such is called *berit*, a covenant. Apparently, the Bible thinks that the redeeming power of marriage consists in personalizing the sexual experience, in having two strangers, both endowed with equal dignity and worth, meet. And the objective medium of attaining that meeting is the assumption of covenantal obligations which are based upon the principle of equality.

Hence, we have a clue to the understanding of the nature of matrimony. All we have to do is analyze the unique aspects of covenantal commitment and apply them to the matrimonial commitment.

Covenantal Commitments

What is the nature of the covenantal contractual commitment in contradistinction to an ordinary civil agreement? In order to have a fuller understanding of the distinctiveness of these two relationships, it would be helpful to consider first that which is common and identical in both obligations, the Biblical-covenantal and the civil.

Both agreements are entered into voluntarily by two parties who act in freedom and by choice. Only two *personae* can enter into a contractual agreement, be it of a metaphysical-Biblical or civil nature. If A looks upon himself as a free person while considering B as a person-object who was created in order to serve A, there is no need for any contractual agreement since the autonomous person may lay claim to the services of the object person without the benefit of an agreement.

Hence, the element of reciprocity is *eo ipso* implied in any contractual agreement. William Blackstone's famous definition of the contract as "an agreement upon sufficient consideration to do or not to do a particular thing" contains the element of reciprocity. Any negotiable instrument (not a contract under seal) is always reached in consideration of an equivalent suffered by one for the promise of another. The Halakhah is in full concurrence with this opinion. Halakhah requires a reciprocal act by both parties binding themselves under an agreement. The legal mode of acquisition called *kinyan sudar*, whereby one party obligates itself in return for an object, the *sudar*, given by the other party, symbolizes mutuality. This law, which is as ancient as Judaism itself, is mentioned in the Book of Ruth.

> *Now this was the custom in former time in Israel, in cases of redemption or exchange: to confirm all things, a man would take off his sandal and give it to his neighbor; and this was the practice in Israel. So when the redeemer said to Boaz, "Acquire it for yourself," he took off his sandal (4:7-8).*

Now let us turn to an analysis of the basic traits of the covenantal agreement which lend the latter its uniqueness. In my view, there are two basic traits by which the covenant is singled out as a unique commitment.

While a civil obligation affects only the property rights of the parties involved in the agreement, a covenantal obligation embraces the very existential experience and places the parties as spiritual personalities in an existential mutual relationship. When God reached the covenant with His chosen community, He was concerned not only with the worldly goods He placed at its disposal, but with the people as people themselves. He claims not only our material but our spiritual possessions as well. He lays claim to body and soul, to perception and thought, to experience and idea. God owns our very lives, our very essence and existence, our very selves. The covenant was many times sealed with blood. "And Moses took the blood and sprinkled upon the people and said, 'Behold the blood of the covenant which the Lord hath made with you concerning all these words'" (Exodus 24:8). God, through the covenant, acquired unlimited ownership of our very selves. We became His people in the absolute sense of the word. It is self-evident that since mutuality is an indispensable element of definition of any agreement including the covenantal, the personalistic aspect of the latter applies to the commitment assumed by God vis-á-vis His people as well. He is our God.

Hence, the chosen community lays existential claims to God as its God. The community belongs to God, and at the same time God belongs to the community. There is ontological reciprocity in the covenantal contract in that each party incurs metaphysical obligations and acquires metaphysical rights. The covenantal ontic agreement is an act of reciprocal giving and accepting at a personalistic level. "I will take you to Me for a people and I will be to you a God" (Exodus 6:7).

The covenant stands out as a unique obligation because of another characteristic trait, namely, the permanency and constancy of the relationship assumed. Let us analyze what permanency and constancy mean within the context of the covenantal community. Historical development *per se* is synonymous with steady change. Nothing in history persists; nothing is unalterable. There are no fixed positions in history — political, economic, cultural or religious. Everything is in a state of flux, or metamorphosis. Old forms are discarded for the sake of new ones which in turn will become old and obsolete and be cast off for the sake of newer ones. History is continuous becoming, steady transformation, and it reminds us of the old imagery of Heraclitus — of tide coming and receding, always taking something along with itself or bringing something new to the shores.

The covenant introduces into the historical ever-changing reality an element of persistence or constancy. Through the covenant the God-man drama becomes protected from the arbitrariness of destiny. Something permanent is brought into the historical occurrence. Within the covenant community relationships retain their identity no matter how powerful and how staggering the forces of historical changes are. Whatever may transpire, however overpowering the historical event, the historical covenantal community will never sever its relationship with God. The law of historical movement applicable to finite reality forfeits its validity when related to the covenantal community where finitude is dovetailed with infinity. This steadfastness and loyalty is the most characteristic feature of the community's act of faith.

Faith's Covenant

Abraham, the Knight of Faith, knew the secret of this kind of loyalty. Countless generations after him have demonstrated the same ability to believe, to be attached and dedicated to an old covenant which many a time has weighed heavily on our frail shoulders and which quite often has appeared to the human eye to be out of context with historical realities. This kind of loyalty and faith is anomalous; it is, to use the Platonic-Kierkegaardian term, a Divine madness, a passion from which our people cannot liberate itself. Of course, this loyalty is nurtured by a great all-enveloping, all-overwhelming and all-consuming love between God and His charismatic community. It is nurtured by a love which does not fade with the passage of time and our failure to find a rationale for our paradoxical historical experience.

We read in the Song of Songs (7:1), "Return, return, O Shulamite; return, return, that we may look upon you." The *Midrash Rabbah* interpreted this strange dialogue between an anonymous interrogator and the love-intoxicated Shulamite as symbolic of the unique steadfastness, fidelity and commitment exhibited by the charismatic community toward God. Return, O Shulamite, from your absurd engagement to your beloved, since even the strongest of bonds is dissoluble. Times have changed. History marches on. The covenantal union is no longer beneficial. On the contrary, it has become a source of misery and distress. The interrogator suggests the termination of the old covenantal relationship binding the Shulamite to her beloved. The Shulamite, however, does not attempt to rationalize her absolute loyalty and her unqualified dedication to her beloved. She admits that her loyalty and dedication are a mystery even to herself. It is futile to debate or to analyze her unswerving loyalty because she acts like one who, under the sway of a great ecstatic experience, has plunged into a never-ending dance whose very rhythm is intoxicating. In short, the covenantal community is metahistorical as far as it takes up fixed positions amid ever-changing historical events.

In view of the above-mentioned Biblical equation of the marriage union with the covenant, we may say that within the matrimonial covenantal community, a relationship prevails that is similar to that characteristic of the metaphysical-covenantal: total commitment and unchangeability. In other words, the two unique traits of the covenant are indicative of the matrimonial community as well.

Even in a community like the matrimonial, afflicted as it is with all the frailties and imperfections of the human performance, the mutual relationship of the two partners is of an absolute nature that encompasses not only property rights, but existential rights as well. The partners belong to each other in a peculiar way; they are united by a personal bond which reaches deeply into the most hidden spheres of the human personality. The matrimonial agreement asserts itself in total commitment, in unqualified involvement. Judaism is in disagreement with both the Catholic and the secular interpretation of marriage. On the one hand, marriage, according to Judaism, need not be solemnized by any cultic or sacerdotal act at all. It need not be a mystery in order to gain acceptance. If marriage is to be sanctified, then, Judaism maintains, man is the only one who may and can sanctify it.

There is, according to the Jewish view, no need for a supernatural act of Divine grace to remedy or redeem the sexual activity of man. The natural becomes personal; the vulgar refined; and the profane sacred — not by the intervention of God, but by that of man. Man was summoned by God to purge and to redeem himself and to raise the instinctual and the natural to the level of the personal and meaningful.

On the other hand, marriage is not merely a civil institution, a *quid pro quo* arrangement pertaining to property and pleasure by two individuals starved for erotic love and a convenient life. Of course, the marriage community is established by human beings. It is a human institution created by the mutual consent of both parties. Yet, its human origin does not diminish its metaphysical meaningfulness. Marriage is more than a formal community or a useful partnership. It is rather a covenantal community, which is nurtured by the awareness of absolute belonging to each other. Married life is an existence in fellowship, togetherness. In it, man finds completeness and existential fulfillment. The story of the first marriage in Genesis confirms this thesis, "And Adam said, 'This is now bone of my bones and flesh of my flesh; she shall be called woman because she was taken out of man'" (Gen. 2:23).

The marriage, like the covenantal union, distinguishes itself by a deep sense of loyalty and faith. Erotic love, as an emotion, lacks constancy and permanence. Fundamentally, it is an orgiastic experience, by its very nature transient. The desire for variety and change constitute the very essence of sexual love. The lover, the Don Juan, moves excitedly from love to love. Driven by an uncontrollable force, he must always give up on love in order to be able to enjoy another. What he would want to do is to have every possible love experience at one instance and drink madly out of the cup of love experience to the dregs. Identity and monotony undermine the very essence of the Eros. The madness to enjoy passing pleasures pushes the Eros along the path of excitement and adventure. The Eros knows no repetition. It searches for new forms of beauty, new faces, new smiles, and new passions. It excites in the new, showing contempt for old.

Marriage, charged with the task of redeeming the erotic experience, tries to free the latter from the whimsicality of the Eros and from the capriciousness of the aesthete. The task of marriage is to teach man to find love in identity and continuity.

Marriage is basically supposed to accomplish the redeeming of the sex life from the aesthetic and hedonic and its conversion to an ethical moral experience whose intensity is not weakened through repetition. While the central category of the aesthete is one of the moment, that of the ethicist is of continued action. Hence, marriage, seen from the artistic vantage point, is but a transient affair; however, while observed under the aspect of the moral law, it acquires the ability to survive the changing moods of the Eros.

Within the frame of reference of marriage, love becomes not an instinctual reaction of an excited heart to the shocking sudden encounter with beauty, but an intentional experience in reply to a metaphysical ethical summons, a response to a great challenge, replete with ethical motifs. Love, emerging from an existential moral awareness, is sustained not by the flame of passion, but by the strength of a Divine norm whose repetitious fulfillment re-awakens its vigor and force. The marriage partners, by imitating God who created a world in order to be concerned with and care for it, extend the frontiers of their communal living to their offspring, and by questing to love someone who is yet unborn, defy the power of erotic change and flux. The ethical yearning to create and share existence with someone as yet unknown redeems *hedone* by infusing it with axiological normative meaning and thus gives it a new aspect — that of faith. Since our eternal faith in God is something which defies rationalization, the mutual temporal faith of man and woman united in matrimony is just as paradoxical. History does not warrant our unswerving religious faith; likewise, utilitarian psychology denies the element of faith in the marriage institution.

Marriage is, as we said, indeed a covenant; and when the prophet Hosea portrayed the eternal bond between God and Israel in glowing ecstatic words, he exclaimed that Israel is betrothed to God in faith, in justice, and for all eternity. "And I will betroth you unto Me forever; I will betroth you unto Me with righteousness and justice, and with lovingkindness and mercy. And I will betroth you unto Me with faithfulness; then you shall know the Lord" (Hosea 2:21-22). This idea of total commitment finds its expression in the Halakhah: any stipulation which frees the husband from a duty which the marriage act implies is invalid if it affects not property rights but the personal union (Kiddushin 19b).

The Meaning of Covenantal Marriage

What is the substance of the ethical norm that is supposed to guide the matrimonial community and is responsible for the latter's transformation into a covenantal community? The marriage institution finds its expression in a metaphysical-personal fellowship, in existential togetherness. However, this idea of a covenantal marriage community, if spelled out in practical halakhic terms, has a sixfold meaning.

First, *a covenantal marriage is a sacrificial community*. Sacrificial action is required from both parties. The term sacrificial should not be understood in a colloquial sentimental sense but in that of catharsis, signifying carnal withdrawal from easily attainable pleasures. The main motif implied in the marriage vow is the sexual commitment between pleasure-loving I and pleasure-loving thou. The prohibition against adultery is the basis of married life according to Halakhah. If one would stipulate in the marriage agreement that adultery would be permitted, the stipulation would be null and void. To marry means to give up freedom of choice with respect to one's sex gratification. Since the culpability of sexual activity manifests itself in the depersonalization of the thou, variety in one's sexual life is the most depersonalizing and vulgarizing factor. Therefore, exclusiveness in sexual life represents the very essence of the sexual ethos. The conquest of the powerful instinct of sexual promiscuity hallows the sex union. However, the catharsis in sexual life according to Halakhah does not exhaust itself in the prohibition of extramarital sex relations. Its demands are by far greater. The very intimate sex relationship of husband and wife is disciplined by Halakhah. Strict laws of separation have been formulated which drastically reduce the sexual activity of the couple and the Halakhah is persistent in its demand for full implementation of those restrictive laws. For only withdrawal and self-discipline purge and redeem the primitive and vulgar sex drive — a biological pressure which is common to man and beast.

Second, *a covenantal marriage is a hedonic, pleasure-oriented community*. Judaism did not overlook or underestimate the physical aspects of marriage. On the contrary, once sacrificial withdrawal from the sinful erotic paradise of change and variety is completed, the natural element in marriage comes to the fore. The two partners owe each other not only fidelity, but also full gratification of their sexual needs. Refusal or failure by one of the partners to satisfy the conjugal rights of the other is sufficient reason for divorce. Each one must observe these laws of consortium with regard to the other. The marriage must not be converted into an exclusively spiritual fellowship. Marriage without carnal enjoyment and erotic love is contrary to human nature and is to be dissolved. The ethic of marriage is hedonistic, not monastic.

The conjugal rights which are mentioned in the Torah have to be complied with by every husband in accordance with his physical capacity and occupation. The wife may prevent the husband from taking extended business trips which interfere with the fulfillment of his connubial duties. He may leave town only if she permits him to do so. She may also enjoin him from changing trades, should the change result in less frequent cohabitation. Withholding of the conjugal rights is forbidden, as it is written, "her food, her raiment and her conjugal rights he shall not diminish" (Ex. 21:10). In case of illness or incapacitation, a waiting period of six months is granted. If, at the conclusion of this period, the physical condition of the husband does not improve, he must either obtain her consent or else divorce her and pay her the value of the *ketubah* (Maimonides, *Hilkhot Ishut* [Laws of Marriage] 14: 1, 2, 7).

Interesting is another law that is indicative of our realistic approach to the marriage institution.

> *If a woman prevents her husband from having sexual relations with her, she is called a moredet, a rebellious wife. [Beit Din] inquires of her why she rebelled. If she said: I dislike him and cohabitation with him is impossible for me, [Beit Din] forces him to divorce her. For a wife is not a prisoner such that she must consort with a person whom she despises (Ibid. 14:8).*

There is no doubt that Judaism holds that the sex instinct, besides serving other purposes, is an important drive in itself when it is raised to a higher personal level. Sexual activity is also committed to fostering and promoting love-sentiments by making two free individuals depend upon and help each other in the hour of physiological need. There is an element of *hesed* involved in a sexual life organized and redeemed through catharsis.

In support of this thesis, theologians always employ the argument from the non-periodic character of passion. The fact that the sexual desire in humans, in contradistinction to animal drives, is aroused continually and is not confined to certain periods, proves that sexual life is legitimate even when it is divorced from other goals (cf. Emil Brunner, *The Divine Imperative*, p. 367). Halakhah generally opposes birth control for reasons completely different from the ones advanced by the Catholic church. God approves of the *hedone* involved in the sex-act for its own sake. We object in general to birth control because any sex-life can be enjoyed only if man is ready to accept responsibility for the pleasure he derives from it. Marriage is an institution based upon responsibilities. Yet those responsibilities are not confined to the woman one marries but extend to the potential offspring of this marriage. Why am I entitled to deny existence to the unborn?

Third, *a covenantal marriage is a natural procreative community*. Whatever one may say about the purpose, the teleology, of marriage, we must admit that both husband and wife have been provided by the Creator with inalienable rights to parenthood. The latter is not only a norm but a right as well. The marriage partners are entitled not only to give to and accept from each other but also to make it possible for the other partner to fulfill his or her desire for a child. This is the way in which marriage was planned by the Creator, and no one has a right to deny this privilege to either of the parents. If a husband makes his wife use contraceptives, she can bring suit for divorce against him. "If he imposes on her a vow to behave during the sexual intercourse in a manner which will prevent her from conceiving" — they end the marriage in a divorce (Maimonides, *Hilkhot Ishut* [Laws of Marriage] 14:5).

Elkanah was wrong in saying to Hannah: "Hannah, why do you weep? And why do you not eat? And why is your heart grieved? Am I not better to you than ten sons?" (I Samuel 1:8). He did not understand the yearning for love, for self-sacrifice and suprahuman devotion in which a woman finds self-fulfillment. Marriage is consummated only in a community of three.

Fourth, *a covenantal marrriage is a cooperative community*. Husband and wife are bound by mutual civil and economic duties. They form an economic unit. Usually, human separateness and selfishness are demonstrated by one's economic activity and acquisitive efforts, by the ruthlessness of the competitive temper, by placing emphasis upon the possessive pronoun. When the Bible depicts Nabal of Carmel, his avariciousness and parsimony, it stresses the possessive form which he used in the inconsiderate answer he gave to David's emissaries:

> *And Nabal answered David's servants and said: "Who is David? And who is the son of Jesse? There be many servants nowadays that break away every man from his*

master. Shall I then take my bread, and my water, and my flesh that I have killed for my shearers and give it unto men whom I know not whence they be?" (I Samuel 25:10-11).

It is no wonder that the acquisitive instinct appears in the child at the same time that he begins as a separate entity to divorce himself from his surroundings. In other words, possessiveness manifests the first unconscious budding of individuality. We know that historically the whole idea of the full autonomy and dignity of the individual as the king of the universe burst forth with the emergence of capitalism, a social order born out of the human acquisitive spirit, out of man's unlimited selfish fantasy which is committed to the production and possession of material goods.

If man and woman join an existential community and are eager to live in fellowship, the precondition for such a life is the abandonment of the economic barriers separating the individuals. A joint economy, or a household, is essential for the liberation of the individual from his insane seclusion as a separate being shut in within his goods and possessions.

We need not go into details with respect to the economic obligations of the marriage partners. However, this economic community is very important for the success of the marriage. What is important psychologically is the fact that the family constitutes an economic unit in which both are dependent upon each other. The husband, according to the law, is the provider, and the wife is the housekeeper. The husband must support and sustain the wife and she in turn is supposed to run the house. Each one fulfills an assigned task, and they need each other. Two people form a complete economic community. The unworkability of some modern marriages is attributable to the fact that, in many cases, the economic community does not exist. Both the husband and the wife provide, and each one is independent of the other. They are economically uncommitted to each other; there is no cooperative effort. It is a business partnership rather than an economic community.

Fifth, *a covenantal marriage is a community of affection and appreciation*. I am speaking not of erotic love but of gratitude and mutual indebtedness. Besides physical attraction, husband and wife must feel friendship for each other. They should share joys and sorrows since they both are challenged by a common destiny. Emotional togetherness is indispensable in matrimony because their existences merge into one experience.

While on the lower level of sexual activity — either as an it-it contact or an I-it erotic experience — the performance does not involve any value judgment or act of approval. Community-love, like any other feeling of sympathy, is identical with axiological [evaluative] appraisal. At this level — the pandemic, the vulgar and carnal — man and woman cast upon each other an appraising gaze to ascertain whether or not the thou is physically capable of satisfying the other's need. There is a *pragmos*-judgment, a cool business-like assessment of the physical charms of the thou. Neither rejection nor acceptance in an axiological sense is involved. Since at this plane the male and the female do not establish any personal relationship — the contact is technical — there is no opportunity given for axiological judgment. But in contrast to this non-axiological relationship, the erotic love which compels the individual to turn to the thou as a person in his independence and reality, with all the power born out of incessant craving for a fellowship, operates with a value system or axiology of its own. The erotic love turns into friendship and as such it expresses itself in value judgments.

One cannot form a friendship unless he finds in it the realization of a value long cherished by him. If the I disapproves of the thou, no friendship is possible. An existential community can only be realized if there is approval of the thou whom one intends to join; I must discover the thou, recognize him as real and approve of him as good, as a person worthy of my love and friendship. Basically, love expresses itself in commitment, a relationship of dependence; it is an affirmative attitude taken towards a strange existence which works itself out into a desire for self-transcendence. When a man feels love for a woman, he *eo ipso* approves of her. The eros gazes passionately at the other self. He is enraptured at the spectacle of the thou and somehow feels that contact with the thou bolsters his own ego. When a young boy proposes to a girl, he begs her to accept him, to approve of him. He tells her that without her company his life is meaningless, trivial and dull. Such a confession is often not a figment of a sickly fantasy but an objective description of one's state of mind. Love is an enriching, meaning-giving, and uplifting experience, because the lonely individual finds approval by another lonely person, and existential approval is elevating and inspiring. The lack of it might shatter a life.

Axiological approval is a manifestation of *hesed*. The individual who is weary of carrying the existential load alone, weary of his secluded, shut-in egocentricity, finds another self with whom he wants to share his very existence which bursts forth with the elemental power of an active volcano. Each partner goes out of hiding to meet the other. Within the community which is formed, they share not only sexual pleasures but more than that, destiny and existence itself.

The laws pertaining to mourning can only be understood in the light of the destiny community. Husband or wife mourn if one of them dies. Mourning symbolizes a torn emotional unity, love which has no outlet, despair at the incompleteness of one's existence, at something which was torn out of one's very existence.

Sixth, *a covenantal marriage is an educational community*. The household is a school where a child receives his most important training to face the challenges with which life presents him in his adulthood. In education, the distinction of man manifests itself. Man must refashion and recreate himself through education. The latter is the mold in which his natural and innate powers are recast and actualized. God provided man with a great potential, with whose actualization he was charged. By planned and wise exercise of his capacities he can make them useful to himself and to the world. While the animal is in full possession of his powers right at birth and does not have to capture them through a series of steps, man must make an acquisitive effort in order to avail himself of these qualities. This series of steps we call the process of growth and development.

The *Zohar*, besides ascertaining the fact that the process of growth and development is alien in the animal kingdom, explained the unique position which man occupies with regard to his emergence as a human.

> *Come forward and take a look. When an infant is born he is not endowed with Divine power before he is circumcised. With circumcision, a higher spirit begins to stir in him. When he grows up and is well versed in the Torah, the Divine spirit is activated more. If his theoretical knowledge is translated into actions and he observes the laws of the Torah, he becomes inspired by this spirit and ascends to greater heights. If he is fortunate to marry, to beget children and to teach them the law to walk in the ways of the Holy King, then he attains fulfillment and perfection as man. In contradistinction to man, the animal has all its powers at the hour of its birth that it possesses when its life comes to a close (Zohar, Parashat Emor 91b).*

Education is equated by the *Zohar* with an act of liberating man from immediacy and naturalness, from the it-status to the acquisition of an I-awareness, an act of raising himself from a mechanical to a spiritual existence, of transcending himself as a factum [natural reality] and gaining freedom as a free agent. What man acquires is the *it'aruta di-le-eila*, the "high stirring."

This process of growth and development finds its full realization in the creative role that man assumes. Procreation and the raising of a child is the supreme task of man, and only in its fulfillment does he find existential growth. The parent enters a new realm, that of education. He is not only a natural father or mother of the child (at a biological level) but he is also the teacher and guide of the child. He helps the child to free himself from a primitive state of biological existence and to take possession of himself. Every father and mother is the educator of the child, and as such they are engaged in a very creative mission — by far more important than the natural act of bringing forth the child, since the former is a spiritual and intentional act, while the latter is accomplished in a mechanical manner and because of a primordial irresistible drive.

If man imitates God by creating life, this happens in the field of spiritual, not of natural, life. The fertilization of the ovum is as automatic a performance as the process of pollination in the world of plant. If, as we have stated before, man's redemption from an incomplete existence, from the disastrous experience of loneliness and forlornness, can only be consummated by the formation of a threefold community of I, thou, and he, through the Divine act of creation which loving man brings to fulfillment — then with the natural birth of the child the creativity of man has not ended; it has just begun. Man's community is completed only through bringing up of the child, developing his inherent powers, providing him with moral values and befriending him with his Maker. I don't have to waste too many words expounding the halakhic approach to the educational mission of the parent. It was incorporated into the first portion of *Shema* containing the basic tenets of our faith. "These things which I command you today shall be put on your heart, and you shall teach them to your children ..." (Deut. 6:6-7).

Maimonides, in defining the idea of *kabbalat ol malkhut shamayim*, the acceptance of the yoke of Heaven, total commitment to Him, which represents the main motif of the commandment of reciting the *Shema*, writes as follows: "What is he supposed to recite? The three sections, *Shema, Ve-hayah im shamo'a* and *Va-yomer*. One reads first the section of *Shema* because it contains the precepts of unity of God, love for Him and the study of Torah ..." (*Hilkhot Keri'at Shema* [Laws of Reading the *Shema*] 1:2).

Man's involvement with God is only realizable if he is ready to commit his offspring to God by imbuing them with Torah knowledge and Torah ideals. Maimonides writes in *Hilkhot Talmud Torah* [Laws of Torah Study] (1:1-2): "It is the duty of the father to teach his young son Torah as it is said: 'And ye shall teach them to your children to speak of them' (Deut. 6:7).... Just as it is a man's duty to teach his son, so it his duty to teach his grandson, as it is said: 'Make them known unto thy children and children's children' " (Deut. 4:9).

In the Aggadah, God Himself appears in the role of teacher. Every day God spends time instructing young children. Physical creation, sustenance of Being as such, are not enough. When one helps children find themselves by taking hold of their inherent aptitudes and acquainting them with the eternal verities which give man a sense of rootedness — only then is the creative gesture of God completed. Father and mother are not only a procreative natural community, but a creative teaching fellowship whose importance can hardly be overstressed and exaggerated.

At this point we may parenthetically mention the problem of the childless couple. Since existential completeness is possible only in a community of three personae — I, thou, and he — the married couple which was not blessed with a child never rids itself of the loneliness experience which is characteristic of a shattered and imperfect existence.

The answer to this problem is quite simple in light of what was said about the educational community which the parents and child form. Procreation is not creation. The latter is realized not in the fertilization of an ovum but in the formation of the child's spiritual personality, in fostering his or her good qualities and trying to sublimate the child's primitive desires and smooth out his rough edges. This can be accomplished not only by natural parents but by a couple to whom the happiness of natural childbirth was denied. They can become teachers and educators of children and by so doing fulfill their mission and find existential fulfillment in a creative act of education.

Judaism has advanced a new doctrine of teaching. Education is not just a technical activity. It is a soul-performance, an existential involvement of two strangers, an imparting not only of formal knowledge but of a total self-experience, of an ontic awareness. It expresses itself in the emergence of a new fellowship, within which master and disciple share one great adventure, that of creation. Therefore, the union of teacher and disciple does not terminate with the end of actual instruction. The community outlasts the physical nearness of these two individuals; it contains something of the covenantal community. The ideal of the scholar is shining in the Jewish firmament. It outranks every other image, that of king, priest and prophet. The role of the High Priest was defined by Malakhi as consisting not of cultic but of educational duties: "The law of truth was in his mouth and iniquity was not found in his lips; he walked with me in peace and equity and did turn many away from iniquity. For the priest's lips should keep knowledge, and they should seek the law at his mouth for he is the messenger of the Lord of Hosts" (Malakhi 2:6-7). King David was depicted by the Aggadah as a scholar, devoting his time to the study of the law and the dissemination of knowledge. The Prophets found their place among the *hakhmei ha-masorah*, the sages of the transmission. "Moses received the Torah at Sinai and transmitted it to Joshua, who transmitted it to the Elders, who transmitted it to the Prophets ..." (*Avot* [Ethics of the Fathers] 1:1).

There is love for and identification with each other in this community of knowledge. Socrates spoke of the teacher as a midwife who merely helps the child to rediscover himself. This metaphor is in agreement with the Socratic-Platonic viewpoint that all learning is recollection (*anamnesis*), a reawakening of something which is dormant in the pupil. The teacher does not give anything of himself. All he does is bring out whatever the pupil possesses. The task of the teacher is not a creative one, and there is no intimate drawing toward each other involved in teaching. The existential embrace within which pupil and teacher find themselves ontically happy and enjoy a full life is missing in the Platonic philosophy. Judaism saw the teacher as the creator through love and commitment of the personality of the pupil. Both become *personae* because an I-Thou community is formed. That is why Judaism called disciples sons and masters fathers. Maimonides writes *(Hilkhot Talmud Torah* [The Laws of Torah Study] 1:2):

> *This obligation [of teaching Torah] is to be fulfilled not only towards one's son and grandson. A duty rests on every scholar in Israel to teach all disciples, even if they are not his children, as it is said, "and you shall teach them to your children" (Deut. 6:7). The oral tradition teaches: "Your children" includes your disciples, for disciples are called children as it is said: "And the sons of the prophets came forth" (II Kings 2:3).*

Our Talmudic sages stated, "Whoever teaches his friend's son Torah acquires him as a natural child" (Sanhedrin 19b).

When the letter *hei* was added to Abram's name, he became Abraham, the father of many nations, the spiritual father of all he taught (Gen. 17:5). Natural procreative Abramic parenthood was denied to the childless couple, yet the creative Abrahamic parenthood is a challenge which everyone is summoned to meet.

Judaism did not recognize the Roman institution of adoption since the Roman concept is directed toward substituting a legal fiction for a biological fact and thus creating the illusion of a natural relationship between the foster parents and the adopted son. Judaism stated its case in no uncertain terms: what the Creator granted one and the other should not be interfered with; the natural relationship must not be altered. Any intervention on the part of some legal authority would amount to interference with the omniscience and original plan of the Maker. The childless mother and father must reconcile themselves with the fact of natural barrenness and sterility. Yet they may attain the full covenantal experience of parenthood, exercise the fundamental right to have a child and be united within a community of I-thou-he. There is no need to withhold from the adopted child information concerning his or her natural parents. The new form of parenthood does not conflict with the biological relation. It manifests itself in a new dimension which may be separated from the natural one. In order to become Abraham, one does not necessarily have to live through the stage of Abram. The irrevocable in human existence is not the natural but the spiritual child; the threefold community is based upon existential, not biological, unity. The existence of I and thou can be inseparably bound with a third existence even though the latter is, biologically speaking, a stranger to them.

Divorce

Judaism did not recognize the principle of indissolubility of marriage. We do not consider marriage an irrevocable commitment and we sanction divorce as a legitimate means of terminating the marriage vow. However, one may point to the covenantal character of marriage which implies the element of constancy. Whereas erotic love is whimsical and transient, the marriage based on ethical norms of constancy introduces permanence and sameness. If this is so, why was divorce not rejected by Judaism as undermining the covenantal structure of the marriage-community?

The answer to this problem, it appears to me, should be sought at two levels, the philosophy of the personality and the philosophy of the sacred.

First, the philosophy of the personality. There is a dialectical character to the human personality: the numinous and the kerygmatic.* The numinous is the lonely, mysterious Adam who never met Eve and who can never commit himself to the other self since he does not step out of his unique seclusion. He does not care to become acquainted with the thou; he is inner-directed, and his existence expresses itself in a continuous movement of recoil and withdrawal. The kerygmatic personality, in contrast, is lovesick and communion-questing; he is eager to deliver a message to the other self; he tries to abandon all barriers separating him from the person who stands alongside of him. He wants to engage in a dialogue and communicate with Eve. Numinous Adam is mute; kerygmatic Adam finds the speech as the great means of attaining a communal existence. All human institutions which necessarily embrace two or more people are the outgrowth of the creative activity of kerygmatic Adam. Numinous, lonely man is not involved in any social commitments that kerygmatic Adam takes on. The former always remains aloof, for himself, lonely and free. Adam and Eve became wedded partners; yet only the kerygmatic personality took the vow of fidelity and constancy. Numinous Adam and Eve never contracted matrimony since they never met and were never cognizant of each other.

Marriage, notwithstanding its covenantal character, is not an institution of absolute worth. There is an objective bond, yet it is confined to kerygmatic Eve and Adam who can standardize and objectify their experiences. It does not reach into the very core of the personality, which remains a *mysterium*, a subjective experience inexpressible and outside of all media of externalization and objectification. Only social Adam and Eve are wed-

---

* A dialectical character is one that reflects opposites, in this case numinous and kerygmatic aspects of the human personality. "Numinous" refers to that which is apart from the world of ordinary observation and is inexpressible; hence the numinous personality is aloof or apart. In Rudolf Otto's philosophy, the term is used to characterize the experience of the holy, but the Rav here applies it to the secluded and lonely human personality. "Kerygmatic" means bearing a message, so the kerygmatic personality is social man. —eds.

ded; lonely Adam and Eve have never joined this community. Therefore, marriage is changeable because it does not embrace the whole of man. Only a part of him is engaged in this institution, and that is why disengagement is permissible. Numinous man terminates the social commitment of kerygmatic man. If the vow of fidelity did embrace all phases of the existential drama, then marriage would be absolute and hence indissoluble. As a matter of fact, the metaphysical betrothal of the charismatic community to God, "I will betroth you unto Me with faithfulness," can never be broken or ended. The prophet himself says, "I will betroth you unto Me forever ... and you shall know the Lord" (Hosea 2:22). Why is this betrothal different from the ordinary marriage which may end in divorce? Why is the wedlock between God and Israel eternal and can never shake off the trammels of the Divine law? Because the union of man and God is all-embracing, it penetrates every phase of existential adventure. Numinous, lonely man weds himself to the Numinous Lonely God and communion is established — not only between an objectified externalized I and a Thou. A lonesome existence gives itself, unites itself with its lover; there is fusion of a finite life with infinity, and this union or fusion is not limited to a surface experience but involves everything in man, excluding nothing. God and man are united undividedly and hence eternally. That is why Isaiah asked the famous question, "Thus saith the Lord, 'Where is the bill of your mother's divorcement wherewith I have put her away? ...'" (Isaiah 50:1). The bond between God and Israel cannot be terminated in divorce.

Second, the philosophy of the sacred. Marriage is a sacred institution. The term *kiddushin*, sanctification, attests to the quality of sanctity which is implied in the marital contract. It is endowed with a quality which is both remedial and redeeming. The element of the sacred is an outgrowth of the sacrificial action performed by the married partners when there is an act of withdrawal at the hour of carnal madness and concupiscence.

Sacrifice and holiness are synonymous concepts in Judaism.

Of course, the more alluring the vision of conquest, the stronger the temptation, the more intoxicating the performance, the greater and more heroic the act of retreat — the more the threads of the person practicing it are woven into the fabric of sanctity. The person who masters his passions and takes a vow of faithfulness and serenity in the sexual realm, who is disciplined without accepting a morbid monastic approach to sex, leads a holy life. The institution of marriage makes it possible for the individual to achieve a sufficiency of body discipline that lends to him the quality of sanctity. The very marriage agreement is based on the idea of the sacred; both partners are committed to the attainment of a sacred relationship. If the latter is not achieved, the personal moment which is identical with sanctity is lacking.

If the marriage institution is infused with sanctity, then it may become desecrated. Judaism has always maintained that holiness is not something objective inherent in an object, prevailing independently of the way this particular sacred object is treated. We denied the idea that there is sanctity *per se*, a metaphysical endowment which persists irrespective of man's relationship to the object. Such an approach to the idea of the sacred would border on fetishism and primitive taboos. Sanctity is born out of man's actions and experiences and is determined by the latter. The very instant man adopts a coarse attitude towards the hallowed object — the moment of sacredness is eliminated. Sanctity expresses itself not in the formal quality of the object or institution but in a relationship between the latter and man. It is an experience rather than an endowment. If something is not experienced as sacred, the object or the institution forfeits its uniqueness and numinous character. With regard to property of the sanctuary, the holy objects, the Halakhah formulated the law of *yetzi'ah le-hullin*, desanctification, which may occur due to *me'ilah*, complete desecration through unlawful use of and trespass upon things that were set apart as holy.

The same principle applies to matrimony. If the marriage contract has been violated and an act of adultery committed, the covenantal sanctity of marriage is dispelled and the latter is subject to dissolution. Divorce is only the formal validation of an act of disintegration which took place before, the conclusion of a process of profanation of the marriage institution which divested it of its permanency and constancy. Basically, divorce is warranted only in cases of adultery. However, we must remember that there are various degrees of adultery. There are more vulgar and more refined forms of adultery. Whenever husband or wife sincerely desire to terminate the marriage, an act of betrayal is committed. Only the inner commitment to each other and complete personal unity protects the marriage from vulgarization and defilement. The corruption of the sexual feeling manifesting itself in the dislike which one wedded partner feels towards the other, in the sexual disgust and aversion, is considered as adultery since the element of faithfulness and dedication is missing from the marriage. The mere desire for separation and divorce implies treachery and an adulterous motif which deprives the marriage of its sanctity. If matrimony could not temper or domesticate the sexual drive, then it failed to achieve what is most salutary in married life, and divorce terminates a union which has never attained sanctity. In the light of the above, one may understand the Mishnah (Gittin 9:10) which discusses the Torah's statement that one may divorce his wife if he finds an *"ervat davar"*:

> *Beit Shammai says: A man should not divorce his wife unless he found in her a devar ervah, as it is written, "If he found in her an ervat davar" (Deut. 24:1). Beit Hillel says: even if she spoiled his dish. Rabbi Akiva says: even if he found another who is more attractive than she, as it is written, "and she does not find favor in his eyes" (Ibid.).*

Beit Shammai interprets *ervat davar* in its literal sense of adultery. If the *Beit Din* is unable to ascertain adultery, a divorce is not warranted. *Ervat davar* was defined in strictly halakhic juridic terms; only legal blame is a justifying circumstance for divorce. Whatever does not border on formal adultery cannot be taken into account as a ground for the termination of the marriage. Rabbi Akiva changes the semantics of *ervat davar* and raises its meaning to the moral level. Dissolution of a marriage is permissible if he desires another woman; this very desire is an adulterous thought which cancels the pristine sanctity of the marriage. A sinful wish and inner betrayal of the wedded partner desecrates the covenantal endowment of marriage, although in the eyes of society the marriage appears to be perfect and the partners blameless. It is not the juridic aspect that is decisive relative to the sacred covenant of matrimony, but rather the moral one. If his affections were alienated by an adulteress, if he has become estranged from his mate because she no longer attracts him and he does not cherish her companionship any more — then the dissolution has begun already. The marriage has been desecrated and de-covenantalized. The divorce formally concludes a process that set in long before that.

Although divorce has been sanctioned as legitimate means of canceling a marital contract, the Talmudic scholars (Gittin 90b) deplored the separation of husband and wife, particularly if they were married for the first time.

> *R. Elazar says: Even the Altar sheds tears for whoever divorces his first wife, as it is written, "And this you do again, covering the Altar of the Lord with tears, with weeping and with sighing, insomuch that He regarded not the offering any more, nor received it with good will from your hand. Yet you say wherefore? Because the Lord has been witness between you and the wife of your youth against whom you have dealt treacherously; yet she is your companion and the wife of your covenant" [Malakhi 2:13-14].*

Divorce is identified with treacherous contravention of the marital covenant.

R. Haggai says: When the Babylonian exiles returned from exile, the skin of the women's faces became tanned because of exposure to the sun. Many husbands divorced these and married younger and prettier Amonites. The divorcees would circle around the Altar and weep, as Malakhi [2:13] says, "And this you do again, covering the Altar of the Lord with tears, with weeping and with sighing." God said: Who will accept the offering of such husbands who caused so much moaning and weeping? After you have robbed your wives of their youth and beauty you discarded them (Genesis Rabbah 18:5).

The altar is the metaphor for the Divine Court of Justice before which every downtrodden and humiliated person may bring charges of evil treatment against his pursuer and foe.

If any trespass against his neighbor, and an oath be laid upon him to cause him to swear, and the oath come before Thine Altar in this House, then hear Thou in heaven and do, and judge Thy servants, condemning the wicked, to bring his ways upon his head, and justify the righteous, to give him according to his righteousness (I Kings 8:31-32).

Human Sexual Differentiation

Man and woman represent not only two sexes with natural anatomic and physiological differences but two ideas of personality. As biologically distinct beings, they are called male and female, but they are not typical of the human race alone. In the animal kingdom and also in the world of plants sex differentiation is the basic trait of their structure and morphology. What is characteristic of the world of man is that sex-physiology is transformed into sex-personality. There is a man-personality and a woman-personality. They are two individualities with unique existential experiences. The I-awareness contains the moment of sex-personality. The male knows that he exists as a man, the female — as a woman. They experience themselves in different dimensions. The tremor of being manifests itself differently in man and woman.

In Judaism (if it is not distorted by narrow-mindedness and fanaticism) the doctrine of the sex-personality has come to expression at many levels: at the level of creation; at that of the mystical God experience; and at the halakhic.

God has created man and woman and made them dependent upon each other not only physically (for the purpose of gratification of the sexual instinct) but spiritually as well. Each one finds self-fulfillment and completeness redeeming him or her from the devastating experience of loneliness. However, the marriage union would simply fail to achieve this ontic goal if man and woman were not separate sexual personalities, if there were not existential tension between them. For loneliness, expressing the antinomic character of being, that is, the contradiction involved in the very experience of *"esse,"* of being, can only be ameliorated if lonely man meets lonely woman and in their union the reconciliation of existential differences, the paradoxical *coincidentia oppositorum*, the coincidence of opposites, is realized. Man is redeemed from loneliness only when friendship binds him to another self whom he did not understand before; in love he must discover the "thou" — not alongside of but opposite him, an existential antagonist whom he can only defeat in ontic union. The incompleteness in being is a result of two ontic situations: finitude-infinity and manhood-womanhood singularity. Only in uniting my finite existence with infinity and in sharing my singular man or woman personality with the opposite sex-personality may one hope to extricate himself from the predicament of loneliness. That is why it is difficult for the single man or woman to find compensation in friendship among his or her own kind for marriage, even when the sexual moment is insignificant as is the case with elderly widowers or widows. The strain of being alone can only be eased if two sex-personalities meet. Only then is peace found for the lonely and weary. How beautifully was this idea expressed in Genesis: "And the Lord God said, 'It is not good that the man be alone; I shall make him a helpmate *ke-negdo*, opposite him' " (Gen. 2:18). The help stands not alongside of but opposite him. Only in opposition does man find help.

Jewish mysticism raised the dual aspect of being — femininity and masculinity — to transcendental proportions. In our God-experience we sense already the dual subjective image we have of Him. God is both our Father and our Mother. Masculine and feminine motifs in our approach to and craving for God are of great significance for the understanding of our universal religious experience. The ideas of *Shekhinah* and *Deus Absconditus*, the "Hidden God," reflect the dual character of Being as feminine and masculine. However, Jewish mysticism did not spell out this mystical polarity of womanhood versus manhood within our transcendental consciousness in terms of a mythology. It interpreted the dual ontic motif in abstract philosophical categories. The principles of creativity and receptivity, acting and being acted upon, energizing and absorbing, aggressiveness and toleration, initiating and completing, of limitless emanation of a transcendent being and measured reflection by the cosmos, are portrayed by the dual motif of masculinity and femininity within our religious experience. The whole cosmology of Jewish mysticism revolves around polarity in Being. Femininity, *Shekhinah*, has been imprisoned within the orderly yet restricted universe, while masculinity, *Yesod*, is transcendent, above and beyond concrete reality. Jewish mysticism has thus resolved the pantheism-theism antinomy* which troubled our religious consciousness since the dawn of our history.

God is both within the cosmic framework and outside of it. However, within the world, Divinity expresses itself through the

---

* That is, the opposition between the idea that God is identical with the world and the idea that God is separate from the world. —eds.

law or cosmic order. Absolute unconditioned infinity limits and reveals itself to us as conditioned finitude; creation is basically an act of self-limitation and self-transformation on the part of infinity which appears in the disguise of a mathematically determined finitude. On the other hand, this infinity-finitude points toward the beyond, where neither law nor any other determinations restrict infinity and where God in His full transcendence and absoluteness acts upon the world within which He finds Himself. Unconditioned, creative, infinite transcendence and self-conditioned, receptive, finite immanence of God are symbolized by masculinity and femininity. The distinctness of the two sexual personalities is rooted in the mystical doctrine of Divine-cosmic femininity and Divine transcendental masculinity. When these two aspects of Divine revelation all merge, the world will find its fulfillment. About this metaphysical mystery of the absolute union of creation-creator, of law and freedom, of finitude and infinity, revolves eschatology, the vision of the End of Days, the great message of final redemption of the world.

The sexual community is also a fellowship of two unique personalities, incarnating two aspects of reality. The Kabbalah based its doctrine of bi-personalism upon the verse, "And God created man in His own image; in the image of God He created him; male and female He created them" (Gen. 1:27). How can we reconcile these two *prima facie* contradictory statements: man was created in the image of God, and man is a dual being? The answer to this question was offered by the Kabbalists. Sexual differentiation expresses more than a physical property; it manifests an ontic contrast, a dual aspect within the essence of creation, something deeper and more fundamental than natural sexual differentiation which finds its full expression in two bi-existential experiences, in two ideas of personalism.

These two *personae*, the he and the she, find themselves in a strange mutual relation, namely, that of fascinating and daunting, of fleeing from and pursuing after each other. The two basic traits of this dichotomous relationship are shyness and craving. The male and female are embarrassed and attracted by each other. There is love for and also, we may say, fear of each other. There is tension and at the same time we are overawed by the nearness of man and woman. All this indicates the supra-physical importance of the sex-personality.

At the halakhic level, the statement that sexual differentiation represents a bi-personality underlies the halakhic philosophy concerning the complex relationship between the sexes.

There is no doubt that in the eyes of the Halakhah man and woman enjoy an equal status and have the same worth as far as their *humanitas* is concerned. Both were created in the image of God, both joined the covenantal community at Sinai, both are committed to our metahistorical destiny, both crave and search for God, and with both He engages in a dialogue. The narrative in the Bible that both the male and the female were created in the image of God suffices to refute the Greek mythological misogynous tradition which found its echo in Socratic and late Hellenistic thought and in modern misogynies such as those of Arthur Schopenhauer, Otto Weininger, August Strindberg, Friedrich Nietzsche and Søren Kierkegaard.

One of the foremost Christian theologians (Emil Brunner, *Man in Revolt*, p. 356) stated that if human dignity were measured by intellectual accomplishments as the old Greeks thought, then the inferiority of the woman would, if determined by historical realities, be warranted. The Bible, however, sees the uniqueness of man expressed in passional experiences, in his ability to withdraw from positions conquered, in his readiness to sacrifice and to make the movement of recoil, in his giving himself to others, in his craving, as a lonely being, for communion with God; therefore, there is hardly any cogent reason to place the worth of man above that of the female. On the contrary, sacrificial, passional action is more characteristic of the woman than of man. The mere fact that among our prophets we find women to whom God has addressed Himself is clear proof that we never differentiated between the sexes axiologically.

Man and woman are both worthy of communing with God, the highest form of human perfection and self-fulfillment. However, the Halakhah has discriminated between axiological equality pertaining to their Divine essence and metaphysical uniformity at the level of the existential personal experience. Man and woman are different *personae*, endowed with singular qualities and assigned distinct missions in life. Hence, axiological equality should not level up the uniqueness of these two sexual personalities. The contrast manifesting itself in tension and sympathy, in longing for and shying away from each other, and portraying a metaphysical cleavage in personal existence must not be eliminated.

If the distinctive features of the bi-personalism are erased, the blessed existential polarity out of which a rich, fruitful marriage is born is dispensed with, a tragic event of tremendous significance for the welfare of society. If the woman does not experience the particular and unique in her existential awareness, if the man fails to feel the paradoxical and strange in his being masculine, if both are not cognizant of the incommensurability of their ontic patterns, then this *Gleichschaltung*, this bringing into line, impoverishes marriage which was blessed by the Creator with richness and variety. The latter can only be attained if man and woman complete, not duplicate, each other.

❧ The Redemption of Sexual Life

The Sanctification of the Natural

The dignity of the body is not attributable to its comeliness and grace, but to the person's unique aptitude for self-redeeming action. Hence, this *dignitas carnis* is not an aesthetic but a religious category. The sanctity of the soul, of the spiritual personality, can be realized only via the sanctification of the body. The Romans knew of the interdependence between mental sanity and physical health. Judaism added a new dimension to the body-soul relationship. There is not only functional but metaphysical unity as well. A sacred soul can only reside in a sacred body. Or, to be more exact, sacredness of the personality is born of the naturalness of man, not of his transcendence. Only the body's participation in and commitment to sacrificial action sanctifies the personality.

Holiness, *kedushah,* sanctification, is a venturesome undertaking. It is not given as a grant but is created by man. The creative gesture which engenders holiness draws on inner resources contained in the realm of man's naturalness; the holiness of the personality, even though it comes to full bloom in one's spiritual dimension, in his noble, sublime emotions, profound thoughts, great volitions and strivings, is deeply rooted in the physical layers of his existence, in his carnal drives, in his being integrated into the kingdom of nature. Holiness is reclaimed from the primitive in man through redemptive action. Freud spoke of the libido as the life force out of which man's creativity, his psychic and spiritual energy, flow. Judaism considers the body the wellspring of *kedushah.* That is why it focused its attention upon the body.

The reason for such a strange attitude towards *kedushah,* which is basically a transcendental quality, is an obvious one. *Kedushah* is a passional experience born of bewildering and painful events, of struggle and combat with one's self and others. In a word, it is a heroic performance attained only when one's life story becomes an *epos*, a narrative of great and courageous action. Holiness is not won easily, at no sacrifice. It emerges out of sorrow, confusion and inner turmoil. Jacob found it in the thick darkness of a strange night, haunted by fear and loneliness, wrestling with some mysterious antagonist (Gen. 32:24-33). Abraham discovered it after a grisly night enveloped him and a horror of great darkness fell upon him, when the Lord disclosed to him the information that his seed "shall be a stranger in a land that is not theirs, and shall be in bondage to them; and they [the Egyptians] shall afflict them for four hundred years" (Gen. 15:13). Moses discovered it at the hour of turmoil, failure, anxiety, and shock, when the Almighty told him: "Go, get thee down, for thy people have corrupted themselves ..." (Ex. 32:7), when Moses pleaded with God out of despair and misery, "Yet now, if Thou will forgive their sin, and if not blot me, I pray Thee, out of Thy book which Thou hast written" (Ex. 32:32). *Kedushah* is an expression of an existence determined by a sense of great seriousness, bordering on the sacrificial and passional destiny, conscious and heroic in its fearlessness and resolution.

If courage and endurance are the preconditions of a holy life, then the laboratory where the latter can be both tested and fashioned is the realm of naturalness. The miraculous metamorphosis which the body undergoes in its ascent from blind compliance with mechanical instincts to purposeful selective conduct is the fount out of which *kedushah* uninterruptedly streams. Disciplining the body, interfering with its pleasure-seeking drives, organizing them into a meaningful whole, and relating them to a higher frame of reference by refusing to yield to the powerful push of the flesh and by resisting the rush of primitive lust, are attainable only at a high price in terms of self-denial, self-despair and self-sacrifice. Desires unfulfilled, pleasure pursuits interrupted when attainment is in sight, and withdrawal from something fascinating are painful events. Because of the passional character of these experiences they represent the dynamics of holiness. Prayer and the cult ceremonial can never bestow sanctity upon a person, since they are only symbolically sacrificial and they give man more than they demand from him in return. Of course, they are suffused by meekness, humility and lowliness, submissiveness to God and complete surrender; yet if looked upon from the viewpoint of the doctrine of sanctification through sacrificial action, they cannot be considered as passional performances, and they are more uplifting and inspiring than disciplining and harnessing.

The dignity of the body is inseparably knitted with the claims which God lays to it, with the exacting demand made upon it, with the displeasure and discomfort it is capable of enduring if called upon by God. *Respectus carnis*, respect for the flesh, ties in with the fact that *passio carnis*, the suffering of the flesh, is a most sublime act of service. Of course, everybody understands that *passio carnis* is not to be equated with self-torture, mortification of the flesh, or *odium mundi*, revulsion towards the world, the condemnation of natural drives or the deadening of the senses and the repression of the exercise of the natural faculties of man. Nothing of that sort was ever preached by Judaism. On the contrary, it displayed full confidence in the inner worth of the naturalness of man and accepted it with hope and prayer.

Judaism's philosophy of carnal existence is an optimistic one: it foresees its undreamed-of progress and improvement. All it requires of man is to redeem himself, body and soul, by employing the knowledge and technique available to him and by fashioning a great world out of hylic material, formless matter, recreating himself in the image of the Master by understanding what is worthwhile in human existence, how to take advantage of it, and how to elevate it to great heights. Of course, like any creative gesture, the self-forming and self-fashioning of man is a passional experience. Yet the pain involved in this operation is not the paroxysm of death but the travail of birth. The world of man is not denied and destroyed, but renewed and rehabilitated in pain. A new license to life, this-worldliness and happiness is obtained through the anguish of withdrawal, through the throes of giving up and sacrificing. We detest unruly, chaotic, boundless and unsatiated desire — all that does not adhere to the order of a redeemed existence. We wrestle with the flesh whenever the latter is obsessed by the satanic love of an amorphous, disorderly life, of an existence which knows no limits, one which is *hedone*-intoxicated and which desires only to enjoy, no matter what or how. Hence, Halakhah concerned itself with the natural order in man and with the media through which it preserves and develops itself.

The redemption of man's sexual life is central in Halakhah. If not cultivated properly, sexual activity can be a sinful affair of the most crass and devastating consequence. Thus the Halakhah was compelled not only to redeem but to remedy the sexual impulse (*remedium concupiscentiae*). Without halakhic approbation, the sexual act is considered to be unremedied. Solemnization and halakhic ratification is a *conditio sine qua non* for the permissibility of sexual activity. This idea comes to expression in the first blessing of *birkhat erusin*, the benediction of betrothal: "Blessed art Thou, O Lord our God, Who has made us holy through His commandments, and commanded us concerning unions that are forbidden, forbade those who are betrothed to us, and permitted those who are married to us through *huppah* with *kiddushin*."

The Judaic sex-ethic might give the mistaken impression that our approach to sex contains an element of ambivalence. On the one hand, Judaism never recommended sexual restraint nor exalted the state of celibacy or virginity. Whoever has read *The Symposium* by St. Methodius of Olympus, a work that imitates Plato's *Symposium* (the dialogue in praise of friendship and the meaningfulness of beauty) and is written as a conversation between chaste and self-denying virgins, will understand what I mean when I say that such ideas were as alien to Judaism as the mythological elements in Christianity. A celibate life is considered by the Halakhah and the Aggadah as an unblessed state which contravenes a basic tenet of Judaism. God commanded paradisiacal man, "Be fruitful and multiply" (Gen. 1:28). Adam did not meet Eve incidentally, but in accordance with the original scheme of creation. God Himself considered a self-denying solitary life of man or woman as bad, declaring that "It is not good that the man be alone" (Gen. 2:18). Judaism was opposed to any maiming of the natural life for the sake of some transcendental goal, since holiness arises out of the naturalness of man.

On the other hand, Judaism could not approve of the natural sexual life without subjecting it to a remedial process of purification, as it was too well aware of all the evils intrinsic in an unchaste life, in unharnessed and undisciplined sexual practices, in lewdness and sexual lust, in the sordidness and despicability of sexual arrogance and animal-like behavior. If it conforms to Halakhah , the catharsis of the sexual instinct justifies it completely. Halakhah made no concession to the frailty of man or his sinful nature and did not consider marriage as a *frenum et medicina pecatti*, a bridle and a cure for sin. There is no need for the healing power of God to absolve man of the sin which marriage necessarily incurs. On the contrary, marriage was blessed by Judaism with dignity, sacredness and purity. The wedding's *nissuin* blessings, which deal with the dignity of man and his Divine charisma, are very indicative of our attitude towards a purged and remedied sexual desire.

Shame vs. Shyness

Let us now analyze the problem of the unredeemed and redeemed sex life. Let us first understand why Judaism singled out sexuality as the most crucial drive upon whose redemption the whole religious destiny of man depends. The story of paradisiacal man attests to the peculiar reaction on the part of man toward his sexual drive. Before they ate from the tree of knowledge, Adam and Eve were not ashamed of their nakedness. "And they were both naked, the man and his wife, and were not ashamed" (Gen. 2:25). It was only after their sin that they suddenly realize that nudity is embarrassing and then tried to cover themselves with the leaves of the fig tree. Prior to the man's rebellion against God, both were in a state of childish innocence and did not mind their own nakedness. After they ate from the tree of knowledge, the feeling of shame at their own nudity awakened and they felt disconcerted because of it. "And the eyes of them both were opened and they knew that they were naked and they sewed fig leaves together and made themselves aprons" (Gen. 3:7). What caused their mentality to undergo such a fundamental change?

Shamelessness and indifference marked the state of paradisiacal man. Shame, which is synonomous with sensitivity, excitement and tenseness, was the result of the first sin. Shame itself is a painful self-awareness, representative of an innate tendency in man to protect himself from scrutiny. The first manifestation of shame expresses itself in the mild embarrassment felt when one suddenly realizes that he is the center of attention, in the averting of one's eyes or whole head or the attempt to block off one's face from the gaze of others. In this feeling of shame, man's uniqueness and individuality assert themselves. One refuses to allow invasion of the self by others. Infants at the age of eight or ten months display this trait. Man's resentful response to the vulgar curiosity of his fellow man is naturally expressed in the feeling of embarrassment. The individual guards tenaciously the intimate phases of his life and resents attempts on the part of others to penetrate into the personal sectors of his personality, into certain thoughts and visions.

Basically, the feeling which manifests the unwillingness of the individual to expose his total existential experience to public view and the cynical eye of the stranger — to protest the profanation of the sacred personality by removing the veil that separates the inner personal sanctum — is not shame but shyness or bashfulness. This feeling stresses only the sensitiveness of the individual to the observing eye of the thou and reflects the principle of self-reserve and a hesitancy to commit oneself to others about certain stages of one's life by action or speech. This state of mind is connected with the experience of reverence one feels in his or her encounter with something awe-inspiring which brings home the smallness of man facing the great incomprehensible, exalted and mysterious. Humility finds its expression in shyness. The arrogant is never hesitant or reluctant to explicate his views or his feelings and thoughts, and he is eager to pass on his message to others. In Hebrew we call shyness *bushah*. We read in *Avot* [Ethics of the Fathers], "He [Yehudah ben Tema] used to say: The insolent ones go to Gehinom, the *boshet panim*, the shy ones, to the Garden of Eden" (5:24). On the other hand, the feeling of shame is the expression of the moral consciousness, and we apply this term for cases in which moral culpability is implied — particularly when serious disapproval, either by one's own conscience or by others, accompanies the feeling of guilt. In Hebrew we may employ the term *bushah* or, to be more exact, *kelimah*. In this case, shame cannot be equated with shyness or timidness; it is a unique experience of self-criticism and condemnation. "I am timid and ashamed, *boshti ve-nikhlamti*, to lift my face to Thee" (Ezra 9:6). *Nikhlam* has the connotation of feeling hurt, of being affronted, humiliated. "For he was grieved for David because *hikhlimo aviv*, his father has done him shame" (I Samuel 20:34). Shyness is identical with humility, shame with humiliation.

Lonely man is protected against intrusion from the outside by a feeling of shame which prompts him to withdraw into seclusion whenever the arrogant thou tries to dispel the charm of being for oneself; shame expresses a state of insecurity. Disapproval, not existential boldness and faith, comes to expression. The man who has overcome all doubts concerning his self-worth and has found meaningfulness and purposiveness in his life is not as subject to embarrassment as is the person who is still locked in the moral struggle with life's problematics, perplexed and bewildered by the elements of absurdity interwoven in the fabric of his existence.

When man realizes that the factum of existence and the ideal of existence are in sharp conflict, he disapproves of himself and feels embarrassed and ashamed. Basically, shame is due to a feeling of guilt, to an awareness of culpability, to the knowledge that I am not the one I should have been, that I failed to realize what was expected of me, that I lead a disappointing existence. This feeling overcomes us when we engage in self-portraiture.

The mechanism of the latter works at two levels: First, at the level of illusion and aspiration, when the fantasy weaves a romantic halo around an ideal self who was never realized. Second, at the level of facticity, when the I in a detached and objective mood casts a cold, appraising glance at himself as he actually is with all his frailties and deficiencies. This twofold self-viewing stems from a metaphysical experience: man as an idea and man as fact. Plato spoke of the dual order within reality: the order of true being *(ontos on)*, the order of necessity, and the half-being ("between being and not being," *Republic* 479c), or the order of factual incidence, the world experienced by the senses. Judaism, although it did not subscribe to the duplication of reality at the level of things and events, did introduce a dual order in the realm of intelligent man. While the order of non-intelligent existents are locked in their facticity, in the deep slumber of mechanical, insensate existence and inevitable inalterability, the human being is free to act and to forge his own existential destiny in compliance with an idea-ideal which he beholds. Therefore Judaism has not construed an ideal reality for the order of things and events, but it did put a captivating ideal in the possession of man which he discovers for himself and whose fascination is made felt with irresistible force. The beholding of the idea manifests human dignity since the idea represents the *tzelem Elokim,* the image of God. Man always contrasts his real self with the ideal *tzelem*-self. "Man walks only in *tzelem*" says the Psalmist (39:7). *Tzelem* here is usually translated as shadow, *tzel*. But the *Zohar (Emor* 104b) interpreted this word in the original sense: Only the image of God sustains man, inspires him and helps him to walk.

The vision of the potential within man is at times a very purifying, most integrating and most stimulating experience, awakening faith in oneself and hope in the future. It might bring about a rearrangement of the various complex and logical orders within the personality, as in the case of conversion. What prompts the feelings of guilt to assail the self-complacent sinner, what arouses a disquietude in man which results in the recasting and recentering of the personality, if not the dialectical beholding of the self at two levels — the aspirational-visionary and the real? The more pronounced the contrast between these two polar self-appraisals, the more powerful is the guilt feeling and the greater is the remedial energy implied in this feeling. The sinner must compare his present defiled state of existence with the one of the pristine purity of the ideal I. Out of this shock a new man is born.

The awakening of the individual engrossed in viewing an ideal image of himself which floats high above reality in a world of dreams and beautiful visions — the sudden transition from the imaginary to the real I, from daydreaming to a realistic self-appraisal — causes the individual a feeling of embarrassment and shame. That is why man is embarrassed when others spy on him while he is engaged in beholding the alter-ego with whom he identifies himself. Many a time, while trying to forget his real self, man becomes deeply involved with this phantasmic self. Suddenly he is interrupted by the inquisitive glance of the stranger and he realizes how ludicrous it was on his part to let his mind run on in idle reverie since the two selves are so incongruous that to dream of reconciliation of the real I with the ideal is nonsensical. Of course, a minute later man forgets the absurdity of imaginary self-portraiture and becomes lost in abstracted musing about himself — and again, when awakened, experiences the pain of failure. (Of course, this feeling is not always a disjunctive one; many a time it may become a creative force in one's life, inspiring him to great efforts and ventures, as in the case of conversion.)

In the case which we just discussed, the feeling of shame stems from the realization that people reading my thoughts, which ruminate on the fantastic and illusory, disapprove of my daydreaming and of my identification with an imaginary self. They classify such musing as childish and unrealistic. On the other hand, many a time what is now the ideal self was a reality once upon a time. The beautiful vision of the self was a fact in the past; only because of some culpable action on one's part did the self fall from great heights and shrink in stature. In such a case the person compares two real selves, one located in the present and the other in the past. When one contrasts the I of today with the I of yesteryear, the shift from existential approval to disapproval is sharp and sudden, and the shame feeling may shatter the entire personality. Everybody is aware of his own spiritual fall and is ashamed because of the others' disapproval.

In other cases, one's degradation and loss of greatness may not be known to others. In such a case, the person will experience shame because of self-disapproval, because of the fact that others, not being aware of his apostasy or lapse from a higher existence, believe in his goodness even while his real life is corrupted by sin. One's friends and neighbors consider him to be honest, sincere, and trustworthy, but he himself knows that his reputation is a big lie. He is dishonest, false and corrupt; he leads a double life. Dr. Jekyll is always ashamed of Mr. Hyde. A dual personality always feels embarrassed when it gazes at itself. The feeling of guilt and the collapse of the usual mechanism of self-defense result in shame.

In a word, shame is the expression of the moral consciousness or conscience that condemns man because of an unfulfilled norm, an unrealized ideal, an aspiration which did not come true, or a wrong of which one is guilty.

Shame is a dichotomous experience. In the form of shyness, it affords the individual protection from the unjust infringement by others on his privacy. It is born in the realm of numinous man* who lives for himself and protests vigorously against any encroachment by outsiders upon his secluded existential sectors. However, the feeling of shame in the exact sense of the word *kelimah* is rooted in one's social awareness. Disapproval by others spells doom for one's community existence, while approval signifies togetherness and interrelationships. Numinous man feels embarrassed when society tries to desecrate his uniqueness and aloneness, kerygmatic man when society expels him. It is

---

*See note above, p. 62. —eds.

paradoxical, and yet true. I guard my exclusiveness and aloneness as long as society is willing to accept me. The moment I feel
that society is ready to reject or disapprove of me, I experience
spiritual ruin as if the bottom of my existence were knocked out,
and I yearn for communion.

It is typical of the spiritual personality that it wants to
remain in seclusion, alone, even though that loneliness is
painful. Man is involved in an ambivalent feeling. On the one
hand, he searches for the thou and is eager to find companionship; on the other hand, he wants to retain his spiritual aloneness and meticulously watches out against the inquisitive eye
which tries to disturb his privacy.

Shame and Shyness in the Sexual Experience

The term *bushah* has a twofold connotation: shyness flowing
from humbleness in the face of something mysterious and
strange, or shame expressing disapproval and guilt. Both experiences are applicable to sexuality. The statement that Adam and
Eve felt embarrassed because of their nakedness can be interpreted as embarrassment in both senses, shyness and shame.

Let us examine first the sense signifying shame. Sexual
embarrassment, which is one of the most pronounced manifestations of the emotion of shame, displays a multiplicity of
aspects. First, it is always through the feeling of shame that
we experience the sexual drive vibrating through our consciousness in its distortion by evil. An element of culpability
is implicit in any sexual tension. Somehow, man considers his
sexual instinct to be something illegitimate and sinful; thus a
sense of shame awakens with the awakening of the sexual
drive. The guilt-awareness asserts itself in this shame. The
person who is sexually excited feels guilty because of his own
desires and therefore tries to hide them.

It is immaterial whether such an attitude is a result of
social conventions and peculiar religious inhibitions, as many

psychologists and anthropologists maintain, or, as most theologians assert, it is a natural pattern inherent in the human mentality. The identification of the sexual impulse with the weakness of the flesh is characteristic of civilized society. The I is afraid that his carnal passion will meet with disapproval on the part of the thou, particularly if the thou is of the opposite sex. Man desiring a woman is overcome by fear because the sexual experience is a guilt experience, a lust experience. He dreads her disapproval of him, and, paradoxically enough, this fear is based upon an implicit feeling of blameworthiness. This explains the unnatural behavior exhibited by adolescents when their sexual instinct begins to awaken. Burdened with a dim guilt-consciousness, they are uncertain of themselves, and they act as if they owed an apology for budding desires and drives. Such a unique approach to the sexual experience found its most radical scientific formulation in psychoanalysis. There the libido was identified with sinful complexes, with a desire for rape and murder.

Let us understand the moment of culpability in the sexual experience. Although the latter is a purely physiological experience, like the hunger for food, it exhibits unique features. The fact that religion, ethics, and law attempt to regulate this natural-organic need points toward a peculiar quality which is inherent in it. No other physical appetite is associated with guilt of lust; only the sexual pressure is felt in a such singular way. Its powerful impact upon the human mentality works itself out as a paradoxical experience of sin and shame. The fact that there are so many anomalies in sex life while there are very few with regard to other carnal drives attests to its unique character. Crime and sex are so frequently interwoven with each other that the line of demarcation is blurred. Apparently the burden of some secret guilt piled up upon the frail shoulders of man finds its outlet, at times, in real sin.

Natural-Paradisiacal Sexual Life

The uniqueness of the sexual experience finds expression in its erotic nature. In other words, the sexual drive turns into an erotic drive or sexual love. There is no culinary love in the real sense of the word. One may prefer one kind of food to another, but it is absurd to speak of love even on the part of the gourmet for only certain satisfiers of the hunger drive. There is, however, sexual love, exactly what the ancient Greeks called *eros* and the Bible *dodim* or *ahavah ba-ta'anugim* (Song of Songs 7:7). (As a matter of fact, the Greeks "distinguished between a heavenly and a mundane Eros. The primal desire from whom the world is derived enters into the sphere of souls and in an arbitrary daimonic way carries out there his cosmogonic work: he is the great pollen-bearing butterfly of psychogenesis. The Pandemous needs only to stir his wings to let the primal fire be revealed in the body's games.")

We must distinguish between three different forms of sexual life. First, the *natural-paradisiacal*. At this level man is a child of nature, confined within himself, within the God-intended scheme of things, without overreaching himself, stimulated by organic insistencies and demands, and guided by the general functionality of tissue systems. Hence no personal moment is woven into his sex life. The latter is not an activity but a function, not an experience but a form of physiological behavior. There is biological motivation, yet we must not speak of intention or motifs.

Of course, biological need finds direct expression in specific patterns of external conduct. Built up organic pressures, employing psychical media, impel man to behave in conformity with the need and insistence of the organism. It is also true that the anchorage of organic tensions cannot take place without resorting to movement toward a physical goal upon which the physical energies are directed. Moreover, the instinctive drive, which is a push (or, as Henri Bergson liked to call it, *élan*), is an activity in the sense that man, determined by visceral and sensory drives, submits himself to some demand. The sexual experience is associated with a sexual activity that is concerned with releasing the built-up pressures of accumulated organic energy, yet none of the partners involved in this type of activity are aware of a mutual personal relationship. There is only an it-it contact; the whole engagement is automatic and does not differ from the way sex functions in the kingdom of the animal. At this level the gratification of the sex-appetite is a mechanical performance which differs little from the activity of eating which satisfies the appetite for food. At the natural plane, man eats (if eating is a mere physiological function) not as a *persona* but as an organic being; the eating remains imprisoned within the organic sphere of existence without reaching into the personal. The same is true of sexual engagement at the natural level. Under the stress of the hunger drive the animal and man will look for food, while the sexual need will force them to behave in a specific fashion which will eventually lead to mating. In a word, the sexual performance at the natural level takes place between two depersonalized beings, each of whom is impelled to look for the other not as *persona* but as an it.

Instinctive sexual behavior is characterized by some basic traits: there is semantic conditioning of the sex-activity, the sexual movement is endowed with meaning. Of course, this meaning is not an expression of an intelligent awareness. It is automatic rather than subjective, as a personal moment is lacking. Yet the drive itself is inseparably interwoven with a specific objective even though the creature involved in the performance of the movement is not aware of it. It is a commonplace in biology and psychology that the sexual instinct is the means by which the survival of the species is made possible. I intentionally used the term the survival of the *species*, for the instinctive sexual drive is not directed towards the preservation of the *individual*. The latter occupies a peripheral position in the directedness of the sex-instinct. Jean-Henri Fabre, in his work *Souvenirs Entomologiques* (10 volumes, 1919-21), demonstrated that instinctive primordial behavior (not only the sexual) differs from that acquired by self-training (the principle of trial and error) insofar as the former promotes servility to the species as a whole while the latter occupies itself with the individual. The individual will many a time expose himself to discomfort and even to danger in order to carry out some kind of task that the instinct imposed upon him and which in the long run serves the interests of the species. The individual serves only as an intermediate stage for the process of life propagation and reproduction. He is merely a milestone upon the long journey of life emergence. The Greeks' universalism finds application in the biological drive. Security of the species is the motto of the instinctive sexual performance.

The instinctive motivation is all-orientated without discriminating between one and another satisfier. The primordial sex drive which has not departed yet from its original natural path is directed upon all objects in which it may find satisfaction. It does not focus its pressures upon specific objects, nor does it single out certain techniques in order to assign to them a central position in the biological matrix. I would say that there is equalization of satisfiers and methods of satisfaction, and that the attendant circumstances of the consummation of the drive are completely ignored. Whether or not the consummation is accompanied by pleasure or pain is immaterial to the innate impulse, which is not pleasure seeking. That the gratification of the sexual desire is accompanied by an intense feeling of pleasure does not alter the naturalness and organic simplicity of the performance. The animal most probably also experiences a similar state of excitement and satisfaction. Yet such a sexual urge is completely bounded in by biological motivation and pressure and does not express itself in the questing for pleasure. The satisfier is never conceived as a source of carnal pleasure; it is always looked upon as something which can release pressure. In a word, the element of beauty is absent from the original sex-drive. Neither does ugliness weaken the sex-desire nor does comeliness cause the excitement to mount. Two object beings meet and the process of mating takes place.

At this level we are confronted by an internal sex-drive with the sexual activity bursting forth in retrospect and antici- pation. The natural tension created by the accumulation of sexual energy is released and man forgets about the whole performance. There is no memory of the bygone, nor is there anticipation of the forthcoming in the same way as one does not indulge in reminiscences about his last night's sleep and does not think with excitement of the fact that he will again enjoy a good night's sleep. Awareness of the act expires with its con- summation There is a strict equation between need and specification, between organic insistence and compliance. The sexual act does not transcend the bounds of the need and does not become an independent activity to be pursued even when the organic is contented.

Aphrodite Hedonic Sexual Activity

The situation changes completely at the second level, the *aphrodite hedonic*. At this level, man acts contrary to the basic principles of the constitution of nature as it manifests itself in the visceral and sensory drives of man.

First, the principle of equality of the satisfier is contra- vened. Upon repeated experience the drive becomes selective. The general motives (which are at first rather non-specifically related to a class of satisfiers) tend to become more easily and pleasantly satisfied through the action of a specific satisfier than by that of others of the same general class. In conjunction with that a new aspect comes to the fore, canalization of ener- gies in a process directed upon the attainment of objectives which are no longer important to the primordial goal and which were selected by the individual who frees organic functions from bondage to the species and places them in the exclusive service of the individual.

Man becomes aware of his own individual insistencies and directs his energies toward a preferred objective in union with a new principle of selectivity which was discovered by the organism. Learning by associative memory makes man direct his sexual energies towards specific satisfiers which hold out to him the maximum amount of pleasure. New paths of sex-activity are paved by constant repetition and accumulation of experience, and the discharge of the unique sexual tensions produced by the non-selective organism are channeled into such paths. The selection of those paths or methods of realization of the instinctive drives serves one purpose: a pleasant performance. Through trial and error man finds out how to perform his task in the most successful and pleasant way. In other words, addiction to *hedone* is the result of selectivity within the realm of sexual activity. In conjunction with the birth of selectivity, man eliminates natural, automatic meaningfulness and supplants it with a new hedonic purposiveness. He is no more committed to this original purpose — the survival of the species. On the contrary, the act may become a negative factor in the life of the group. Excessive indulgence in and repetition of the sex-activity because of its concomitant hedonic moments leads to biological and psychological anomalies.

What happens is as follows.

Man as an individual emancipates himself. He discovers himself and begins to be self-orientated and self-centered. The individual as an independent entity who is related to no one but to himself steps forward and asserts his role as a sensual being. His cry is: I want to be the master who enjoys his own sensual activities, and not a slave to the group. In a word, at the level of the Aphrodite hedonic sexual activity, the emancipation of the person from an order of necessary, compulsive and mechanical action takes place. The individual gains initiative and freedom of choice. His approach is not mechanical anymore. It assumes a personal character. The I pursues not what nature impels him to do but what best serves his own hedonic interests. The I appears for the first time as a sex-active and sex-conscious person. In sensuality is the I born.

What kind of a person emerges from this hedonic sexual experience? A pandemic one, vulgar and carnal! Let us not forget that this type of sexual activity is fraught with the demonic desire for power. I enjoy the satisfier and *ipso facto* I dominate it. The hedonist becomes egocentric, self-loving and self-adoring. His egotism reaches such proportions that his pleasure manifests itself not so much in the discharge of physical tension as in the knowledge that he dominates the other person who is just as dedicated exclusively to the comfort and enjoyment of the selfish self. Pleasure sensation is identical with the exercise of power over the other person. *De facto* he converts the partner into an it. One of the partners becomes the master-*persona* and the other the slave-object, since the institution of slavery converts people into objects, *personae* into the neuter it. This type of dominion is distinguished by its ruthlessness and insatiability. No barriers are strong enough to stop the demonic person from engaging in his aggressive designs. He does not recognize any other existential area except his own and he enjoys his liberation from all restrictions, a liberation which expresses itself in the depersonalization of others, in transforming them into satisfiers.

Even at this level there is community of man and woman which is based on sympathy between the opposite sexes who are attracted to each other at a personal level. We can hardly speak of solidarity or a personal relationship. The void of indifference expressing the relationship between person, event, or object neuter engulfs them both. He or she is not motivated by the yearning for companionship flowing from the gnawing feeling of loneliness and forlorness of the individual. A is attracted to B because B is attractive, physically comely. The relationship of the male-ape to the banana is the same as its relationship to the female. Both assert themselves in the response of an organism driven by specific pressures to the sudden appearance of a satisfier. With the discharge of the organic tension there expires the relationship as well. The best illustration of such an I-it relationship in the sexual realm can be found in the institution of prostitution. The man who avails himself of the institution considers the woman as an object which serves one purpose only — the gratification of his need. She is an it, a satisfier, a source of animal pleasure and nothing else. At the aphrodite-pandemic level, either the he or the she forfeits personal worth and sinks into oblivion. Sexual function, if performed at the pandemic level, depersonalizes either the man or the woman under the impact of an overwhelming force with which either he or she is identified.

At this level, the pandemic person isolates pleasure from the complex sexual activity and absolutizes it. Pleasure is remembered long after everything else has receded into the background and is also anticipated before the pressures build up. The sexual experience is sought after, worked for, and retained in memory. The bounds within which the sex life was enclosed by nature are transcended and the element of infinity injected into it. Sexual activity turns into a Dionysian cult. One is sex-intoxicated, sex-overwhelmed, sex-dedicated. He quests for infinite hedonic possibilities which his vivid imagination brings before his mind's eye in wonderful colors. He does not want to be satisfied. He seeks a constantly self-renewing sexual hunger, not sexual gratification. The vastness of the desire, the boundlessness of the excitement, the endless number of the satisfiers enchant the pandemic personality. Of course, this type of activity forfeits its meaningfulness and serves no purpose. Man is afraid of the consequences of his sexual activity and tries to prevent nature from completing its task. He gets out of nature the maximum amount of pleasure without giving it anything in return.

At this juncture the crucial issue of guilt comes to the fore. The feeling of culpability expresses itself not in the fact that man did free himself from the order of natural immediacy, from the it-order, but in his attempting to limit the act of emancipation to himself and not trying to free his partner from the same insensate order.

If the sexual impulse is not redeemed and is left in its crudity, the participants in the drama are guilty of an act of mutual exploitation and vulgarization. The corruptions are interlaced and compounded with enslaving a human being, with denying him the most elementary right of personal existence. The person is depersonalized, desensitized and de-emotionalized. The climax of the hedonic sexual union is *ipso facto* an act of objectification of the personal, intimate and unique.

Thus the element of guilt in sexuality is due to the depersonalizing function implied in it. The I depersonalizes the thou. The latter becomes thwarted and dwarfed in the face of the demon of pleasure who overwhelms and crushes his personal singularity.

Powerful man is rebellious and is not ready to submit himself to the original semantics, the true meaning, implied in the act. He wants to deprive nature of its inherent rights on the basis of which it demands from man compliance with its semantics. The sexual urge was distorted by the pleasure-seeking man. Adam and Eve began to feel embarrassed because of their nakedness. Each one desired the other for sheer delight of possession. Sinister longing for dominion, exploitation and depersonalization is a moral wrong.

Moreover, the act of depersonalization is accompanied by treachery — man cheats nature, steals from her all the pleasures she has in store for him, and refuses to fulfill the commitments he automatically takes on while deriving comfort and gratification from nature. He becomes a parasite receiving gratuitous benefits from his host — nature — and repays it with injury or anomalous behavior. The guilt demonstrates itself in man's dishonesty with regard to natural semantics and his reluctance to take on with his indulgence in the hedonic experience responsibilities and duties.

Redeemed Sexual Activity

The third level of sexual life, *redeemed sexual activity,* uranian aphrodite eros, spells a new relationship between man and woman. It places sexuality on a new plane. A new passion for an existence in sympathy, for ontic solidarity and community, asserts itself via a carnal biological medium. The sex-drive represents, at this level, not only an organic but a personal insistence as well. This eternal quest of the unique, lonely individual to flee his solitude and to share his personal existence with others, finds fulfillment via a carnal medium. God, somehow, employs the flesh as the instrument of His will in order to enable a metaphysical craving to become a reality. Mystics of all ages overburdened sexual sensuality with excessive symbolism. The parallel between the lustful kiss of man and woman and the spiritual kiss of the soul in eternity was a commonplace in medieval mysticism. Even our prophets used sexual love as a simile for the transcendental love of God for man. Since time immemorial erotic tension symbolized longing for metaphysical union. A community bound by flesh is *eo ipso* an existential community. The relationship changes from I-it to I-thou. Erotic love tears down the barriers within which the individual is shut in. Erotic love delivers the I from his loneliness and leads him toward the thou.

Of course, erotic love is the cry of the flesh in the night of passion, sensuality and vulgar desires. However, it is also a metaphysical cry. We know that wherever there is erotic love, the lovers are lonesome for each other even when sexual desire is silent. They enjoy each other's company. They like to converse, meditate, dream and rejoice together. *"Ve-ha-adam yada et Havah ishto,* Adam knew his wife Havah" (Gen. 4:1); *"va-yeda adam od et ishto,* Adam knew his wife again" (Gen. 4:25). The Hebrew term *va-yeda* in its sense of knowing each other sexually connotes the metaphysical element involved in the sexual function. The term *va-yeda* points toward an act of cognition or recognition. The I recognizes the personal existence of the thou. The latter becomes real to the I. The private sphere of the I expands through the eros.

If you should inquire as to the essence and meaning of the institution of marriage, I would say that through marriage the miraculous transition from the I-it contact to an I-thou relationship occurs. Marriage personalizes sexuality as the joint experience of the I and the thou, as a community of two individuals driven by loneliness and metaphysical despair to give up their independence and commit themselves to each other. Basically the same drive that brings man to God makes him quest for his companion. Judaism hated promiscuity in sexual life; *zenut*, promiscuity, is perhaps the most abhorrent phenomenon of the heathen world against which the Bible mercilessly fought, because in every form of indiscriminate sex-activity the personal moment is lost and the element of dominion emerges. The I enjoys the it. The experience is not shared with another I; it remains an isolated dreary experience, animal-like in seclusion and loneliness. The pandemic I never emerges from his hiding even though he is physically attracted by the woman.

Sexuality in the Biblical Narrative

We find accounts of all three phases of man as a sexually-minded being in the Biblical story of creation. Let us examine these accounts.

"And God created man in His own image, in the image of God created He him; male and female created He him. And God blessed them and God said unto them, 'Be fruitful and multiply and replenish the earth and subdue it' " (Gen. 1:27-28). If we compare the blessing bestowed upon man with the one granted to the animal, we will notice both similarities and discrepancies. When the Pentateuch tells us that God blessed the animals (aquarian, terrestrial and fowl), it relates that "God blessed them, saying, 'Be fruitful and multiply, fill the waters in the seas, and let the fowl multiply on the earth' " (Gen. 1:22).

The term "blessed, *va-yevarekh*" refers to an instinctive drive which finds its expression in a directed activity. When the Bible recorded the creation of the plant, it did not mention anything about a blessing which was addressed by God to the vegetative world. We are told that the plant is endowed with the biochemical property of regeneration that is inherent in all organic matter. "Let the earth bring forth grass, the herb yielding seed and the fruit tree yielding fruit after its kind whose seed is in itself upon the earth" (Gen. 1:11). There we have a statement of fact, the propensity of the plant for multiplication.

The unique assignment that the Bible termed "blessing," given by God to the animal in contradistinction to the plant, consists of the sexual dynamic which is alien to the vegetative world. In the animal kingdom, the propensity for reproduction expresses itself not in tissue functionality alone but in a biological motivation and a push toward a peculiar sort of activity serving the same end. While in the vegetative realm fruition is carried out automatically without involving the plant in some kind of activity, the animal, prompted by mechanical pressure, "acts" in order to reproduce. In other words, the biochemical insistence which is regionalised in the plant employs the help of the whole organism in order to realize the task assigned to the animal. The latter is provided not only with a capacity but with a drive, push, or mechanical will as well.

As I stressed before, the term blessing, as in *"va-yevarekh,"* implies the addendum which was given the animal in excess of a mere biological aptitude for reproduction. This addition is identical with sexual hunger and tension. *Berakhah,* which always employs the grammatical imperative, singled out the individual animal as the agent of its class. The mechanical will is both directed and generic. The objective of copulation is not the gratification of the sexual impulse but reproduction of the species and clan. The Bible spelled it out in no ambiguous terms. "Be fruitful and multiply, fill the waters in the seas, and let the fowl multiply on the earth" (Gen. 1:22). The species conditions the biological motivation. The individual constitutes only a medium through which the survival of the species is made possible.

With regard to man, the blessing of multiplication refers, as it does in the case of the animal, to the biological will which was placed at the disposal of the species and which manifests itself in the sexual appetite and a violent push toward the latter's gratification. Yet man and animal are alike insofar as there is no personal relationship between the male and female involved in the sex activity. Both behaviors are unrelated and impersonal at the level of it-it contact. They are organic drives translated into instinctive motion, like eating and other organic functions.

While the animal remains forever at this stage and can never free itself of the mechanical it-it contact, man was endowed with the ability to transcend the non-reflective automatism and reach the phase of self-experience. This ability was implanted in man at the hour of creation by singling him out from the animal kingdom in a twofold way.

First, man was granted dominion over nature, "Replenish the earth and subdue it" (Gen. 1:28). Man's rule over nature forms an integral part of his biological push toward expansion and multiplication. The Torah has interwoven man's drive for power with his sexual will. In his gratification of the sex-appetite he finds not only sensual pleasure consisting in relieving organic pressure but another kind of satisfaction as well — the exercise of power. While the animal's expansion does not imply dominion over other species, man multiplies and attains dominion over other species. The reason for this peculiar combination is to be found in the ability of man to develop his biological drive into a technical intelligence which is guided by his associative memory. The knowhow is by far more pronounced in man than in animal. The technological capacity, although not constituting a unique endowment in man, is nevertheless more developed in him than in the animal. It is a gradual differentiation, yet a very important one. The main distinction lies in the fact that whereas man projects his accumulated experience onto the past and frees his associative capacity for a never ceasing process of learning, anticipating and experiencing the unknown, the animal, not apprehending time in its two-directional expansion, neither relates its experience to the past nor anticipates the infinite character of the experience.

In a word, the human personality began to bud in the realm of biological motivation which attains perfection in the form of a technical intelligence. The latter makes it possible for man to conquer his environment; "Thou hast made him to have dominion over the works of Thy hands; Thou hast put all things under his feet" (Psalms 8:7). The awakening of the human personality occurs through his sex-drive. The it-it contact turns into an I-it relationship.

Second, the very blessing was addressed differently to man than to the animal. Reading the story of the creation of man carefully, we will note that the Torah used a unique term with regard to him. While reporting about the Divine blessing to the animal, the Bible employs the phrase "God blessed them saying, 'Be fruitful and multiply ...'" (Gen. 1: 22). But concerning man, a new phrase was added: "God blessed them and God said to them, 'Be fruitful and multiply'" (Gen. 1:28). The extra words "va-yomer lahem Elokim, and God said to them" shed a new light upon man's role within the universe of nature.

The term va-yevarekh alone denotes the embedding into the organic frame of existence specific tensions and insistences, under whose impact both animal and man are driven to act in a certain way. Va-yevarekh does not constitute by itself any norm or law. It exhausts itself completely in the natural dynamics system. The phrase "va-yevarekh otam Elokim lemor" means

"God blessed them as follows" or, as the medieval grammarians interpret, "God blessed them and said." Yet this *lemor* denotes only an act of will; God willed the animal to be fruitful. The term *va-yomer* is used in the Bible to indicate the creative act of God which is identical with His will. "*Va-yomer Elokim yehi or*, and God said 'Let there be light' " (Gen. 1:3). *Va-yomer* does not refer to speech; God could not have spoken to the void of nihility (nothingness). The same is true of the *lemor* when He created the animal; the *va-yevarekh* symbolizes inner tropism, automatism and motivation followed by movement.

However, in the blessing conferred on man the Pentateuch employs a new term "*va-yomer lahem*, and He told them"; the grammatical dative appears for the first time in the story of creation. This term sheds a new light upon man's position in the universe. While *va-yevarekh* denotes the implanting of an inner tropism in man's tensions and insistences under whose impact he is driven to do something, the *va-yevarekh* and *va-yomer lahem* implies already both biological pressure translatable into motion, by virtue of which accumulated energies are being discharged, and the awakening of the personality, of an I-awareness within natural man. Through the dialogue, God addresses Himself to man; God confronts man and speaks to him, and through this conversation it begins suddenly to dawn upon man who he is. Man is spoken to, and through speech he becomes a person.

Fundamentally two transformations take place. First, man discovers himself in the *kerygma*, the message that God passes on to him, in the *logos*, the word, in the communication. Infinity addressed itself to him and in the face of this miracle man found himself. Second, God through His speech advised man of a new grammatical form — the imperative *peru u-revu*. Man is forced not only by an organic push but by a new sort of pressure to act in a certain way. In this terse address the ought was born and, with the emergence of the imperative, the birth of a new personality, the ethico-religious, was announced. New vistas opened up for man. Inner tropism, automatism, and biological motivation are raised to new levels — intelligent patterns of existence, planned movement, conscious deliberate activity, purposive motifs and the questing not for the pleasant but for the decent and Divinely willed. Man's natural existence is good not only because God willed it but also for a different reason entirely. The natural pattern may become ethico-moral; natural man is equipped to redeem his *physis*, his physical nature, and elevate it to great heights. There is a tremendous potential of moral energy within the natural realm. The biological need pressing man for action corresponds to an ethical right inspiring man to act; there is a possibility of uniting the biological *élan* with the ethical motif. The I is born in the imperative — in man experiencing the will of God.

In short, man and animal part at the crossroads at which God's blessing was imparted to them. The blessing conferred upon man was unique in two respects: First, he was granted power over nature, and in power interwoven with sensuality he discovered himself. Second, he was addressed by God in the imperative form, thus suddenly encountering both speech and the ought. In both, in the address and in the challenge aimed at man, the latter found himself. We are faced at this juncture with the birth of the religious personality.

Adam, who was born in sensuality, in his drive and aptitude for dominion over the world he enjoys, found only himself, not the other self. Powerful man does not recognize the existence of the thou since the whole of creation serves him exclusively. He demands from the thou total surrender and depersonalization. The Adam who was bolstered by the charge "Replenish the earth and subdue it" (Gen. 1:28) had no companion; he was insanely shut up in himself. He could not discover Eve as a self.

Adam who emerged out of confrontation with God, with an overpowering will that challenges and summons, who was advised by God and to whom God communicated the mystery of the ought of the norm, found not only himself but Eve as well.

Where the miracle of speech arouses man from his deep slumber of insensateness and mechanical existence he finds not only himself but the other self as well. He becomes aware of himself because he encounters the other I. He experiences himself while a norm is communicated to him, and wherever commitment is required, the person cannot consider himself as world-self, as an all-embracing self, since in such a situation he meets the other self at whom his ethical activity aims.

Man in his sexual life should have risen from the level of inner tropism and forced movement to that of a personal relationship which is founded on communication of *va-yomer lahem* and normative activity. He could have omitted in his sexual life the phase of eros, domination through *hedone*, of hypnotic and orgiastic carnal love. However he chose the way of the pandemic eros of sin, of finding and thou-depersonalizing. He tripped and fell.

How did the pandemic personality develop?

Man and demon met, they confronted each other, struggled — and the demon won. Who is the demon? The serpent! The demonic personality expresses itself in its desire not for common enjoyment but for exploitation. The I remains non-creative. He has neither the desire nor the ability to give, to commit himself to find common interests and needs with the other self. All the I is concerned with is himself. He is completely dominated by a pleasure frenzy. He continues to take, to receive, to enjoy, not giving anything in exchange. The lack of reciprocity is the most basic trait of the demon. The other self fades into oblivion. The demon deals with an it.

Power is an aesthetic category. Questing for power is *ipso facto* a search for pleasure. The metaphysical desire for companionship is completely replaced by the lust for union through absorption of the thou. The serpent is both pleasure-intoxicated and power-conscious. The mere fact that it made an effort to seduce Eve (Gen. 3:1-5) indicates his hunger for power, for the mere attempt to influence others and master their destiny manifests the will to dominate. The erotic personality is masterful and dominating. For the serpent, *Elokim* (always symbolic of omnipotence, of power) is a power-hungry and pleasure-seeking God who created the world in order to enjoy it, and Who finds joy in enslaving it. The idea of Divinity for the demon combines in itself both dominion and an orgiastic-existence. God wanted man for the sole purpose of keeping him eternally in bondage and rejoicing in his ignorance and vulgarity. God is fearful of man the competitor, of man who may find out how to master his own destiny. He does not want man to discover himself and his talents. God possesses a vast technical intelligence; whatever He created is destined to satisfy His desire for power. Therefore, man should revolt for the sake of his own good.

The whole controversy which raged in antiquity and the Middle Ages about the nature of the first sin — whether it consisted in the discovery of sensuality or in rebellion — may satisfactorily be resolved. The aesthetic experience is impregnated with both motifs, the quest for pleasure and the quest for power. The orgiastic enjoyment is rebellious and anti-authoritarian. The serpent wants to play — it matters not with what; to find gratification — it matters not via what medium. He rejects the norm. He frowns upon all laws. The aesthetic appetite is stimulated by a boundless fantasy. The main motif of the aesthetic personality is *hemdah*, the desire for something which is outside of one's reach. *Hemdah* drives man to drink the dregs of the cup of pleasure and wring them out. The quest for infinity, wasted on sensual finite goods, manifests itself in *hemdah*. This limitless passion is sheer revolt against God. If God is all powerful and rejoices in His infinite existence, then any attempt to compete with Him borders on rebellion. It is peculiar that when Genesis describes the deterioration of man in terms of *hamas*, the sin of venality, it uses the term *elohim*.

"And it came to pass when man began to multiply on the face of the earth and daughters were born unto them, the *benei elohim* (lit., sons of the gods) saw the *benot ha-adam,* the daughters of man, that they were fair and they took for wives all which they chose" (Gen. 6:2). The *benei elohim* encountered the *benot ha-adam*. Who were the *benei elohim*? The demonic personalities who craved for power and unlimited opportunities. The sons of the privileged few, of the masters, of robber-barons who thought that they were competing with the *Elokim,* the Almighty. They rebelled against the norm, the moral law. If the woman was fair and aroused desire, they took her prisoner and defiled her human sanctity and dignity. The *benei elohim* were typical of the God-pictures the serpent painted.

It is quite natural that the immediate change demonstrated itself in a new experience — the feeling of sexual shame. Adam and Eve felt embarrassed because of their nakedness. Why? Because each one desired the other not as self but as an It, as an object which may gratify his or her lusting body. Adam was ashamed because he desired Eve not for the sake of her personality but for the sheer delight of depersonalizing and possessing her. The same is true of Eve in her thoughts about Adam. Had the sexual love represented metaphysical longing, the madness would not have appeared at all. If equality and reciprocity formed the essence of the union realized through carnal means, man would not have felt ashamed of his sexual desire. Yet man developed his personality not via the Divine speech and communication but through his desire for power. That is why the sex life became a complicated ambivalent affair. Hate and love, disdain and fascination, are involved in the I-it relationship. The partners must stimulate each other and kindle passion. There is no other bond uniting them except the one of lust and physical attraction. The dignity of the thou plays no role whatever. Only the pleasure derived by the I is relevant. Therefore man began to hide his desire, for it spelled humiliation of the other self. The feeling of shame appeared in the sexual world of man.

The sexual impulse is, of course, a powerful catalyst which accelerates the establishment of the existential community by two adventurous individuals who emerge from their solitude and join each other in their quest for ontological fullness and greatness . The Bible stresses the singularity of this kind of fellowship in which two *personae* different in temperament, thinking, mode of reacting and experiencing, find self-fulfillment in each other by stating, "Therefore shall a man leave his father and his mother and he shall cleave unto his wife and they shall be one flesh" (Gen. 2:24). Oneness of the flesh is a metaphor indicative of complete unity, of a community of souls which comes into existence under the pressure of the sexual urge.

❧ *Parenthood:*
Natural and Redeemed

Natural Parenthood

The Bible tells us that "The man called his wife's name Eve (*Havah*) because she was the mother of all living things (*hai*)" (Gen. 3: 20). But man's name is not identified with fatherhood; he is called *adam* or *ish,* but not *av.* His role as a father was not portrayed symbolically by his name, while Eve's role as a mother was; nothing reflects Adam's task as a father. In contradistinction to Adam's, Abraham's fatherhood did find an expression in his name. God added the letter *hei* to his name in order to make Abraham's fatherhood universal, to make him "a father of many nations" (Gen. 17:5). Why did a change take place when Abraham, the father of our nation, appeared on the scene? Apparently a new idea of fatherhood that was unknown to Adam was revealed to the world with the arrival of Abraham.

Adam was the father of the natural, unredeemed community; Abraham was the father of a redeemed, spiritual community. Adam sinned and acted contrary to God's will; Abraham proclaimed God's word as the highest law for man to abide by. Adam lost the paradise; Abraham wanted to restore the paradise to man. Apparently, the role of the father within the confines of the natural, sinful-egotistic, pleasure-minded and power-oriented community differs from that within the redeemed, covenantal, ethical, love-oriented and humble community. Within the first community, founded by Adam, the father's role is of such minimal significance that it is not worth being demonstrated by the name, while in the covenantal community the role is redeemed and elevated, infused with new meaning deserving of emphasis and mention.

In the natural community, the woman is more concerned with motherhood than the man with fatherhood. Motherhood, in contrast to fatherhood, bespeaks a long-enduring peculiar state of body and mind. The nine months of pregnancy, with all its attendant biological and psychological changes, the birth of the child with pain and suffering, the nursing of the baby and, later, the caretaking of and attending to the youngster — all form part of the motherhood experience. In a word, the woman is bound up with the child and she experiences her motherhood role in all her thought and feeling. The father, if he wants, can deny his fatherhood and forego responsibility. The mother is bound up with the child; the father can roam around forgetting everything. Motherhood is an experience — unredeemed and hence brutish, yet an experience. Physically, fatherhood implies nothing tangible and memorable. The male, bodily and mentally, does not experience his fatherhood.

In short, within the natural community the mother occupies a central position while the father is relegated to a role that is intangible and vague, since it does not imply any restrictive bonds. Motherhood is a fact that is foisted upon a woman. That is why the name of the woman was derived from her role as a mother, while Adam's name has nothing in common with his fatherhood. "Can a woman forget her baby or disown the child of her womb?" (Isaiah 49:15).

Redeemed Parenthood

With the emergence of Abraham and the founding of a new kind of community, the covenantal one, the vague role of fatherhood and the all-absorbing experience of motherhood were redeemed. New commitments were accepted; man began to live not only for himself, but for others as well. He became concerned with the destiny of others, and discovered in himself responsiveness not only to biological pressure but to the call of conscience, through which God addresses Himself to him. The fatherhood idea was redeemed, purged of its orgiastic-hedonic element, infused with life, and turned into a central reality on par with that of motherhood.

What is fatherhood in the covenantal society? It is the great educational commitment to the *masorah,* the tradition, the freely assumed obligation to hand down, to pass on to the child the covenant, a message, a code, a unique way of life, a tradition of *mishpat u-tzedakah*, of justice and charity. In the covenantal community, the father is promoted to teacher, and his role *ipso facto* is shifted from the periphery to the center on par with that of the mother. That is why Adam — as the representative of the natural community — was not aware of his fatherhood. Only with the emergence of the covenantal community and with the formulation of the doctrine of father-teacher was the fatherhood commitment suddenly revealed to us.

Motherhood expresses, as I explained before, a natural, unalterable reality, a factum. The woman becomes involved with her child within the natural community, while the man freely accepts fatherhood only in the covenantal community. However, not only did the role of the male undergo a change in the covenantal community, but that of the female did as well.

Abraham personified fatherhood as a great commitment. Sarah became the first mother in the sense that her motherhood stemmed not only from instinctual involvement due to biological pressure but from free commitment as well. What was Sarah's commitment? The same as Abraham's: an educational *masorah* commitment to hand down and teach the covenant, God's word, the way of a covenantal life of *hesed u-tzedakah*, of kindness and charity.

Mother's job changed into a great mission; her preoccupation with the child was endowed with ethical meaning. She not only nurses the child physically, she brings him up; she assumes the role of educator. Motherhood is not only an experience but a commitment as well. At this juncture motherhood is hallowed on account of another idea which is linked up with the spontaneous free choice of motherhood on the part of the woman in the covenantal community. As "mother-teacher," the woman is no more connected with only the fruit of her womb, with the child she bore. As long as motherhood, like fatherhood, was rooted in biological facticity, its confine was very narrow and extended only to a clan. One can experience biological motherhood only in respect to one's own child. However, when motherhood was transformed into a commitment and being a mother was equated with being a teacher, an apostle of God, the carrier of God's covenant, His prophet, then motherhood, like fatherhood, was elevated to a universal spiritual level. Instead of being just the father and mother of their offspring in a clannish sense, Abraham and Sarah accepted responsibility for the multitudes, for the world community of the committed. The father and mother of the clan were promoted to father- and mother-teachers of the entire covenantal community with all its universal aspirations. The letter *hei* was added to both of their names, signifying a transformation to universality. God promised Abraham that he would be "a father of many nations" (Gen. 17:4) and that Sarah "shall give rise to nations; rulers of peoples shall be of her" (17:16).

Sarah replaced Eve. The freely committed universal mother supplanted the instinctually involved natural mother. Eve was "the mother of all living"; Sarah, the mother of nations and kings. Eve's motherhood consisted in giving life (in a natural sense) to her child. It lacked, however, the element of leadership. Her motherhood was a result of a biological pressure, the consummation of a natural process. Sarah's was due to a great vision, to a new mission she took on. She and "all the persons they had acquired in Haran" (Gen. 12:5) — her children/pupils — formed a covenantal community, one founded on education, a living tradition and commitment. Sarah redeemed the motherhood experience by taking a factum, a natural reality, and changing it into a commitment. Passive involvement became an active commitment; natural entanglement was elevated to a normative choice. The woman herself rose from a receptive to an active role. And the most important dimension which was added is that of universality, the capacity to assume motherhood vis-á-vis all children.

No more should a childless couple feel desolate and forsaken because the Almighty has not blessed them with an heir. The barren woman may lack the natural motherhood experience, but she can attain covenantal if not natural motherhood by choice, by commitment, by helping others, by contributing toward the strengthening of the covenantal community, by exposing children of other parents to the word of God. The Romans — to whom the idea of covenant was alien, who, in spite of their advanced technological achievements, never freed themselves from the bonds of the natural community — tried to compensate the childless man and woman by establishing the institution of adoption. Judaism did not need to create such an institution. The letter *hei* added to Abraham's and Sarah's names symbolized the exalted idea of covenantal fatherhood and motherhood, one which is realized not through natural but through spiritual-educational media which transcend the boundaries of a clan and extend into the open spaces of universality.

The Need for Sacrificial Action

However, any act of redemption is bound up with sacrificial action. A physiological reaction changes into meaningful hallowed action at any time the individual displays courage and the ability to answer the violent, orgiastic, hypnotic call of nature in the negative, thus incurring pain and suffering because of his refusal to cooperate with biological pressures that have not found their total release. Judaism identified sanctity with sacrifice, this identification being reflected in the status of utter and immutable sanctity, *kedushat ha-guf*, assigned halakhically to a *korban*. One cannot hallow anything unless one is ready to surrender, give up, and be defeated.

Let us analyze from this viewpoint the redeeming passional action of the covenantal mother.

Motherhood *per se*, even at the level of naturalness, is described by the Bible as a passional experience. On the one hand, the woman pays a much higher price than the father for engaging in sex. While the father is permitted by nature to walk off free, the mother becomes burdened with responsibilities for many long years. She loses her freedom and ability to order her life in accordance with her desires. In fact, she must give the whole of herself to the child. To be a mother — even at a natural level — means to shift all other responsibilities and concerns to the periphery. Even the most primitive motherhood experience is fraught with pain and suffering.

On the other hand, the woman, discriminated against by nature and charged to carry the heavy load of motherhood alone, is not ready to give up her role as mother and cast off the burden. This compulsive will in the woman to be a mother at all costs emphasizes the pathos in her role. The tragedy of the woman becomes the more pronounced the less she can avoid it. The woman in the Bible yearns for a child with her heart and soul and is not able to suppress the urge for motherhood. The experience would not be so sorrowful if it could be dispensed with, if the woman felt happy without it.

However, the Bible denies that such a possibility exists. The woman wants to be a mother; she cannot get along without involvement in this kind of a passional experience. The longing for children, for a home, for the parent-child community, is by far more intense in the woman than in man.

The lot of the unmarried woman is by far more miserable than that of the unmarried man. The impact of sexual loneliness upon a woman is more devastating, both physically and mentally, than it is upon a man. The woman finds herself in a paradoxical predicament. On the one hand, she craves a husband and child; on the other hand, this longing, which penetrates into the very depth of her personality, can be fulfilled only by means of pain and suffering.

The story of creation describes this role in a short verse. "To the woman He said, 'I will greatly multiply your sorrow and your conception. In sorrow you shall bring forth children; and your desire shall be to your husband, and he shall rule over you'" (Gen. 3:16). In other words, the desire of the woman is tragic, masochistic. On the one hand she yearns for children, a husband and a home; on the other hand, she pays the high price (in terms of her freedom, safety and leisure) for the attainment of this desire.

With the emergence of the covenantal community and the change of the mother role from an inevitable experience to a free commitment, the passional component of this experience and the tragic dichotomy were redeemed. I say "redeemed" and not liquidated or eliminated, since there is no power in the world which can nullify God's will. The pain and suffering involved in being a mother can never be eliminated. However, it is subject to redemption, to infusion with meaning and purposiveness. While Eve suffers, her passional experience is absurd, purposeless, a waste of energy and human feelings. While Sarah suffers, her experience is hallowed as a sacrifice for a great, exalted idea: the perpetuation of the covenantal community.

The Yearning for Children

Let us analyze the covenantal mother and her redeemed passional experience.

She wants a child. Her yearning for children is perhaps more powerful than that of the mother in the unredeemed natural community. Rachel exclaimed in utter despair, "Give me children; if not I shall die" (Gen. 30:1). Hannah's story (I Samuel, chapter 1) is replete with tenderness, human tragedy, suffering and faith. She is a woman in distress, a woman who thought that she had lost everything in life, that she had been completely forsaken by God and men, a woman who felt a great poverty, the absurdity in living. She sought relief in prayer, for from a human viewpoint, the situation she found herself in was hopeless. No doubt her yearning for a child was by no means less intense than that of Eve. Yet there was a basic difference. Eve's yearning for a child was not related to a great goal. It was purely egotistic, instinctual, primitive desire. Eve wanted to be a mother because she felt a need not only to be loved but to love, to shower someone with affection.

As long as this desire is not redeemed and purged of its instinctual elements, a mother wants a child only to satisfy her desire for loving and caring for someone. She wanted a child because she was in need of giving vent to emotional pressure, to gratify a *per se* good instinctual drive, that is, to shower someone with love. What this leads to was irrelevant for Eve. The purpose is fulfilled in dandling, hugging, or kissing anything.

However, in the covenantal community the urge to love is purged of its egotistic instinctual elements and turns into a need to serve, to sacrifice, to participate in the great adventure of being a people of God and a messianic community. The woman is no more a dandling, playing mother. She is a mother who teaches, educates, trains, and consecrates the child to God.

The covenantal mother's desire and craving for a child flow from the deep recesses of her personality where God's image is engraved. She tries to imitate the Creator. Jewish mystics asked: Why did God create the world? Does God, the Almighty, infinite, eternal, omniscient and transcendent, need a frail, finite, transient, and conditioned world? Yes, they said, He needs the world in order to have somebody on whom to practice kindness and mercy, in order to let somebody share in the great I-awareness of being, in order to give love and bestow *hesed*. God did not need the world for Himself. He wanted it in order to give man the possibility of attaining greatness.

So, too, the covenantal mother needs a child to make happy, to have the latter join the great community of the covenant, to serve the great cause, to consecrate the child to God. She is required to surrender her child. Jewish covenantal training is basically identical with an act of consecrating the child to God. A mother can be affectionate — Judaism has never condemned the manifestation of love by a mother. But covenantal mother has to withdraw from her child; her total possessive claims are curtailed in the covenantal community. For dedication to the covenantal cause and unlimited affection are mutually exclusive.

Hannah is the woman who proclaimed that motherhood asserts itself in consecration of the child, in giving him away, in surrendering him to God. "O Lord of hosts, if Thou wilt indeed look on the affliction of Your handmaid and remember me and not forget Thy handmaid but wilt give to Thy handmaid a man-child, I will give him to the Lord all the days of his life..." (I Samuel 1:11). And what did Jewish mothers do throughout the millennia if not exactly the same thing that Hannah pledged? What does a Jewish mother do now when she brings her child to a yeshivah?

Jews introduced a system of public compulsory education 2100 years ago, while the so-called Western world was roaming the forests in Northern and Central Europe. "It was enacted to establish teachers of young children at every city and town, and to bring the children to them at the age of six or seven" (Bava Batra 21a). The child used to be taken away from the embrace of his mother at a very tender age and brought into a new world of Torah, teaching and training. Even now a Jewish child leaves home early in the morning and comes home late in the evening. When Hannah said, "For as long as he lives he is lent to the Lord" (I Samuel 1:28), she did not mean that he would retreat into some cloister; she did not think of physical solitude or a monastic life. Judaism has always opposed an unnatural life. What she had in mind was a life of service to God by serving the covenantal community. We are all still practicing this.

Let us recapitulate. In the natural community, the woman is involved in her motherhood-destiny; father is a distant figure who stands on the periphery. In the covenantal community, father moves to the center where mother has been all along, and both together take on a new commitment, universal in substance: to teach, to train the child to hear the faint echoes which keep on tapping at our gates and which disturb the complacent, comfortable, gracious society.

Two Complementary Missions

There is a distinction between mother's and father's mission within the covenantal community, since they represent two different personalistic approaches. Father's teaching is basically of an intellectual nature. Judaism is to a great extent an intellectual discipline, a method, a system of thought, a hierarchy of values. In order to be acquainted with all these aspects, one must study, comprehend, acquire knowledge and be familiar at least with its basic principles. Let me confide: it is not too easy a task. The teaching must be strict, exact and conscientious. If the father cannot accomplish it all by himself, he must see to it that his child obtains the necessary instruction.

However, Judaism is not only an intellectual tradition but an experiential one as well. The Jew not only observed but *experienced* the Shabbat, the Jew *experienced* Rosh Hashana and Yom Kippur. He did not only recite prayers on those days. The *seder* was not just a ceremonial, but a great *experiential* event. There is beauty, grandeur, warmth, and tenderness to Judaism. All these qualities cannot be described in cognitive terms. One may behold them, feel them, sense them. It is impossible to provide one with a formal training in the experiential realm. Experiences are communicated not through the word but through steady contact, through association, through osmosis, through a tear or a smile, through dreamy eyes and soft melody, through the silence at twilight and the recital of *Shema*. All this is to be found in the maternal domain. The mother creates the mood; she is the artist who is responsible for the magnificence, solemnity and beauty. She tells the child of the great romance of Judaism. She somehow communicates to him the tremor, the heartbeat of Judaism, while playing, singing, laughing and crying.

Leadership in Times of Crisis

While intellectual involvement is important, in times of crisis and distress the experiential commitment is indispensable. Were it not for the mother, the Jews would not have been able to defy and to survive so many crises which threatened to annihilate our people. Again the contrast between the natural and covenantal mother is striking.

The natural woman, Eve, becomes involved involuntarily, not only in natural motherhood, but also in many human situations. She is vulnerable to the smooth but evil tongue of the serpent, sinks easily into her receptive role, into her quest for pleasure, and loses her independence of mind and will. She cannot resist the satanic persuasive arguments and false promises. "And the woman saw that the tree was good for food and that it was pleasant to the eyes ... she took of its fruit and did eat ... " (Gen. 3:6). The natural mother, Eve, abandoned her freedom of choice based on critical scrutiny; she let herself be easily hypnotized by the serpent, seduced by him. She could not rise to the heights of a courageous personality; she yielded. In crisis, she displayed weakness, confusion and fear.

By redeeming the motherhood experience, Sarah restored the dignity of the woman. A new task was given to her, namely, to rise *heroically* in moments of dismay and spiritual chaos, when man, notwithstanding his great intellectual prowess, finds himself entranced and is about to fail in the implementation of his fatherhood commitment.

The mother in times of crisis assumes the role of her husband's keeper, his guardian and teacher. In the covenantal community, motherhood is a more powerful spiritual force than fatherhood. The shy, modest, reserved mother turns into an active personality whenever critical action is called for.

Man's mind roams about in a world of abstractions and twisted ideas. He is at times too critical, too skeptical to realize the simple truth which brooks no interference from the oversophisticated intellect. That is why the Bible has always portrayed the woman as the determining influence, saving the male from committing grave errors. She quite often changed the course of destiny.

The woman is a crisis personality. In normal times, when routine decisions are reached, the man makes up his mind and the Biblical woman follows him. However, in times of upheaval and transition, when the covenantal community finds itself at crossroads and the choice of alternative courses of action is about to be made, a choice that will shape destiny — it is then that the mother steps to the fore and takes command. The greatness of the man expresses itself in everyday action, when situations lend themselves to logical analysis and discursive thinking. The greatness of the woman manifests itself at the hour of crisis, when the situation does not lend itself to piecemeal understanding but requires instead instantaneous action that flows from the very depths of a sensitive personality. "God gave woman *binah yeterah,* an additional measure of understanding over men" (Niddah 45b).

Motherhood and the Covenantal Community

Sarah is responsible for the survival of the covenantal community. Abraham had two sons, Ishmael and Isaac. The covenant was confined to Isaac and not given to Ishmael. Why? Because the mother of Ishmael was Hagar, and the mother of Isaac was Sarah.

Let us just read the Biblical text pertaining to the event of the covenant and the birth of Isaac.

> *And when Abram was ninety-nine years old, the Lord appeared to Abram and said to him: "I am the Almighty God; walk before me and be perfect, and I will make My covenant between Me and you and will multiply you exceedingly ... As for Me, behold my covenant is with you, and you shall be a father of many nations. Neither shall your name be called Abram, but your name shall be Abraham, for a father of many nations have I made you ... And I will establish my covenant between Me and you and your seed after you in their generations for an everlasting covenant, to be a God unto you, and to your seed after you"* *(Gen. 17:1-7).*

We do not yet know whether God refers to Isaac or to Ishmael. However, God qualifies his statement by saying: "As for Sarah, your wife, you shall not call her name Sarai, but Sarah shall be her name, and I will bless her and give you a son through her, yea, I will bless her that she shall give rise to nations ..." (Gen. 17:5-16). The covenant is restricted to Sarah and her offspring, and does not include Ishmael. Abraham feels embarrassed and he begs God that Ishmael may also be admitted to the covenant. "O that Ishmael might live before Thee" (Gen. 17:18). God, however, rejects Abraham's plea and He says: "Sarah, your wife, shall bear you a son indeed, and you shall call his name Isaac, and I will establish My covenant with him for an everlasting covenant, and with his seed after him. As for Ishmael I have heard you. Behold I have blessed him ... But My covenant will I establish with Isaac whom Sarah shall bear unto you ..." (Gen. 17:18-21).

God lays emphasis upon Sarah's role in the realization of the covenantal society. Abraham's offspring are not taken into this esoteric community if their mother happens to be Hagar and not Sarah. Later, when Sarah demands the expulsion of Ishmael, and Abraham is not eager to comply with her request, God tells him in terse terms, "Let it not be grievous in your sight because of the lad, and because of your bondwoman; in all that Sarah has said unto you, hearken unto her voice, for in Isaac shall your seed be called" (Gen. 21:12).

Rebecca is responsible for the covenant being transmitted to Jacob instead of Esau (Gen. 27). Isaac had contemplated entrusting the spiritual heritage to his oldest son. At the hour of crisis Rebecca intervened and thereby determined the historical destiny of the covenantal community. She sent Jacob to Haran to marry her nieces. Miriam is responsible for the emergence of Moses as a leader and redeemer of his people. If not for her, he would have never been imbued with great passionate love for his poor brethren. She suggested to the princess that a Hebrew wet-nurse be employed for the infant, preventing Moses from disappearing in anonymity and ignorance. "And his sister stood afar off, to know what would be done to him ... Then said the sister to Pharaoh's daughter, 'Shall I go and call for you a nurse of the Hebrew women ... ,' and the maid went and called the child's mother" (Ex. 2:4,7,8).

Similarly, Deborah saved the people from oppression and slavery when she organized the rebellion under the military command of Barak (Judges 4-5). And the Aggadah relates that the women refused to contribute to the Golden Calf *(Pirkei de-Rabbi Eliezer* 45) while they gave generously to the Tabernacle (Ex. 35).

The woman is both a demonic and Divine crisis personality. Eve and Delilah represent the woman-demon; our matriarchs, the Divine individuality. The destiny of mankind and of the covenantal people was shaped by the woman.

The Book of Proverbs dedicated its last section (31:11-31) to the woman of valor in whom the heart of her husband trusts. Valor as a trait of the feminine personality was born in the covenantal community where motherhood, instead of being a factum, became a challenge and an ideal.

The Tragedy in Motherhood

And yet the story of the Biblical woman, the covenantal mother, ends with a tragic note. The very moment she brings her job to a close, the instant she completes her task, when the crisis is over, she returns quickly to her tent, draws down the curtain of anonymity and disappears. She is outside of the hustle and bustle of the male society. Abraham sits "in front of the tent" (Gen. 18:1). His name appears in the press and many know him; he is the leader, the father, the teacher; his lips drip honey; he enlightens the minds; he fascinates the passersby. Hardly anyone knows that there is a Sarah, humble, modest, publicly shy. Somewhere in the tent is the person who is perhaps responsible for all the accomplishments credited to Abraham, for all the glory that is bestowed upon Abraham, who is superior to him, who leads the leader and teaches the teacher and guides the master, who inspires the visionary and interprets his dreams.

Sarah, the Biblical woman, is modest, humble, self-effacing. She enters the stage when she is called upon, acts her part with love and devotion in a dim corner of the stage, and then leaves softly by a side door without applause and without the enthusiastic response of the audience which is hardly aware of her. She returns to her tent, to anonymity and retreat. Only sensitive people know the truth. Only three travelers inquired about her. These travelers were not ordinary people whose eyes see only the surface. They were the angels of God. Their glimpse penetrated and apprehended the image of the true leader, teacher, prophetess, to whom everything should be credited. Nonchalantly they remarked, "Where is Sarah, your wife?" (Gen. 18:9). In other words, we know that without her you could not play the part that God assigned to you. Where is she? Why do not people know the truth? Why has she been just trailing behind you? Why did she not march in front of you? After all, the covenant cannot and will not be realized without her. Abraham answered tersely, "She is in the tent" (Gen. 18:9). Indeed she is enveloped in mystery.

It is quite interesting that although Abraham survived Sarah by thirty-eight years, his historical role came to an end with Sarah's passing. Isaac leaves the stage together with Rebecca. Jacob relinquishes his role to Joseph with the untimely death of Rachel. Without Sarah there would be no Abraham; no Isaac were it not for Rebecca; no Jacob without Rachel.

And yet, and here the tragedy manifests itself with all its impact, we say, "God of Abraham, God of Isaac, God of Jacob," but not "God of Sarah, God of Rebecca, God of Rachel and Leah," even though they had an equal share in *Borei Olam*, the Creator of the World.

The Halakhah was cognizant of the greatness of the covenantal mother when it formulated the rule that *Kedushat Yisrael*, one's status as a Jew, can be transmitted only through the woman. The Halakhah was also conscious of the loneliness and the tragic note in the feminine commitment when it accepted a contradictory rule that the child takes his father's name and family status.

The Duality of Fatherhood

A question arises in the Mishnah and Tosefta Bikkurim whether a proselyte may, when praying, address himself to God as "our God and the God of our fathers." The Halakhah has accepted the viewpoint of Rabbi Judah in the Jerusalem Talmud (Bikkurim 1:4) that the proselyte may recite the fixed text of the Bikkurim portion, including "which Thou didst swear unto our ancestors" (Deut. 26:15). Maimonides writes, relative to this problem: "The proselyte brings [*bikkurim*, his first fruits] and reads [the portion in Deuteronomy 26] for it was said by God to Abraham, 'and you shall be a father of many nations' (Gen. 17:4). Thus he [Abraham] is the father of the entire world that enters under the wings of the Divine Providence" (Maimonides, *Hilkhot Bikkurim* [Laws of the First Fruit Offering] 4:3).

Maimonides did not interpret the phrase "a father of many nations" in the sense of natural fatherhood, that Abraham will be naturally fruitful and fertile, the progenitor of many peoples. He saw it rather as denoting another kind of fatherhood, the spiritual. Abraham is the father of all those who gather under the wings of the *Shekhinah,* the Divine Presence, of those who cleave to the God of Israel and commit themselves to His teachings. The change from Abram to Abraham is symbolic of the transition from the relationship of biological progeny and offspring to that of metaphysical father/teacher and child/disciple.

When a man begets a child who is biologically his, a natural being becomes an Abram. This role is not a distinct privilege bestowed upon man exclusively. Procreation is a natural function of man and beast alike. But fatherhood that is rooted in the great idea-experience surpasses by far fatherhood due to a natural process of fertilization of the ovum. This message was conveyed to us through the covenant with Abraham. The covenant freed our ancestor from the natural restrictions of nature and widened his fatherhood experience to universal proportions. Whoever in the hour of enlightenment decides to return to God is embraced by Abraham as a beloved child.

In a word, fatherhood is a double experience, a natural and a personal-metaphysical one. At the first level, man is procreative and sues for a status of fatherhood which is doomed to failure because he will never develop the proper relationship with his offspring. He will have to resign himself to unmitigated contempt on the part of the son or daughter, as the young will always resent and despise the old; or he may have to establish a veritable tyranny in his home, a result of a meaningless and absurdly resentful relationship. At the second level, father and child form a relationship which adds a new quality to their existential experience. They form an ontic community, a community of being, within which man is relieved of the loneliness which lashes him with untold ruthlessness and existential insensateness. Only within this fellowship is real fatherhood found.

However, when I speak of the Abrahamic fatherhood which is attained through education, I understand the latter not only in terms of technical training of the child, of the development of his aptitudes and talents, of actualizing the child's full natural potential, of exercising his or her innate physical and intellectual capabilities. However important and essential this type of education is to the full realization of the child, the idea of Abrahamic fatherhood implies a new dimension, one which is to be found beside the realm of education as it is understood by philosophers and pedagogues. The service Abraham rendered to Isaac did not consist in educating him in skills and aptitudes in the Platonic sense, in bringing out what already was endowed in him, but in introducing him to a new existence, a covenantal, redeemed one. Abraham ushered Isaac into the covenantal community consisting of four *personae*, I, thou, he (lower case) and He (upper case). Abraham revealed to Isaac the regenerating Law of God, or His ways. Abraham became a part of the scheme of revelation of God's Law. While education aims only at being human, Abraham is within finitude involved with Isaac as to the latter's *trans-humanitas*. He gave him something which lies beyond and above the finite reality. He discovered for him the idea of self-transcendence and self-redemption, of catharsis.

"For I have known him that he shall command his children and his household after him that they shall keep the way of the Lord, to do righteousness and justice, so that the Lord may bring upon Abraham that which He had spoken of him" (Gen. 18:19). Fatherhood expresses itself in a testamental act, in transmitting the great experience and law of *revelatio Dei*. Not only does the father prepare his children for life, not only does he adapt them to an existing reality, as the naturalistic theory interprets the educational activity, but he also commits them to a higher transcendental reality. The fatherhood of Abraham is covenantal and was firmly established at the Mount Moriah with the *Akedah* drama, his willingness to sacrifice Isaac (Gen. 22). Many a modern father who tries to give his children an excellent technical education fails to become Abraham, to re-experience his fatherhood in letting his children discover a new reality of a committed, redeemed existence.

Clan and Nation

When God changed Abraham's name from Abram, He changed his task as well as that of his children. Abraham's role was changed from that of a private person, an individual, into that of a father of a nation. The land was granted not to a father of a *clan* but to a father of a *nation*. The promise was related to a nation: "I have made you the father of many nations ... I will make nations come out of you" (Gen. 17:4,6). He will no more be just the head of a clan, of a tribe or many tribes. He will be the father of a nation, of an aboriginal covenantal entity. The father personifies the nation; he is a nation disguised as an individual. Abram denotes the natural link, the father of a family;

Abraham signifies the existential link between a father and his offspring when he experiences ontological unity, oneness of being, and comity, as if he lived in them in a future generation, as if he will continue to exist through them. A nation is not a clan. It is an entity *per se*, a personality, an individuality. It is not an collective thing integrated of the many, but an aboriginal unity. *Keneset Yisrael*, corporate Israel, is a being. It exists in the same manner as I, you and he exist. For instance, we believe that the promised land belongs to us. To whom? To me, to you, to him? To all of us? No! It belongs not to one of us, nor to all of us in partnership! It belongs to *Keneset Yisrael* as an individuality, an original being. *Keneset Yisrael* may encompass all of mankind, since everybody can join through *gerut*, conversion. No racial legitimation is required.

Once the children of Abraham will form a nation, once Abraham will be elevated to the father of a people, a nation, another question arises: who will be the mother of the nation? A clan can be formed by having a common ancestor, either a father or a mother. It is a purely biological blood link. A nation, however, is not dependent upon a blood relation. A nation has a common father-teacher. The father of a nation passes on to future generations not just genetic characteristics but a spiritual heritage, a way of life, a morality, an accumulation of values — in a word, a great world, a specific existential experience; he wills his own self to the generations, creating a sense of ontological unity, "...that he shall command his children and his household after him that they shall keep the way of the Lord, to do righteousness and justice" (Gen. 18:19).

The Torah has emphasized that both father and mother were created in the image of God and that both of them express themselves by using their respective image-consciousness in a unique way. Together they reflect the total glory and majesty which God invested in them. Hence, the nation cannot come into existence and become God's own nation unless the nation receives the moral code from the mother as well as the father. God speaks to his people either as a father or as a mother. He entrusted teaching to both. Hence, a nation must have a mother.

That is why the Torah tells us that Sarah could not bear a child (Gen. 11:30, 16:1). Without her, there will be no birth of a nation. The whole covenant would have been null and void if Sarah had not been involved. Abraham turned into a spiritual father, a universal teacher, or into an idea; so did Sarah. She became a mother of people, not a mother of a clan. She was transformed into an idea. Of course, she will teach her children the same moral code that Abraham formulated. However, she will interpret the same code in the unique style which only a mother knows. Abraham interprets events in his individual fashion. Sarah interprets events and things under the aspect of involvement and sharing.

How beautifully the Torah tells us the story of a father whom God charged with the mission of forming a nation and who could not implement his assignment because Sarah, the choicest of all women, could not join him since she was barren. God had to resort to a miracle in order that a charismatic nation be formed. Sarah *will* be the mother of the nation. "I will bless her and give you a son through her. I will bless her that she shall give rise to nations; rulers of people shall issue from her" (Gen. 17:16). The Almighty reemphasized that without Sarah there will be no covenant with a nation. The great historic task was entrusted to two people. They reflect the greatness of man *in toto*. Through them the great nation will achieve completeness.

Kibbud u-Mora: The Honor and Fear of Parents

Outward Action and Inward Experience

There are few Biblical norms that regulate the obligations of children toward their parents. One norm was disclosed to us by God in the Decalogue, the other is contained in Leviticus. We are commanded in *kibbud* and *mora*, to honor and to fear our parents. In the Decalogue we come across the precept of *kibbud*: "Honor your father and your mother as the Lord your God has commanded you, that your days may be long and that it may go well with you upon the land which the Lord your God gives you" (Deut. 5:16; see also Ex. 20:12). The precept of *mora* finds expression in Leviticus (19:3): "You shall fear every man his mother and his father." The precepts of honoring and fearing were enumerated among the 613 *mitzvot* as two separate commandments, since they are related to two different acts.

The norms of *kibbud u-mora* consist of two components: outward action and inward experience. Under the aspect of outward action, the Halakhah developed a normative science and a technique of good conduct on the part of the child towards his or her parents. This normative and technical discipline introduces fixed, statutory standards of good behavior with which the son or daughter must comply. The realization of the norm concerning external action is attained with the formal correspondence of one's actions to the formal halakhic criteria. If the action is legalistically correct, the norms of *kibbud u-mora* are considered to be fulfilled. The Halakhah, when viewed from this angle, does not demand the intrinsically good deed, a deed which expresses good will, an inner commitment, an emotional attachment or relatedness. Outward action which is just incidentally good has been sanctioned by the Halakhah, notwithstanding the "neutral" motivation responsible for this particular behavior. The right or good deed may be the consequence of a morally irrelevant decision conditioned by circumstances lying outside the ethos, and yet still sustain halakhic significance and worth.

Under the aspect of inward experience, *kibbud u-mora* are raised from the level of technique — technical discipline — to that of an experience. A novel element is injected into the performance — the motivation, the causative inner situation of man, the all-pervading mood. The deed becomes the agency through which experience speaks, the objectified intimate feeling which reveals the very recesses of personal existence. The good will becomes externalized, noble desire presses into action, and the organs of acting are inspired by restlessness. The tense muscle is then an experience concretized, the feverish movements of the hand are a thought turned into nerve tissue, and the whole of external man — an ecstatic soul made visible. The deed in such a stage consists not just of acting but of acting out something deep-seated, hidden in the inaccessible recesses of the human personality. The *pe'ulat mitzvah,* the mitzvah performance, becomes a dramatic gesture, a soliloquy — or rather a colloquy — telling a marvelous tale of the boundless existential distances and unexplored spaces of man, his dilemma, contradiction and self-redemption.

At the level of *kibbud,* action becomes then the agency through which the inner commitment of child to parent speaks, and thus formal relationship turns into ultimate relatedness, mechanical distance into spiritual closeness, and the separateness of two *personae* is supplanted by an existential union. Wise action toward one's parents becomes sincere and meaningful action.

Outer and Inner as Independent Fulfillments

We must state that these two aspects, the outer and inner, are not interdependent. One may act wisely toward one's parents — so that, from the viewpoint of *kibbud u-mora* techniques, the behavior is irreproachable and meets all standards of decency and propriety — while he personally remains emotionally indifferent and completely uninvolved in the very action which takes place. The child is rich and generous and showers his parents with gifts and favors. Materially they lack nothing since the child attends to all their physical needs. Yet he does not love them nor does he feel attached to them. His relationship, if we may speak of it, is one of cold civility and courtesy — the precept associated with external action is fulfilled, while the experience of *kibbud* is lacking. This unimpeachable behavior is a result of good breeding, excellent manners, and natural politeness. If I may use idiographic terms,* I would say that his "good conduct" is due to a "habit of mind" and not to conviction. He himself may be wary of all feeling of reverence, averse to all doctrines glorifying parents and contemptuous of all emotions of loyalty, love, devotion, and so forth.

---

* Terms referring to the separate and distinctive features of the individual personality
  – eds.

On the other hand, let us take the case of a person who loves his parents and feels committed to them, but has not been furnished by Providence with the proper material means to provide them with food and shelter. He is poor, a day laborer who barely earns a meager livelihood and is unable to support his father and mother and spend time with them. The external aspect of *kibbud* is not realized by him, even though this omission is due to unfriendly circumstances which are beyond one's control. Yet, as to the experiential component, he certainly developed the proper approach to his parents, one of love and respect.

There are also many who, in spite of the fact that their hearts overflow with love and tenderness for their parents, cannot act out their feelings. Various psychological blocks and inhibitions prevent them from expressing their inward life in outward symbols of action. They are handicapped by a sense of shyness; they are embarrassed by the arrogant intrusion of the outside upon their privacy. They simply refuse to open up their inner world and let action spotlight their most intimate experiences. They remain impersonal and therefore allegedly cold, violating the technical principle of *kibbud*. Others, eager to manifest their inner experiences, fail to do so because they lack a sense of coordination between the emotion and expression, intention and deed, thought and grammatical formulation. They are hampered by a certain clumsiness in demonstrating their inner world, and hence quite frequently they do or say just the opposite of what they intended to express through word or action.

The same is true of *mora*. One may be a coarse person and not be able to observe the halakhic etiquette which is binding upon the child. One's language is vulgar, he is uncouth in guise and gesture, his manners are uncultivated. He lacks the ability to control his anger. It is self-evident that from time to time he may commit an infraction of the norm of *mora* by uttering the wrong word or giving his parents an ugly look. Yet, in spite of the fact that he is unrefined and rude, in spite of his awkward exterior, his heart might be tender and kind, might inwardly experience fear and admiration for his parents. The opposite is also possible. The child is by nature a polite person, has inbred excellent manners and polished phrases, treats his parents with courtesy and civility. Formally his relationship is immaculate. Yet inwardly he feels contempt for them and considers himself superior to the old folks. He actually only tolerates them, notwithstanding all the niceties he accords to them. In either case only one aspect of the precept finds its fulfillment, while the other is violated.

The Halakhah has adopted a tolerant attitude toward all these people. Of course, the ideal realization of *kibbud u-mora* can only be attained when the external act and the inner experience, the outward and the inward, complement each other. However, the people whose intentions are good even though their outward behavior does not reflect their inner mood, or, vice-versa, individuals who act in accord with the practical code of *kibbud u-mora* out of sheer habit and technical training while their soul abides in the bleak and dreary realm of neutrality, are not to be condemned as violators of the *kibbud u-mora* obligation. The latter norm fluctuates, like certain mathematical functions, between a maximum and minimum boundary. Judaism, with its realistic approach to human nature, has always been tolerant toward its frailties and limitations and did not expect the average Jew to attain the perfect harmony between his inner and outer orders. As it has always rejected the theory of the esoteric character of the religious act, it had to give an opportunity to every normal person who is in command of his deeds to share in the realization of the Divine commandment of *kibbud av va-em*. A similar attitude has been adopted by Judaism toward many halakhic precepts.

Halakhic Norms: Their Rationale and Implications

The formal, practical, normative component of *kibbud* summons man to serve father and mother; it is a call to the service aimed at the promotion of physical and mental well-being of the parents. It is basically an act of welfare service. The practical normative aspect of *mora* finds its expression in a halakhic etiquette which regulates the formal relationships between parent and child, even though this particular decorum is not correlated with an inner feeling.

The Talmud says: "What is implied in the principle of honoring one's parents? One is to provide his parents with food and drink, lead them into the house and out if they are old or infirm" (Kiddushin 31b). Maimonides writes:

> *What does kavod imply? It means providing them with food and drink, clothing and covering, the expense to be borne by the father. If the father does not have the funds and the son does, he is compelled to provide. He must support his parents in accordance with his means, conduct his father in and out and perform for him such personal services as disciples perform for their teacher, and stand before him as he stands before his teacher (Hilkhot Mamrim* [Laws of Rebels] *6:3).*

Again, the Talmud there spells out the basic components of the *mora* relationship. "What is implied in the commandment of *mora?* One is not to sit or stand in his father's place, contradict his words or decide contrary to his opinion." Maimonides repeats the Talmudic passage almost verbatim:

> *Mora requires that the child not stand in the place in which his father usually stands, or sit in his place, or contradict his words, or decide against his opinion, or call him by his name either during his life or after his death. When referring to his father, one should say: "My father my teacher" (Hilkhot Mamrim* [Laws of Rebels] *6:3).*

The practical components of *kibbud u-mora* are easily identifiable and lend themselves to precise formulation: *kibbud* equals welfare service, *mora* equals observance of proprieties. However, the subjective aspect of *kibbud u-mora*, the inner experiences, elude strict interpretation and classification.

In order to gain some insight into the structural patterns of the human experiences of *kibbud u-mora*, we are compelled to inquire into the ethico-philosophical rationale and metaphysical implications of these norms. We deem it both allowable and necessary to delve into the live religious consciousness and search for new dimensions within which we may find the certitude afforded by genuine analysis.

But before we try to inquire into the essence of the inner experience, let us state again that such an experience is halakhically relevant. *Kibbud u-mora,* as I have said before, represent not only a halakhic discipline but a romance as well. The subjective component of *kibbud* is indicated by the mere fact that the Torah availed itself of the term *kibbud* instead of employing the usual Biblical phrases for charitable service, such as, "You shall relieve them," "Open your hand to your parents," "Let them come into your gates and eat and be satisfied," "You shall surely help them." We find proof that this assumption is correct in the Talmudic passage:

> *It is said "Honor your father and your mother" (Ex. 20:12) and it is also said "Kabbed et Hashem me-honekha, Honor the Lord with your substance" (Proverbs 3:9). Thus Scripture compares the honor due to parents to that due to the Omnipresent (Kiddushin 30b).*

It would be absurd to suggest that the precept of *kibbud Hashem me-honekha* signifies the furtherance of God's welfare. Such an interpretation would border on the blasphemous. The identification of *kibbud av* with *kibbud Hashem* refers to an inner experience, one which in all probability manifests itself in a feeling of tender love and compassion for the parents, in a unique subjective approach to father and mother, in an act of relatedness to and identification with them.

Utilitarian Motivation for the Ethical Deed

The norms of *kibbud u-mora* may be seen under three different aspects: the pragmatic; the ethical; and the ontic. These three different motifs have one idea in common: the self-insufficiency and helplessness of the individual, of which the Torah has taken cognizance in the story of the creation of Eve. The idea of interdependence of individuals is basic in Judaism. A man who is only for himself, whose activities and concerns are confined to an isolated life and a self-centered existence, who makes no effort to meet the thou in a spirit of friendship, mutual assistance and cooperation — such a person is doomed to failure. Hence compliance with the principle of *hesed* is not only mandatory but useful as well with respect to the furtherance of our own good. Judaism has never felt embarrassed by this utilitarian motif, if and when it helps man to reach the ethical decision. Our world formula (in contradistinction to the Christian ethic) has not rejected the naturalistic system of morality, despite the fact that it has been the lodestar of most agnostics.

Judaism accepted the here-and-now order of things and events, and sanctioned the creative efforts of man to shape his own destiny and conditions of physical existence and to promote his material welfare. It did not divorce the ethical motif from the human being's utilitarian nature. Moses already emphasized the pragmatic element in a life dedicated to God and His word. He stressed many times that through the service of God man may find the supreme good, even though the term "good" conveys to him worldly happiness and joy. We may say that the law was given to Israel in order to provide them with a way of life that would assure them well-being and this-worldly fulfillment. "And the Lord commanded us to do all these statues, to fear the Lord our God, for our good always, that He might pre-serve us alive, as at this day" (Deut. 6:24). With regard to the precept of honoring the parents the Torah speaks of the practical relevance of the compliance with this law.

Secularistic ethical materialism reduced the ethical conscience to a condensed interpretation of an anthropological experience and the norm to natural desire, denied the existence of morality as an absolute factum, and attempted to dispense with the moral "ought" and its pressure upon natural man as a singular non-natural awareness. In contrast, Judaism has accepted the norm-*pragmos* as a full-fledged Divine imperative revealed to us in the mysterious encounter of God and the charismatic community. The compulsive power of the norm, its transcendental character and unconditional duty-awareness of the individual or the community, have not been diminished in any way because of the fact that the fulfillment of the moral law aims at the promotion of the interest of the doer and is found to be useful. It is honorable and moral to serve others while I desire my own good and happiness. This only superficially resembles the approach of Aristotle's eudaemonistic theory or Mill's utilitarianism.* When it is thoroughly examined we come across cardinal differences between philosophical and religious ethical pragmatism.

Loneliness and Interdependence

What is the utilitarian motif of the ethical deed? In order to answer this we must introduce the idea of human loneliness and creatureliness. Man was not provided with independence at the hour of creation. He is not a self-sufficient being who could gratify all his physical drives without employing the help of others. The Creator willed man to feel helpless while in seclusion and to be constantly in need of companionship. He cannot

---

*A eudaemonistic theory is one in which happiness is the greatest good. John Stuart Mill's utilitarianism refers to the theory that the moral quality of an act is determined by the amount of pleasure or happiness it produces. —eds.

alone emerge victorious from his combat with his environment. "It is not good that the man be alone; I shall make him a help-mate opposite him" (Gen. 2:18). Kohelet says: "Two are better than one: because they have a good reward for their labor, for if they fall, the one will lift up his fellow; but woe to him that is alone when he falls for he has not another to help him up. Again if two lie together, then they have heat; but how can one be warm alone. And if one prevail against him, two shall withstand him; and a threefold cord is not quickly broken" (Eccl. 4:9-12) In a word, the lonely person is helpless; he cannot sustain himself. The mere existence of a society in which the individual finds his place within the framework of a coordinated effort to meet the challenge of the struggle for existence corroborates the thesis that the position of the lonely person is untenable.

The Midrashic scholars availed themselves of a strange hom-ily in order to express the idea that interdependence prevails in nature as well as in the human community. The Midrash says as follows relative to the verse, "If thou lend money to any of My people that is poor by thee, thou shalt not be to him as an usurer; neither shalt thou lay upon him usury" (Ex. 22:24):

> Come and see how all of God's creations borrow from one another. The day borrows from the night and the night borrows from the day ... The moon borrows from the stars and the stars borrow from the moon ... The light borrows from the sun and the sun borrows from the light ... Hokhmah (wisdom) borrows from binah (under-standing) and binah borrows from hokhmah ... Heaven borrows from earth and earth borrows from heaven ... Hesed (lovingkindness) borrows from tzedakah (righ-teosness) and tzedakah borrows from hesed ... The Torah borrows from the mitzvot and the mitzvot borrow from the Torah ....(Ex. Rabbah 31:15).

There are no isolated, shut-in events or things at any level within the order of creation. There is interdependence in the astral world, there is interaction between the transcendental and finite existences, there is mutual relatedness within the realm of ethico-religious values. In short, everybody and everything is influenced and affected by something or somebody from the outside. The idea of *hesed* rests upon this premise. If one is utilitarian-minded, he should realize that to be charitable is practical and useful. Even the simpleton may figure as follows: Now I am mighty, rich and capable of supporting others, and the thou is dependent upon me. However, destiny is whimsical and changeable. In the future the roles might be reversed, and I, the now independent and powerful person, shall find myself in dire need, and he who petitioned me for help might be in a position to lend me support in time of trouble and crisis. Therefore, I must come to his assistance now in order to make it possible for me to appeal to him tomorrow when I shall need help.

The Torah says:

> *If there be with you a poor person, one of your brethren, within any of your gates in the land that the Lord God gives to you, you shall not harden your heart, nor shut your hand from your poor brother but you shall open your hand wide unto him and shall surely lend him sufficient for his need in that which he wants .... You shall surely give him, and your heart shall not be grieved when you give to him ... for the poor shall never cease out of the land; therefore I command you, saying, "You shall open your hand wide to your brother, to your poor; and to your needy, in your land ..." (Deut. 15:7-11).*

You cannot foresee future events and you are unable to predict the revolutions of the wheel of fortune. Today, your brother is poor and he needs your support; tomorrow the situation might change and you will stretch out your hand to him. People remember favors and do not forget injustices. Poverty will not cease out of thy land; who will share it the next day, one does not know, therefore did I command you to extend a helping hand to your poor brother. Later you will be compelled to appeal to him, and he will reciprocate. "Cast your bread upon the waters, for you shall find it after many days. Give a portion to seven and also to eight, for you know not what evil shall be upon the earth" (Eccl. 11:12).

The Talmudic sage Rabbi Meir was credited with a beautiful aphorism as an annotation to the verse, "It is better to go to the house of mourning than to go to the house of feasting for that is the end of all men, and the living will lay it to his heart" (Eccl. 7:2):

> He who eulogizes the deceased, will be eulogized at his death; he who buries the dead, will be buried when he will pass on; he who carries the coffin, will be carried by others [when his body will be ready for burial]; he who mourns for others will be mourned by others (Moed Katan 28b).

In other words, dare not abstain from visiting the house of mourning and attending the dead even though it is a very difficult and unpleasant task. Death is the common destiny of every human being. At present you are the survivor; you outlived your brother and you are summoned to take care of the burial arrangement for him. Tomorrow you will depart from life and others will treat you exactly in the manner you treated your fellow man.

The Utilitarian Value of Kibbud Av va-Em

Since the general norm of *hesed* implies a utilitarian theme, there is good reason to assume that the commandment of *kibbud av va-em* is also provided with a similar motif. Indeed, the Torah concludes the command to respect one's parents with the promise "that your days may be long and that it may go well with you ... " (Deut. 5:16). The very precept of *kibbud av va-em* was evolved from the deep-seated awareness of our human interdependence and individual insufficiency. The parents give a part of themselves to the child; they rear him and supervise his growth from birth to maturity with unlimited devotion and superhuman sacrifice. It would be impossible for anyone to reach adulthood without being guided by others, usually by the parents. Sacrificial action on the part of the father and mother provides the child with the proper upbringing and education. At this stage the child is the recipient of favors, the parents the givers and doers.

Time passes on. The children grow up; the parents have aged. The tender weak child is a strong adult, physically, mentally and socially. The parents, powerful and efficient a score or two scores of years ago, are now old, feeble and helpless. They need the assistance of their child — not long ago their little baby, whom they kissed and hugged. The Judaic law states unequivocally: help thy father and mother for purely selfish reasons. The law is very practical and makes reference to our human experience. It is pragmatic and addresses itself to egotistic man: observe the law, for by observing it you are furthering your own interests. To honor father and mother and to serve them is not only a good act but a prudent one as well. The child, who finds pride and joy in his youth, strength and ability, now will have willy-nilly to encounter the experience of old age, of physical frailties and mental incapacity, and will not be able to lead an independent existence without the assistance of his children. If he will treat his parents rightly, similar treatment will be accorded to him by his children.

At this stage, the precept of honoring and fearing requires external action on the part of the child. He must provide the parents with food, clothes, shelter, medical and nursing care, since at some future date he will ask his children to do those same things for him. On the other hand he must not insult, give affront to, or humiliate his old father and mother, even though at times their conduct is bound to embarrass and provoke him or to arouse ridicule. Let him tolerate mutely their absurd whims, their infantile desires, their strange mannerisms which reflect senility, and try to gratify their needs. The son must not become angry or excited at the sight of an old mother offending him in the presence of great exalted men, or of a father throwing money into the sea. He might find himself in a similar situation and would not like his children to abuse him or to restrain him from doing those things in which he will childishly find delight.

Gratitude and Ontic Awareness

We may say that the *pragmos* may serve not only as a causative agent but also as an experiential motif endowing action with inner meaning and worth. God wills us to try to be successful, to attempt to realize our ambitions and to care for and to protect ourselves against all kinds of hazards. The awareness that good begets good, that noble deeds breed nobility and that consonance with propriety is appreciated and rewarded, is a worthwhile experience. Through it you discover that the other fellow is real. Your parents do exist.

It was precisely for this reason that the Halakhah had to raise the norm of *kibbud u-mora* to a higher level, that of ethical idealism. At this level we reiterate the thesis that the human being has been denied absolute autonomy of existence and that therefore he cannot build an isolated existence but must always depend upon and expect help from his fellow human beings. The premise is the same as in the utilitarian philosophy. However the conclusion is different. While from the pragmatic viewpoint we urge man to display kindness to others in order that he may lay claim to similar treatment whenever he will be in need of help, at the level of ethical idealism we do our duty without anticipating any reciprocity or reward. The action is not only prudent but also good, unselfish, and detached from any utilitarian impulse. It is based upon the feeling of gratitude.

In the feeling of gratitude, the experience of ontic fellowship comes to expression. Not the physical but the human existence of the I is dovetailed with the existence of the thou. The I manifests an awareness of belonging to someone else, a knowledge that my existence is irrevocably tied up with the other self, who stands alongside of me. Bahya ibn Pakuda, in *Duties of the Heart*, (*Sha'ar* 3, introduction) traces the whole spectrum of religious and ethical feelings to the gratitude experience. The awareness of grateful indebtedness is the very core of religious and moral thinking and feeling. Acknowledgment of an act of kindness and the grateful acknowledgment of its beneficial impact upon our lives lies at the root of every religious and moral act.

Thus *kibbud av va-em* is placed in a new dimension, namely that of gratitude — the experience of existential solidarity with which we are bound together and from which it is impossible to drift away. The child is indebted to his parents out of grateful appreciation for everything that they have done for him selflessly and disinterestedly. He feels that his relationship to them is an indestructible fact and that he belongs to them and cannot break away from them. If he did attain some success in life — the achievement is mostly due to the sacrifices and loving care of his parents. Hence he is under obligation and must pay his debt of gratitude to them. However, we emphasized that *hakkarat ha-tov*, gratitude, signifies not only the duty of repaying a favor received but an act of recognition and axiological appraisal, a value judgment, a feeling of being indebted and a sense of obligation as well.

We speak quite often of displaying our gratitude to God. (The Bible considers this motif as basic in our relationship to

Him. Some incorporate the principle of gratitude as a fundamental precept into the *hesed* system.) Yet it would be fallacious and primitive to say that our gratefulness expresses itself in reciprocating and doing something for the Almighty in payment of our indebtedness as if our service were to be useful to Him. Gratitude expresses itself not mainly in deed but in thought and feeling, in an inner experience, in the establishment of a unique relationship between the benefactor and the I who enjoyed his kindness and friendship. This relationship is essentially ontic. Gratitude means going out of ourselves toward the thou, placing ourselves in a unique relation to our benefactor, and letting him share with us our most precious possession — ourselves.

I am whatever I am because of a series of circumstances, influences, various determinants. Someone was perhaps the greatest influence in my life, one who helped shape my personality. I know that person extended to me a helping hand when I was in need, that he guided and comforted me in times of crisis, that his words of encouragement and his assistance made it possible for me to emerge victorious from all encounters with hostile and cruel elemental forces. This relationship gives rise to a new ontic perspective. The self is not the exclusive property of the person himself. The benefactor contributed to the development of my self, my talents, abilities and skills, possibly more than I myself. Participating so prominently in the formation of the I, the benefactor acquired a part of the I. The I belongs both to myself and to the thou to whom I owe a great debt. Thankful appreciation denotes the acknowledgment of a creative effort on the part of my benefactor, who became involved in my existential destiny.

This peculiar ontic partnership — which resulted in the inclusion of the other in my ontic awareness — brings us to a second point, namely, that no action, inward or external, should be exclusively I-directed. Any concern with oneself points at the same time towards the other. I free myself from an egocentric and greatly exaggerated, erratic anxiety about myself, and I begin to care (which is a sane and good experience) about myself as related to the other. Desires, hopes, regard and love are not self-centered any more. They are communally directed to where I and the other find ourselves communing.

The interdependence between the I-self and the other-self is spelled out not in terms of practical living — physical service and joint production of economic goods — but in metaphysical accents on an existence in solidarity and sympathy. At the level of ethical idealism, the self-insufficiency and incompleteness of the individual which manifest themselves in gratitude are experienced in his very ontic awareness. He is not only helpless but also lonely. He feels the restrictive power of an isolated and solitary life. He belongs to the other self not only economically but ontically as well. He feels attracted to the thou because the thou is entangled with him in the same fate and destiny.

Gratitude reconciles the person to the idea that there are no isolated hemmed-in existences; there is no ontic seclusion. The sense of gratitude liberates us from the abnormal state of self-directedness and brings solitary man face to face with another lonely being. True gratitude means an existence turned outwards, an acceptance of responsibilities for and gracious giving to the other, an awareness that wherever I am the other trails behind me like an everlasting shadow. In short, gratitude is not only an ethical but an ontological experience, an awareness of the other's being.

Gratitude creates a sense of inner relatedness and existential togetherness between parent and child. The Talmudic maxim conveys the idea of ontic partnership most succinctly: "Our Rabbis taught: there are three partners in a person, the Holy One, Blessed Be He, the father, and the mother ..." (Kiddushin 30b). In gratitude one discovers the reality of the other not in a practical but in an ontological sense. The other encroaches upon my privacy and individual separateness.

"Love Your Neighbor as Yourself"

As a matter of fact, the commandment of *"ve-ahavta le-re'akha kamokha*, and you shall love your neighbor as yourself" (Lev. 19:18), expresses the idea of ontic relationship. The noun *"re'akha,* your neighbor" signifies a co-existent companion, a co-worker — in short, one with whom you are connected and co-related. Why did the Torah command us to love the other like ourselves? Why did the Torah stipulate that the kind of love which we must give others should not differ from the love we are bestowing upon ourselves? What does the *"kamokha,* as yourself" mean? The answer has already been formulated. The *re'a,* the neighbor, is a part of ourselves, a co-participant in our ontic endeavor — for we are all joined to one another. When we turn to ourselves, desiring to serve ourselves we *eo ipso* move toward the other with whom we are linked through an existential fellowship.

We said that at the idealistic level the norm of *kibbud* is based upon the idea of gratitude. We then arrived at a conclusion that the norm of *ve-ahavta le-re'akha* rests also on the same experience. One must feel gratitude not only to his parents but to his neighbor as well. Now a new question arises: What has the commandment of *kibbud* added to the norm of love for the other self? What is the unique element in the norm of *kibbud u-mora?*

In order to answer this question we must first analyze the commandment of *ve-ahavta le-re'akha kamokha.* Three interpretations of this precept may be advanced: First, you must not do to others what you do not want others to do to you. This formula, employed by Hillel in his conversation with the proselyte who asked him for a short aphorism in which all Jewish ethics can be summed up (Shabbat 31a), recognizes the distinctness of the I, his separateness, and does not ignore his specific rights. The I ascertains his position and comes into his own before any relationship to the other is developed. According to Hillel, the Torah never demanded from man to desire for others whatever he would wish for himself. This would be unrealistic and contrary to human nature. The I must remain a distinct identity endowed with unique rights and privileges. Thus the commandment of *ve-ahavta* was interpreted in purely negative terms, as an injunction against inflicting harm upon the other — as a prohibition against action which I would resent bitterly if aimed at me. The thou here reaches equality with the I and stands alongside of him. The I discovers that the other self is as real as he is. When the reality of the other self not as a physical object but as a personality is established, the latter commands the respect of the I. He is enjoined from violating the dignity of the *re'a*.

A second interpretation, quite different from the one offered by Hillel, is found in Maimonides' Code:

> *The following positive commands were ordained by the Rabbis: visiting the sick, comforting the mourners, joining a funeral procession, dowering the brides, escorting departing guests... These constitute deeds of lovingkindness performed by the person for which no fixed measure is prescribed. Although all these commands are only on Rabbinical authority, they are implied in the precept, "And you shall love your neighbor as yourself"; that is: What you would have others do unto you, do unto him who is your brother in the Torah and in the performance of the commandments (Hilkhot Avel* [Laws of Mourning] *14:1).*

The norm has been filled with a positive moment. One is not only enjoined from doing harm to his neighbor but is also required to do good to him, to help and to stand by him in trouble and in suffering. The qualification of *"kamokha,* as yourself" has the following connotation. Do your neighbor all the favors which you expect others to do to you. The positive aspect of this maxim is apparent.

The reality of the thou must be experienced by me. He *is* and he stands alongside of me. Yet another motif comes to the fore: solidarity. The distinctness still prevails. However, I see myself outside of the existential sphere of the other self. I must respect him and treat him with compassion, sympathy and understanding; yet, the I and my neighbor, even though related, are not identical. Only a bond of ontic solidarity is formed.

A third explanation of the commandment is possible: Do for your neighbor whatever you are willing to do for yourself. This is the most difficult norm. The aim is high and exalted. The idea of community existence is born. The very barriers in which the I was imprisoned are torn down for the others who enter into it. No longer is there a boundary separating the I from the thou. The I emerges from his retreat and joins an existential community with the thou. The closed cycle of individual existence is broken. The other is not an alien existence; he is related to me metaphysically and we both participate in the creation of a together-being. The commandment of *ve-ahavta le-re'akha kamokha* is based upon the mere fact that he exists and that this existence is part of the ontic union. These three maxims represent, indeed, three basic approaches of the I to the thou.

The first interpretation, phrased in the negative, says that the I must recognize the existence of the thou, I must see the thou as real. This act of acknowledgment contains *ipso facto* a contractual relationship with the basic clause that guards the rights of the other in the same manner as I want my prerogatives to be protected from unjust infringement. The relationship is of a *juridic* nature. There is a solidarity awareness; yet solidarity is not to be equated with community. We must not speak of a union. The autonomy has not been completely eliminated. One considers the thou as the other self who is not to be equated with the I. The ontic realms are still separated even though they are not completely closed to each other. There is communication and interaction between them; the narrowness of the existential individual has disappeared. The spaces are wide. Yet no existential union has been formed as yet. The thou has not entered the I, nor has the I been admitted into the thou. The second — the Maimonidean — interpretation points toward a higher level of interhuman relationship. The latter is raised from an awareness of neutral facticity to an awareness of ontic solidarity. The third notion proclaims "union of being." Individual existence ceases to be solitary. It becomes a community existence, a fellowship of *hesed*, rooted in an awareness of unity.

The Talmudic controversy between Rabbi Akiva and Ben Petura revolves essentially about this problem: What does the norm of *ve-ahavta le-re'akha* seek to establish? Is it a mutual relatedness to and recognition of the other, a partnership, solidarity, or love?

> *Two are traveling on a journey and one has a pitcher of water; if both drink, they both die, but if one only drinks, he can survive. The son of Petura taught: it is better that both should drink and die rather than that one should witness his companion's death. Until Rabbi Akiva came and taught, "'Ve-hei ahikha imakh, that your brother may live with you' [Lev. 25:36] — hayekha kodemim le-hayyei haverkha, your life takes precedence over his life" (Bava Metzia 62a).*

Ben Petura subscribes to the third maxim; Rabbi Akiva to either the second or the first. Rabbi Akiva's statement stresses the distinct character of "*imakh,* with you." Your existence should be coordinated with your brother's; there must not arise a barrier separating you from your brother. He must stand alongside you. Yet it does not summon the I to bring about a full merger of the selves.

In light of Rabbi Akiva's interpretation of the norm *ve-ahavta*, we may grasp the unique element in the precept of *kibbud av*. While the bond between the I and the other self is one of ontic solidarity and comradeship, only the parent-child ideal relationship is translated by the Halakhah into an existential community. The ethical implications of a relationship which is based on love are tremendous.

The Ontic Unity Between Parent and Child

There is an ontic union, a unity of being, between parent and child; the child's self-awareness must include father and mother. The child must experience ontic oneness, a sense that he is irrevocably bound to his parents and that this unity is an indestructible fact from which he cannot break away. Hence one's inner self-experience — expressed in terms of love, self-regard, self-esteem, and concern with and worry about himself — extends its frontiers into parts unknown, to another existence, which in this case happens to belong to the parent. The principle of community as to abstention and positive action reigns supreme. I must accord to my parent whatever I think is due to me, be it physical care, peace of mind, or love and regard.

The bond between parent and child, once the latter reaches maturity, is completely divorced from any hedonic, egocentric motivation and can only be interpreted in terms of love of a higher quality, which is rooted in the awareness of unqualified unity on the part of both parent and child. There is a steady outpouring of the heart of the parent toward the child, and conversely there is a continual act of identification of the child with the parent.

In a word, the norm *kibbud* is interpreted in categories of love: to honor means to love; and the latter manifests the experience of ontic unity, of a thou union.

The Search for Roots: Finite and Infinite

There is an existential give-and-take relationship between parent and child. Each depends existentially on the other. The dependence between parent and child is reminiscent of the dependence prevailing between a tree and its roots. What chance of survival has the tree whose roots have died, and of what use are the roots if the tree has been felled? Suspended in midair is the child who has drifted far from his origin — his parents. He must feel a devastating loneliness. He must burn with a thirst, since the cool crystal-clear waters of the well-spring from which he removed himself in a fit of rebellion and anger are at an almost endless distance from him. Vice-versa, one should endlessly pity the parents who in their mad rush for success and riches, lose their child, for all the riches that were assembled turn into dreadful poverty; and a bright day full of fragrance, song and color turns into a dreary and cold autumnal night. The Halakhah has emphasized time and again the unique nature of the parent-child relationship. In fact, it has introduced into it a transcendental motif and equated it with the relationship binding man to God. The origin-perception is characteristic of both.

Finite man searches irresistibly for his ontic roots, the roots of his being. He questions himself, he keeps interrogating his mind and soul, inquiring of them, whence comes his paradoxical existence; whence the beauty, joy and ecstasy of being just a human being who unlike the animal transcends the biological natural dimensions; whence the sweet assurance that one *is*. The answer is quite often slow in coming. But, when it finally does come, it strikes man with elemental force; it is straight and unequivocal. In fact, the answer does come in the form of a real *"ursprung* (source)" revelation or in the form of a living perception rather than that of a lifeless abstract conception. Suddenly, the darkness dissipates; the horizons become brilliantly illumined. Man sees God and, while seeing Him, he comes upon his ultimate true ontic root.

Yet, the encounter of man and God can only occur if man, in his quest for the great ultimate and eternal root, is also concerned with his little, conditioned and transient this-worldly roots. Only after finite man recognizes and acknowledges his dependence upon someone in the here-and-now world, does God bestow upon him the illuminating consciousness of the dependence upon the One and Only root. The quest for the root is not only a transcendental adventure, but a human adventure as well.

Thus, man seeks the great ultimate root of all being in Infinity and finds it in God; he also explores at the same time the finite realm, moving along all its paths in his search for the limited and conditioned root of being. And in so doing, he discovers his parent. As we likewise have already stated, Judaism, with its characteristic sense of realism, considers the root quest within here-and-now reality to be the reflection of the primary search for the absolute origin or source beyond the bounds of sensuous reality. The Jew learns to confess his faith in God and his impassioned yearning for Him by telling the story of people whom he loves and with whom he seeks to identify himself. Judaic faith and theology are linked with finite experiences and meaningful human relations. By developing proper structures of human relations, the Jew learns how to love, revere and commit himself in an ultimate manner to God. When the child finds his finite-conditioned origin in his father or his mother, he *ipso facto* discovers his infinite and ultimate origin in God. However, it is impossible to discover the mysterious transcendental origin if the individual is not acquainted with the origin-perception of belonging to and being rooted in something or someone within the range of the finite and tangible world.

Man and Self-Denial

As the term of our inquiry we seek the definition of *mora* experience, whereby we may differentiate between this term and *kibbud*. The question is a simple one. What more can the Torah demand from the child than a union in love with his parent, equal care and devotion?

I believe that a passage in the Maimonidean Code contains the clue to the understanding of the experience.

> *To what lengths should the duty of kibbud av, of honoring the parents, extend? Even were they to take a purse of his, full of gold, and cast it in his presence into the sea, he must not shame them, manifest grief in their presence, or display any anger, but rather must accept the Divine decree without demur.*

> *To what lengths should the duty of mora, of revering them, extend? Even if he is attired in costly garments, presiding over a congregation, and his parents come and rend his garments, strike him on the head, and spit in his face, he must not shame them. It behooves him to remain silent, to fear and revere the King, King of Kings, who has thus decreed... (Maimonides, Hilkhot Mamrim* [Laws of Rebels] *6:7).*

Both situations are mentioned in the Talmud (Kiddushin 32a and 31a, respectively). The phrase used by Maimonides is identical in both cases: "To what lengths should the duty extend?" However, Maimonides discriminates between these two cases; the first one he classifies under the category of *kibbud*, the second under that of *mora*. Of course, we wonder what the criterion of this distinction is.

Let us analyze both happenings in terms of the human power of endurance and sufferance. Both cases call for great willpower, self-control and emotional restraint. It is not easy to let senile parents destroy property or to acquiesce to their heaping abuse on themselves and their children. To behave with stoic calmness and casual indifference is very difficult. Both episodes attest to a powerful moral character, and to the mastery one exercises over his emotions. Yet if one should ask me which of these two events was more indicative of the moral strength of the person involved in those unpleasant experiences, I would say the second one. It is much easier for one to witness a senseless waste of money than to suffer humiliation and be reviled in the presence of people whose respect he is most eager to command and whose contempt and disdain he fears.

This heroic deed transcends by far the limits set by the norm of "love thy neighbor like thyself," even those set by Ben Petura's interpretation, that is, the awareness of the I-thou union in love. One would never subject himself to public contumely and ridicule, though he may waste his money and throw a handful of golden coins into the street in order to enjoy the excitement of the crowd throwing itself on the gold and to enjoy the peculiar reputation of being extravagant and exotic. In a word, the first episode demonstrates equality; the parent should be treated with the same magnanimity and liberality as one is accustomed to accord to himself. If there is a possibility that one may under certain circumstances resort to similar erratic tactics, then he is enjoined to tolerate such strange conduct on the part of his parents. However, if he would *never* knowingly behave in a like fashion even under the stress of the most unfriendly events, then the toleration of such whimsical conduct cannot be based upon the norm of *kibbud*. The latter demands equal love but not preferential treatment; it says that one must practice indulgence of parents' strangest whims as long as such whims might make *him* act in a strange fashion.

The norm of *kibbud* never recommended unlimited tolerance toward a parent who exceeds all bounds of normal behavior. To display patience and perseverance toward a parent who has completely lost his control mechanism for discriminating between right and wrong, decent and indecent, the Torah had to introduce the norm of *mora*. The latter advances a new element: sacrifice. The ideal of self-denial for the sake of the parent has emerged with the norm of *mora*. I must place myself in his service unreservedly. My commitment to him is unqualified, my duty supreme. The norm of *mora* summons me to even take on the burden of his suffering. *Mora* demands not equality but reverence, which in turn expresses itself in self-giving to the parent, in placing him above myself, in assessing my relatedness to him as something sacred and indispensable for my own being, in experiencing a unique dependence upon him which can only be understood if placed within a metaphysical transcendental realm.

Yet we must pause to inquire into the philosophical background of this strange and unique idea. The norm of *kibbud* with all its ramifications can easily be interpreted within the framework of human interrelationships. The union in love, the existential community, the sharing with others, however distant and sublime these goals might appear to be, do not transcend the bounds of finite human fellowship and communion. The Halakhah had perhaps tried to idealize individual and social relations, since *de facto* no one can put the other on par with himself. The element of self-love and self-regard will always be present even in one's dealings with father and mother. Yet the image of selfless love which embraces another existence is an ideal within the frame of finite reference.

In contradistinction to *kibbud, mora* is alien to the class of feelings which accompany one's contacts with his fellow man. It is essentially a category borrowed from our religious life, where we finite beings encounter infinity.

Two Types of Fear

Let us probe into this problem a little more deeply. The medieval philosophers spoke of two emotions of *yir'ah*, of fear. The first is *yir'at ha-onesh,* fear of punishment. At this level, fear is equated with fright, and it manifests itself through inner agitation and alarm caused by forebodings and the anticipation of injury or punishment. The second is *yir'at ha-romemut*, fear of the exalted, or *yir'at ha-kavod,* fear of majesty. Here, fear is identical with the feeling of awe arising from one's encounter with the infinite, mysterious, unknowable and wholly other. This type of fear is not based on prescience and anticipation of consequences but on the awareness of the infinite, incomprehensible and exalted which is (to use Rudolf Otto's words) "quite beyond the sphere of the usual and intelligible" and which fills us "with blame, wonder and astonishment." The commandment pertaining to the fear of God refers to both emotions of fear — fright and awe.

Maimonides writes in his *Sefer haMitzvot:*

> *He has commanded us that we are to fear Him and that we are to be in awe of Him, so that we may not be like those unbelievers who walk in the stubbornness of their hearts and in a spirit of contrariness. Instead we are to be in fear of His punishment at all times (Positive Commandment 4).*

In his Code, he interpretes the norm of *yir'ah* in different terms.

> *And what is the way that will lead to the love of Him and the fear of Him? When a person contemplates His great and wondrous works and creatures and from them obtains a glimpse of His wisdom which is incomparable and infinite, he will straightway love Him, praise Him, glorify Him and long with an exceeding longing to know His great name, even as David said, "My soul thirsts for God, for the living God" (Psalms 42:3). And when he ponders these matters, he will recoil affrighted and realize that he is a small creature, lowly and obscure, endowed with a slight and slender intelligence, standing in the presence of Him who is infinite in His knowledge ... (Maimonides, Hilkhot Yesodei ha-Torah [Laws of the Foundations of the Torah] 2:2).*

In *Sefer ha-Mitzvot* he introduced *yir'at ha-onesh*, in *Mishneh Torah* — *yir'at ha-romemut*. Both viewpoints are correct insofar as man's relationship is concerned. However it would be absurd to maintain that the Torah commanded the child to display fright and alarm with respect to his parents. The painful emotion of fright has no place within the parent-child relationship. It is hardly possible that the Torah has been trying to instill in us a feeling of insecurity and agitation with regard to our parents. This would be utterly ridiculous.

What the Torah meant with its commandment of *mora* is an inner relationship of admiration, profound veneration and awe. One must revere his parents; they should arouse in his soul a craving, a longing, a deep, fearful love, a tremor and a great joy. These characteristics do not belong to the sphere of human mundane experiences. They stem from our transcendental awareness and are exclusively within the realm of man-God confrontation. By commanding the child to fear his father and mother, the Torah introduced a new dimension into an inter-personal human relationship, namely, the transcendental. It whisks us far from the array of modes of action, thought and feeling of the material-human universe, into the transcendent pure realm of a higher consciousness, by which we become aware of the great mystery of being. In fear man transcends himself and moves on to a higher existential order. The conscious self becomes suddenly aware not only of standing alongside of his parents, but of the great mystery transcending everything and everybody. Our relationship to our parents reflects this mystery awareness and the sense of absolute dependence upon that great unknown. Somehow we shift our relatedness to them into a new perspective, to a new plane which is the meeting place between two realities — the human and the transcendental, man and his origin, creature and creator.

What is the mysterious element involved in the parent-child relationship that engenders a feeling of awe? Parents are, after all, finite beings, as are all humans. Why should they be treated with a reverence which should be due only to the Creator? The answer is implicit in the question and has already been suggested: the *mora* relationship to a parent must not be torn out of the context of relations to God. There is a secret unity beneath the surface diversity. Relationship and relatedness to a parent hides in its essence man's longing and craving for God; there is a final oneness in our surrender to parent and God. In fearing the parent, one stands in awe and tremor before God himself, before the "Before," the source of his existence; in giving parents respect and reverence one adores and worships God.

There is in the fear of a parent the great tremor which an approach to God causes, the rapturous trance, even an overwhelming stupor in the face of the unknown. Hence the mysterious component in the experience of fear of the parent alludes to the beyond, to a transcendental world.

Keneset Yisrael and Eternal Life

The awareness of being is a communal one; otherwise the individual becomes lost in his misery and wretchedness. Judaism has apprehended — long before existentialist thoughts and works spelled it out — the indissoluble bond between being and nonbeing, life and Death, existence and nihility.

Judaism has given ample expression to the anxiety feelings present in man. No psychiatric therapy will cure them, since they form part of his conscious selfhood. This anguish is rooted in the dual awareness of a finite conditioned existence, bounded on all sides by an abyss of nothingness; in the feeling of loneliness, of a being cast out and thrown with dizzying speed to its doom. The fear of death is a potent motif in Judaism.

How did Judaism approach the problem of death? The human personality was raised to a level above the world of decay and disintegration and placed in a transcendental world. The spiritual reality of man is of Divine origin and hence cannot cease to exist. The personality is invested with all the greatness of a true being, and hence is indestructible.

However, immortality is not something that is given the individual in his own right, merely on account of his existence. After all, man has been placed within the order of concrete thinghood where existence is just the preamble of non-being, life — the path to the valley of the shadows, where all creatures are subjected to the tyranny of the law of becoming and decaying.

If man wants to defeat death and to scoff at nihility he must somehow elevate himself above this order of meaningless existence and come close to the order of eternity. In order to gain a pass to everlasting reality he must represent God. He must remember God, become His *shaliah*, His ambassador. He must carry His message and convey it through action. He must become the medium through which God addresses himself to the world, the instrument of revelation. The ideal of prophecy must find at least partial realization in all of us.

This is possible only if the individual Jew includes himself in *Keneset Yisrael*, the community which was burdened at the dawn of history with the Divine logos and ethos, God's word and ethical system, and whose very historic existence is unconditionally consecrated to one goal only — the fulfillment of the covenant through a commitment to a singular *modus existentis*, a mode of existence willed by God. Only when the individual joins this community which is claimed by God, may he lay claim to a deathless existence. Only through identification with the origin may one gain eternal life. It is interesting that the term *karet*, cutting off — which, according to *Hazal*, our Sages, refers to severance from the transcendental order of existence — is mostly linked in the Bible with the expression *"me-adat Yisrael*, from the community of Israel"* (Ex. 12:19) or *"mi-kerev amma*, from the midst of her nation"* (Lev. 17:10). Judaism identified the termination of existence with cutting off the self from the community, for the individual strikes roots in eternity only by abiding within its confines. The great mystery involved in the relationship of child and parent is related to the fear of man vis-á-vis his short-lived sojourn as a being in the sense world and to his quest for permanence. Steadfastness can be achieved only through service which unites man with Being in eternity. This dedicated service can be realized within the community only when the individual joins the great march of *masorah* and *kabbalah*, with its perennial handing down of something great and sublime, its uninterrupted process of teaching and learning, of giving and receiving God's word, law and vision. Each individual is admitted to this fellowship only through his parents who transmitted to him the mysterious testament in order that he may forward it to his successors, thus uniting him with the abstract *makor* and *takhlit*, the source and the purpose of a metahistorical drama of gradual fulfillment of a promise and a vision.

Whoever feels this passion experiences the bliss of belonging to such a society. He fears God and his parents because through them he gains access to a higher order.

"My child, heed the discipline of your father, and do not forsake the instruction of your mother" (Proverbs 1:8).

❧ *Torah and Shekhinah*

Father and Mother

The Talmud relates:

> *Rebbi [R. Judah the Prince] said: It is revealed and known to Mi She-amar Ve-hayah Ha-olam, He who decreed and the world came into existence, that a son loves his mother more than his father because she sways him by her tender words, (meshadalto bi-devarim). Therefore, Ha-Kadosh Barukh Hu, the Holy One, Blessed Be He, placed the obligation of love of the father before that of the mother [in Ex. 20:12 and Deut. 5:16, "Honor your father and mother"].*
>
> *And it is revealed and known to Mi She-amar Ve-hayah Ha-olam, He who decreed and the world came into existence, that a son fears his father more than his mother*

because he teaches him Torah; therefore, Ha-Kadosh Barukh Hu, the Holy One, Blessed Be He, placed the obligation of fear of the mother before that of the father [in Lev. 19:3, "You shall fear every man his mother and father"] .(Kiddushin 30b-31a).

One phrase worth analyzing in the above quoted passage is the appellation, "He Who decreed and the world came into existence," instead of the usual "Holy One, Blessed Be He" or "*Ha-Makom*, the Omnipresent," which are often employed to refer to God. As a matter of fact, the attribute "Holy One, Blessed Be He" occurs in the second part of each of the statements. Apparently, the introduction of a new designation was intentional rather than incidental.

The explanation, I believe, is simple and irrefutable. When the Baraita speaks of God as the legislator whose authority must be respected and whose norm is unqualifiedly and universally binding, the term "the Holy One, Blessed Be He" is used; God is holy, He is the source of holiness, and therefore He requires of man to be holy. In other words, "the Holy One, Blessed Be He" means the God of holiness, which is the highest norm in our law-system and the generic name of the moral law.

However, when we refer to God as the creator, omnipotent and omniscient, Whose will is embedded in organic as well as inorganic matter and Who in His inscrutable wisdom devised the original scheme of creation with all its dissimilarities, antinomies, contradictions and paradoxes, we call Him *"Mi She-amar Ve-hayah Ha-olam*, He Who decreed and the world came into existence."

In the second part of each observation, when we speak about the norms concerning the obligation of a child vis-á-vis father and mother, the description of *Ha-Kadosh Barukh Hu* was employed; in the first half of each observation, when we deal with the striking contrast between the paternal and maternal relationship to the child, revealing the deep gap between the role the father plays in the life of the child and that played by the mother, we use the attribute of *"Mi She-amar Ve-hayah Ha-olam."* This emphasizes that the distinctiveness which marks each relationship — paternal as well as maternal — was willed by the Maker. Father and mother should each act in singular fashion.

The Torah, in narrating the story of the creation of man, employs the most mysterious of metaphors. "And God created man in His image, in the image of God He created him, male and female He created them" (Gen. 1:27). We are mystified by the inclusion of the physiological fact of sexual differentiation in the story of man created in God's image. It is obvious that the difference between man and woman, Adam and Eve, asserts itself not only in biologico-physiological sex-differentiation but in personality-differentiation as well. The Torah speaks not only of sexual differentiation but of bi-personality. The spiritual essence of man differs from that of the woman, and this divergence in their metaphysical spirituality finds its expression in the incommensurability of the motherhood and fatherhood experiences. In what does this incommensurability manifest itself? The Baraita has defined the basic distinction between paternal and maternal love as, "she sways him by her tender words, *meshadalto bi-devarim*," while "he teaches him Torah."

What is *shiddul devarim*? Literally, the phrase means to convince, to persuade, to win over, to sway, to placate. However, the literal meaning is misleading in this context, since it could suggest to us that father and mother are competing for the affection of the child, as if the parent-child community hallowed by Judaism as the first natural community created by God were torn asunder.

I would prefer, therefore, to deviate a bit from the literal meaning and translate the term as having the connotation of being affectionate, of playing with the child, and showering him with love and tenderness. I cannot help associating the Talmudic phrase *meshadalto bi-devarim* with the import of the Biblical phrase *yeled sha'ashu'im* (Jer. 31:19), a child with whom one plays, with whom one laughs, jumps, dances, sings and cries.

In contradistinction to maternal love which consists of *shiddul*, embracing, dandling, playing — the father is engaged in a different activity, teaching him Torah. He passes on knowledge to the child. In other words, the father disciplines the child while the mother affectionately plays with him. "My child, heed the discipline of your father, and do not forsake the instruction of your mother" (Proverbs 1:8).

I want you to understand: the Baraita does not speak of father and mother, but of types — father types and mother types. The real father may have certain characteristics which belong to the mother-type, and the mother may act like a father. The Baraita is speaking of so-called *"deyoknaot,"* prototypes, archetypes.

Here a question arises. The contrast between father's and mother's relationship basically portrays two successive periods in the child's life. It is not, *prima facie*, a contrast at all. The mother dandles and plays when the child is very young, whereas father enters the scene as educator and disciplinarian at a much later stage, when the child begins to mature. At that phase, the mother discontinues playing with the child and most probably restrains herself from showing her affection. The child simply outgrows all this. In short, mother's outpouring of love and father's stern discipline at first glance relate to two successive periods. We do not understand where our sages found a basic discrepancy between the paternal and maternal relationship.

Apparently, the mother never stops dandling her child. She never ceases to be affectionate and loving even though the child is a full-grown person, an adult. If she does not engage in it physically, she is preoccupied with all this inwardly, in thought. In other words, the Baraita concerned itself not with actual manifestations of tenderness on the part of the mother and actual disciplining on the part of the father, but with inward attitudes, spiritual approaches, and personalistic patterns, which might at certain times assert themselves in two different kinds of activity vis-á-vis the child.

In order to understand the contrast we will introduce another Baraita: "The father is dutybound to circumcise his son, to redeem him [if he is a firstborn], to teach him Torah, to teach him a craft — some say, to teach him to swim too" (Kiddushin 29a). The mother has been relieved of all these educational duties vis-á-vis her son. (See Kiddushin 30b.) What is the message of this Baraita?

Again, the law is rooted in the fundamental incongruity of the two concerns, paternal and maternal. Of course, both relationships are genuine, deep-seated and intimate. Yet the teleology or purpose guiding father in his efforts to help his child is not identical with that which is stimulating mother. Neither are the images of the child which father and mother behold the same. The discrepancy expresses itself in, if I may use a Heraclitean-Hegelian term, a dialectic of movements — that is, father and mother move in two opposite directions.

Father keeps on moving away from his child; mother continuously moves toward him. Father's love is manifest in a movement of recoil, mother's love in the leap forward; father is preoccupied with disengaging himself from, mother with attracting herself to, the child. Father's concern expresses itself in an act of gradual detachment, mother's in that of enhancing the relationship. Let me explain this. Father is basically a teacher, a leader; he gives advice, he offers opportunities, he blazes the trail for his offspring. However, he expects the children to learn to act on their own, to utilize the counsel they are given gratuitously, to take advantage of the opportunities and finally to attain complete independence and maturity.

In contradistinction to the father, the mother holds onto her child, refusing to let go; her desire is to be always a part of him. She can never perform an act of withdrawal. On the contrary, she surges steadily forward to her child. For the mother, no matter how old and independent the latter is, the image of the baby, the memory of an infant held in her arms, the picture of herself playing, laughing, embracing, nursing, cleaning, and so forth, never vanishes. She always looks upon her child as upon a baby who needs her help and company, and whom she has to protect and shield.

As a matter of fact, the mother can never forget the biological fact that her child was once a part of her, that she gave him her blood and that she brought him into the world with suffering and pain. When she says: "My baby," she means to say: "Once we were one body. I gave you life. We together were involved in the same organic processes." Neither can she ever dismiss from her mind the sleepless nights during which she in anguish watched over a sick feverish child; she remembers all her prayers and vows because of him.

"The words of King Lemuel (Solomon); the burden wherewith his mother corrected him. What my son? And what, *bar bitni*, son of my womb? And what, *bar nedarei*, son of my vows?" (Prov. 31:1-2). The mother of Lemuel, Batsheva, addressed herself to King Solomon with these words. She came to reprimand him after he had married the daughter of Pharaoh. He was then the great king, the most powerful and famous ruler in the Near East, respected and admired by all. And yet for her he was the baby of old, the baby of her womb, the baby of her vows.

Two Forms of Remembering

The difference between the two parental relationships to the child, the father's and the mother's, is due to a more basic divergence in the act of remembering.

There is a progressive image memory which moves with the stream of time-consciousness. It retains thoughts, impressions, perceptions, and so on. It is basically a technical reproduction of knowledge. However, this reproduction is limited to the projection of a pale image, a still picture, a lifeless copy of what transpired in the past. What one remembers does not interfere with the present; the memory does not cross the frontiers of time dimensions. The past, where the event lies, is dead; the present is alive. The progressive image memory cannot change it.

There is, however, a non-progressive and timeless event memory which captures and imprisons the experiences themselves and quickens bygones with new life. One endowed with such an event-memory not only remembers the past but relives it. The latter strikes him with enormous force, infusing images with life, converting old pictures into realities. This memory makes man retreat either into the dark night of loneliness or into the bright daylight of affection and love. Some people are fortunate not to possess such a capacity for reliving, for reexperiencing. But those who are blessed or cursed by Providence, which endowed them with the power of confronting the past as if it were the living present, know what I mean.

The father belongs to the people whom Providence has spared by giving them a progressive photo memory. He remembers that his child was once a baby. But it is just a recollection — a pleasant one, to be sure. Now the child is an adult, and the father treats him like one.

The mother, however, was provided with timeless event-memory. Not only does she remember her baby, but she lives through the various stages of the child's development, from its earliest infancy on, and clings to it. "Is not Ephraim a dear son unto me or a child that I dandle, for whenever I speak of him I do remember him" (Jer. 31:19). *Prima facie*, the sequence in the verse is wrong. First one recalls an episode, and only following the reproduction does one discuss it. You do not speak of somebody whose image is hidden in a latent memory and has not been reproduced. The order should have been reversed: Whenever I *remember* him I *speak* of him.

It is obvious that the prophet refers to the experiential

memory, to the capacity of living through a seemingly forgotten past, of restaging and reenacting the great drama of motherhood which is perhaps the most exalted emotion both in its moments of illuminated joy and in those of black and despairing ecstasy. Whenever I see Ephraim I think of him as I remember from years back: when we together had a wonderful time, playing, laughing, jumping, running, and he was then so innocent, so pure, so babyish.

In short, the love of father consists in helping the child to free himself from paternal authority, in moving away from him, while mother's love expresses itself in steady intensification of her emotional attachment, in surging toward her child.

The Halakhah entrusted education to the father — and what is the educational gesture if not an act of granting independence to the young person and training the latter to live with dignity and responsibility and in freedom? The father was charged with this task because it fits into the framework of paternal concern. The mother was relieved of the educational duties since she instinctively resents her child's adulthood and the independence that education is supposed to promote and foster.

Let us emphasize the capacity for mental growth. The fact that man is teachable and educable is part of the unalterable law that God pronounced at the emergence of Eve: "Therefore shall a man leave his father and mother, and he shall cleave unto his wife" (Gen. 2:24). Since a human being responds to the educational gesture, the aboriginal parent-child community is only a transitory phenomenon. With the child's reaching maturity and *ipso facto* acquiring freedom, the parent-child community disintegrates and is superseded by the matrimonial community. The father, paradoxically, works hard in order to liquidate the very community which he formed and of which he is an integral part. The mother, however, has never reconciled with this Biblical decree and resists any effort aiming at the dissolution of the parent-child community. She clings courageously and tenaciously to that community whose liquidation would spell disaster. She refuses to accept her destiny and to surrender her baby to another woman. She resents, and at times her resentment borders on enmity towards her daughter-in-law, since the latter is the one who is blamed for destroying the community. The tension between a woman and her daughter-in-law is proverbial in all languages. The Halakhah is also aware of the conflict. The mother-in-law and daughter-in-law are included among the five women whose testimony is not accepted to establish that a woman's huband has died (Yevamot 117a).

God's Love

We have mentioned before that the two incongruous concerns for the welfare of the child represented by father and mother are rooted in the metaphysical idea of *imago Dei*, of *tzelem Elokim*, of the image of God. Apparently, the two modes of love-manifestation can be found in God's relationship to the covenantal community. God acts as both our father and our mother. Of course, we humans cannot comprehend His ways and can never foresee what concern God will display in a particular situation and at a certain time. Yet both modes of loving, caring and helping, are manifested by the Almighty. He is our disciplinarian: "the Lord your God disciplines you just as a man disciplines his son" (Deut. 8:5). We invoke him as *Avinu Shebashamayim*, our Father in heaven. We also have trust and faith in Him in a manner reminiscent of the child's trust in its mother. In fact, God is our mother, the *Shekhinah*. "As one whom his mother comforts, so will I comfort you" (Is. 66:13). "Surely I have pacified and stilled my soul like the suckling on its mother's breast; like a suckling is in me my soul. Let Israel wait for the Lord from this time forth and forever" (Ps. 131:2-3). Every sensitive Jew knows that at times we run to the Almighty for advice and encouragement just like a confused, frustrated and disappointed child runs to its father, while at other times we cling to the *Shekhinah,* just like a child who, in utter despair, hides its head in shame in his mother's lap, finding there solace and comfort. May we call God both Father and Mother? Certainly yes!

> *The disciples of R. Yohanan ben Zakkai said to him: Master, bless us. He said to them: May it be God's will that the fear of heaven shall be upon you like the fear of flesh and blood. His disciples said to him: Is that all? He said to them: If only you can attain this! (Berakhot 28b).*

In other words, the relationship of God to us and our relationship to Him lend themselves to description and interpretation in finite human categories. The Jew has learned to confess his faith in and impassioned love of God by telling the story of people whom he loves and with whom he seeks to identify himself. Judaic faith and theology are linked with finite experiences and meaningful human relations. By developing proper human relations structures, the Jew learns how to love, revere and serve God.

If it is correct to speak of our relationship to God in terms of general human relations, it is certainly proper to visualize our approach to the Almighty in terms of the child-parent community.

> *It is said, "Honor your father and your mother" (Ex. 20:12) and it is also said, "Kabbed et Hashem me-honekha, Honor the Lord with your substance" (Proverbs 3:9). Thus Scripture compares the honor due to parents to that due to the Omnipresent (Kiddushin 30b).*

The Baraita does not merely *parallel* the honor and fear that one is obligated to display towards one's parents with the honor and fear due to the Almighty. The Baraita rather *identifies* the two acts. When one honors or reveres his natural parent, father or mother, he, *ipso facto*, honors or reveres God.

Maimonides (*Hilkhot Yesodei ha-Torah* [Laws of the Foundations of the Torah] 2-4 and *Guide of the Perplexed* I:72) expounded the idea that every phenomenon in nature, big and small, organic and inorganic — in a word, the whole cosmic drama — manifests the ceaseless inner quest of creation for the Creator. This inner quest, Maimonides thought, is the prime source of cosmic dynamics. If the flight of the bird, the roar of rolling tide, the fall of the stone, the flexibility of one's muscles, and so on, however mechanical and scientifically determinable, represent the movement of the world to its Maker, if "from the ends of the earth are his praises sung" (Is. 42:10), then the vital powers of man, such as falling in love, reverence, kindness and charity certainly belong to God. Man, like the bird, keeps on leaping forward to his Creator.

There is only one great love. This single love belongs to the Single One. In loving father and mother, a person is really in love with God, whose glory shines through two elderly people. The finite love, if I may use Platonic imagery, is just a reflection of the boundless love one at times unconsciously feels for the Almighty. What is transient fatherhood and motherhood if not a reflected beam of light coming to us from beyond the frontiers of the cosmos, and what is paternal or maternal concern if not an echo of the great concern of the Almighty?

"Whenever Rav Yosef heard the footsteps of his mother, he would say: Let me rise because the *Shekhinah* is coming" (Kiddushin 31b). Behind every mother, young or old, happy or sad, trails the *Shekhinah*. And behind every father, erect or stooped, in playful or stern mood, walks *Malka Kaddisha,* the Holy King. This is not mysticism. It is Halakhah. The awareness of the *Shekhinah* results in the obligation to rise before father and mother.

Hence the analogy is legitimate as well as enlightening. God is our father, teacher, legislator and master. He shows us the way to perfection and greatness, the paths of a true life; He handed down to us the Torah, and endowed us with absolute freedom of choice to live either in compliance with or in opposition to the Torah. He charged us with responsibility, and He expects us to display independence in decision and courage in action, as well as to combat, we ourselves, evil and wickedness. God as father is at an infinite distance from us. We call Him *Avinu She-ba-Shamayim,* our Father in Heaven; He abides in the recesses of transcendence, beyond the flying nebulae and the uncharted lanes of the cosmos. Of course, He watches over us, determines our destiny and directs our actions. Yet He is not present in our midst. He dwells in eternity and infinity, beyond the *arafel,* the cloud of the numinous mystery. The Divine paternal emphasis, like that of the natural finite father, is on freedom, on man's responsibility and ability to perform the most arduous tasks all by himself, since man is a free, mature and powerful being. The principle of *behirah hofshit,* of free will, reigns supreme in paternal relationship at both levels, at the natural and transcendental.

However, there is another side to the coin. No matter how free a man is if seen under the aspect of the original scheme of creation, in the course of time and history he gradually becomes the slave of circumstances, an obedient servant of his milieu. He loses his courage and forfeits the heroic capability of defying everything and everybody. Temptation is too strong, sin fascinates, unredeemed vulgar beauty attracts with an irresistible force. Man is in need not only of a Divine law but of Divine help and cooperation as well; He is in need not only of a father who teaches and commands but also of a mother who takes her child across the busy street. He needs a mother who should do for him what he has to accomplish.

In moments of relapse to lower spiritual and mental levels — when freedom of decision is forfeited — Father says let him free himself from this apathy, from this trance of senses and faculties. My child is an adult, He says, a mature person. The free will can overcome any opposition. Father despises weakness, hates cowardice. Only Mother, hearing the plea of Her "baby," comes down to be together with *bar bitni u-bar nedarei,* the child of Her womb, the child of Her prayers and vows. She helps him to walk along the winding paths of our this-worldly existence. Neither sin nor disobedience nor rebellion can sever the bond uniting Mother and Her baby. The older the child is, the more socially and economically independent, the more prominent, the more helpless he appears to be to Her, the more She thinks he needs Her help — the more intense becomes the love which draws the *Shekhinah* Mother to Her child. The *Shekhinah* is always present. The name is indicative of Her presence: *"Ha-shokhen ittam be-tokh tum'otam,* who dwells with them in the midst of their impurity" (Lev. 16:16).

Our sages knew of the antithetic nature of man.

> *R. Hama said in the name of R. Haninah: But for these three following verses the feet of Israel's enemies [a euphemism for Israel] would have slipped [i.e., they would not be able to defend themselves on the day of judgment]. One is: "Whom I have wronged" (Mikhah 4:6); a second, "Behold as the clay in the potter's hand so are ye in My hand, O house of Israel" (Jer. 18:6); the third: "And I will take away the stony heart out of your flesh and I will give you a heart of flesh" (Ezek. 36:26) (Berakhot 32a).*

Rashi explains that God admits that man is not completely free "since He created in them the evil impulse" (Ibid., *s.v., nit-motetu).*

In other words, we deal here with an antinomy [contradictory situation]. The thesis says: man is adult, free and independent. He should do everything by himself. The antithesis states: man is a child, weak and helpless; he is in constant need of mother who will help him reach the proper decision and engage in worthy action. Father accepts the thesis, Mother — the antithesis. The inner contradiction in the idea of free will might have caused Maimonides — who so eloquently expounded and formulated this concept (in, for example, *Shemonah Perakim* [Eight Chapters], chapter 8, and *Hilkhot Teshuvah* [Laws of Repentance], chapter 5) — not to include it in his thirteen *ikkarim*, the table of the basic tenets of faith in his introduction to the commentary to *Helek* (Sanhedrin chapter X).

Hashra'at Shekhinah

Let me venture some reflections on the centrality in the Halakhah of the idea of *hashra'at Shekhinah*, the indwelling or resting of the *Shekhinah*, the Divine Presence.

We may say that the whole idea of *kedushah*, of holiness, in its application to *kedushat makom*, the sanctity of a geographic spot *(kedushat mikdash vi-Yerushalayim,* the sanctity of the Temple and Jerusalem), or to some time entity *(kedushat Shabbat ve-Yom Tov,* the sanctity of the Sabbath and Festivals), or to the personal status of some people *(kedushat kohen ve-kohen gadol,* the sanctity of the priest and High Priest), or to the act of hallowing life itself in accordance with the precept of "*Kedoshim tihyu,* you shall be holy" (Lev.19:2) — the whole idea is nurtured by the awareness of the presence of the unseen *Shekhinah*. The departure of *Shekhinah* rescinds *kedushah*. The controversy about whether the *kedushah* of the Land of Israel is retained after the exile *("kiddesha le-sha'ata, kiddesha le-atid la-vo")* revolves about one problem: May we say that *Shekhinah* has awaited our return to Jerusalem and Temple Mount for two millennia? Wherever the awareness of standing before God has been extinguished, *kedushah* is gone and with it *simhah*, happiness. Mourning, *avelut*, then commences. The very gist of mourning consists in the desolate feeling of absence of the *Shekhinah*.

Of course, I cannot within the framework of this paper engage in a detailed analysis of the idea of *hashra'at Shekhinah* as it is reflected in a variety of halakhic laws. All I want to do is to single out two aspects of this idea which, in my opinion, have great relevance to the modern observant Jew.

Let us first analyze several paragraphs in Maimonides' Code:

> *Laws concerning talmud Torah comprise two affirmative precepts, the first being to study the Torah ... But it is the duty of the father to teach his young son Torah ... If a son has not been taught by his father, it is his duty, as soon as he realizes his deficiencies, to acquire knowledge for himself, as it is said, "That you may learn them and observe to do them" (Deut. 5:1). And so too you will find that study in all cases takes precedence over practice since study leads to practice ... (Hilkhot Talmud Torah* [Laws of the Study of Torah], *headnote and 1:1,3).*

> *If a man wishes to learn Torah and has a son who needs instruction, his own requirements are to be satisfied first. But if his son has better capacity and greater ability to grasp what he learns, then the son's education takes precedence. Still, though his son takes precedence, the father must not wholly neglect the study of Torah. For, just as it is incumbent on him to teach his son, so is he under obligation to obtain instruction for himself. A man should always study the Torah and then marry ... (Hilkhot Talmud Torah* [Laws of the Study of Torah] *1:4,5).*

It is obvious that Maimonides has stated the case of *talmud Torah* in clear unequivocal terms. One is duty bound to study for himself and to teach Torah to others.

In view of the above, halakhah 8 comes to us quite as a surprise:

> *Every Jew is under an obligation to study Torah whether he is poor or rich, in sound health or in pain, in the vigor*

of youth or very old and feeble. Even a man so poor that he is maintained by charity and goes begging from door to door, as also a man with a wife and children to support, are all under the obligation to set aside a definite period during the day and at night for the study of Torah, as it is said, "You shalt meditate therein day and night" (Joshua 1:8) (Hilkhot Talmud Torah [Laws of the Study of the Torah] *1:8).*

The question which comes immediately to the fore is a simple one: Why was it necessary for Maimonides to duplicate? He has already defined the *mitzvah* of *talmud Torah* in the previous seven paragraphs, parts of which I quoted before. Why repetition and redundancy?

Apparently, Maimonides speaks of two distinctive performances. In the first seven paragraphs he deals with the performance of acquiring knowledge, of training the mind in the methodology of Torah, in interpretation, exposition and conceptual analysis, precise application, *et cetera.*

In paragraph 8, Maimonides speaks of an entirely different duty. One is under obligation to set aside a definite time for the study of Torah. The general precept of *talmud Torah* is not concerned with programming, with arrangements in terms of a fixed schedule. Whether one is systematic or disorganized is irrelevant. What counts is the result: the amount of knowledge one acquires, the development of intellectual prowess, the exercise of talents. Decisive is the scholarship one masters, at both levels, quantitative and qualitative. The method he may have employed is unimportant. He might have studied in spurts at random without setting up a program. The relevant question is: *what* did he accomplish, not *how* did he accomplish. However, in halakhah 8 emphasis is placed upon the "how," upon the way in which he studies. Halakhah 8 is out to achieve orderliness. It wants that the process of *talmud Torah* be systematic, well organized, that definite hours be set aside, and that the tightly organized schedule be kept at all costs. Tardiness, procrastination, delay, and change are considered a grave violation even though the loss was recouped later by devoting to study an equivalent number of hours.

As a matter of fact, Tosafot (Sanhedrin 7a, *s.v. ela*, citing Shabbat 31a) imply that on the day of judgment one is interrogated about two things in respect to *talmud Torah*: whether or not he was engaged in the study of Torah; and whether or not *kavata itim la-Torah*, whether he set up and kept a fixed schedule for *talmud Torah*.

At best, the law pertaining to *kevi'at itim*, establishing specifically fixed times and dates, is *prima facie* enigmatic. The question is simple. Why is it necessary to set aside definite hours? What difference does it make how one studies as long as he puts in long hours and as long as the results are good? In respect to other *mitzvot* no rules have ever been formulated about regularity and orderedness. Why should *talmud Torah* be different from other *mitzvot*? Why is a person compelled to answer two questions pertaining to *talmud Torah* on the day of judgment? One question is concerned with the "what," the other with the "how."

At a second glance, it begins to dawn upon us that what appeared at first as incomprehensible reflects an exalted idea which aspires to transcend intellectual formalism and rise to a sublime drama of faith. In this drama we will see presented, under veils, the adventures of restless man, adult and child. Apparently, *talmud Torah* is a dual activity. At one level, the mind is preoccupied with the study of Torah. As such, it is a regular intellectual performance which fits into the framework of the classical formula of learning. At this level, the relationship prevailing between Jew and Torah can be compared to, or rather equated with, the universal subject-object encounter which takes place in any intellectual performance. In essence, the encounter is purely functional, and, using Martin Buber's jargon, exhausts itself in "I" facing "it," which means the absence of relationship.

At the second level, *talmud Torah* becomes a total performance claiming the whole of the personality, and it cannot, as a total performance, be pressed into the classical formula of learning as an I-it confrontation. It is rather, to use again a Buberian phrase, an I-thou relationship. *Talmud Torah* is not just acquisition of knowledge but a personal meeting of the Jew with the Torah. At this level, the Jew cannot just walk into the *beit ha-midrash* unannounced and unexpected and study Torah in his leisure time. As long as the Torah is an it, an object, one can act vis-á-vis an "it" at random; the scientist opens up the door of the laboratory, walks in and picks up the test tube. If the Torah, however, is a "thou," one must arrange a meeting, make a date with her. Otherwise she will not wait for him.

The Jew has a rendezvous with the Torah. Maimonides placed enormous emphasis upon the sanctity of this rendezvous, the significance of keeping the engagement. Neither pain (*ba'al yissurin*), nor hunger or abject poverty (*ani*), nor the dreariness and desolation of old age (*zaken*), nor the aggressive excitement of youth can serve as an apology for breaking the engagement with the Torah.

If an hour was designated, the appointment made, the meeting arranged, no excuse is good enough to disappoint the Torah. Any delay, no matter how potent the reason was, is a violation of the precept of *ve-hagita bo yomam va-lailah* (Josh. 1:8), studying Torah day and night. Punctuality and promptness concerning the rendezvous a Jew has with the Torah are a prime prerequisite. After all, the command of *ve-hagita bo yomam va-lailah*, to engage in the study of Torah at night and day, was addressed to Joshua who was the commander of the armed forces, the king, the chief justice and the successor of Moses. He certainly was a busy man.

The question arises again. Why is it important that the Jew have an engagement with the Torah? What is in general the gist of the idea that the Jew-Torah relationship is an I-thou rather than an I-it encounter? One may say the Torah is a book, a discipline, a doctrine, a Law, a method that I can master, but not a living person whom I must meet. Is the whole halakhah of *kevi'at itim* pure imagery, a flight of human fantasy, an allegory, a mystical vision which recedes fast with the daybreak of reality, or is it something more than all these things? I believe the second alternative is true.

A Rendezvous with Mother Shekhinah

It is self-evident that the halakhic emphasis upon a rendezvous with the Torah and the significance of punctuality and promptness in keeping this rendezvous is to be understood as referring to someone else who trails behind the Torah, namely the *Shekhinah*. God, the *Ribbono Shel Olam*, in this case disguised as Mother *Shekhinah*, never separated Herself from Her daughter; veiled in humble anonymity, She accompanies Her daughter princess, the Torah. She is present wherever Her princess happens to be. Can one meet the Mother *Shekhinah* alone without having a date with Her daughter? No! Whoever is eager to invite Mother *Shekhinah* must first set up a meeting with Her daughter, the princess. She always accompanies her; she is the princess' mother, the princess' friend and the princess' chaperone, who does not leave her out of sight. By dating the daughter, one dates the mother as well. "Moses received the Torah from Sinai" (Avot [Ethics of the Fathers]1:1). The Mishnah does not say "The *Kadosh Barukh Hu* gave the Torah to Moses at Sinai." Why? Because Torah and *Shekhinah* are inseparable. The *Shekhinah* never divorced Herself from the Torah. The latter is still *Torat Hashem*, Her word, Her beloved princess. They never parted company. She lets Moses and Her chosen community share in the great adventure, in the wonderful unitive love affair of *Shekhinah* and *Torat Yisrael*. "When two sit together and engage in Torah, God's *Shekhinah* rests upon them" (Berakhot 6a).

The *mitzvah* of *talmud Torah* begins as an intellectual activity which requires exertion, concentration, absorption, a trained logical mind. The aim of this activity is acquisition of knowledge. However, once the activity is initiated it turns into a great total experience of meeting *Shekhinah*, of having a rendezvous with God. The Jew studying Torah is like a traveler who, within sight of the initial goal, stops to take a breath and then continues with new strength upon his endless journey toward an unknown destination. Knowledge alone, at first very much desired, does not satisfy any more; he is in love with the *Shekhinah*.

In this context another problem is resolved. Have all Jews an equal share in Torah, or is the share proportionate to the accomplishment, to the amount of knowledge one possesses? On the one hand, we know the singular importance we ascribe to *talmud Torah*. On the other hand, we also know what Moses proclaimed: "*Torah tzivah lanu Moshe, morashah kehillat Ya'akov*" (Deut. 33:4). The whole congregation of Jacob owns the Torah — the scholar and the ignorant have the same rights and prerogatives!

The process of learning Torah is both esoteric and exoteric.* At the esoteric level the brilliant mind accomplishes more, the dull — less. This cannot be helped. No process of democratization can change the character of education from esoteric into exoteric. There is an aristocracy of the brains, an institution which Congress cannot abolish — an intellectual gesture is esoteric. However, when we come upon the second aspect of *talmud Torah* — as a rendezvous with the *Shekhinah*, as a meeting with God — the act of *talmud Torah* becomes exoteric and completely democratized.

Let me explain: when Maimonides enumerated various kinds of situations in which one must, in spite of staggering difficulties, comply with his fixed Torah schedule, he has indirectly conveyed

---

* Esoteric means restricted to a small group, while exoteric means open to the public. — eds.

a new idea, namely, the experiential component of *talmud Torah*. The feeling of the presence of the *Shekhinah* is determined not by accomplishment but by effort. The act itself is redemptive, hallowing and inspiring, regardless of who is engaged in it, be he a genius, be he a dull person; if *talmud Torah* even at the experiential level had an esoteric character — the worth being determined by achievement — how could Maimonides warn us against delay? If results count, a change of time may be beneficial. It may raise the quality of the performance. A person who is hungry or in pain cannot concentrate. The time he spends in study is a total waste. And yet Maimonides insists that the engagement be kept. Let us ask ourselves: What is the use of study without obtaining the regular benefits of the intellectual exercise? Wouldn't it be more profitable to postpone the "date" for a short period of time and resume the study of Torah after all physical handicaps have disappeared? The answer to this question was given already, and it is terse and clear.

In respect to the rendezvous with the *Shekhinah* through the study of Torah, centrality has been assigned to the effort; the results are of marginal significance. The worth of the meeting between man and *Shekhinah* is determined by the sincerity of the commitment, by the intensity of the dedication, by the warmth of the encounter, by the love and passion of the God-questing individual, and not by the brilliance of the performance. The *gaon* and the dull person, the great mind and the simpleton, share in the redemptive hallowing experience in accordance with the effort — *"lefum tza'ara agra,* according to the labor is the reward" (*Avot* [Ethics of the Fathers] 5:26).

Believing and Searching

At this juncture, at which halakhic thought and vision, halakhic abstraction and spiritual perception, merge into one, at the frontier of knowledge and illuminated intention, of objectivity and subjectivity, of Divine intellectual disciplines and an exciting romance with the *Shekhinah*, a new *mitzvah* emerges. Let me elaborate a bit. In my opinion, there are two *mitzvot*: *emunah ba-Shem*, belief in the existence of God, and *bakkashat Elokim*, the search for God.

The *mitzvah* of *emunah ba-Shem* was formulated by Maimonides in *Hilkhot Yesodei ha-Torah*. The first precept of Judaism is *emunah ba-Shem*. We all are acquainted with the first paragraph in the Mishneh Torah: "The basic principle of all principles and the pillar of all wisdom is to realize, *leida*, that there is a first Being who brought every existing thing into being. All beings . . . exist only through His true existence" (*Hilkhot Yesodei ha-Torah* [Laws of the Foundations of the Torah] 1:1).

What is the semantics, the meaning and significance, of the term *leida*? Of course *emunah*, belief in God, faith and trust in His absolute, true reality, omniscience and omnipotence, the absolute conviction that He is the only one to whom we are committed unconditionally; Him we will serve, by His will we will abide. This cardinal precept is categorized under the verse of "*Shema Yisrael*, the Lord is our God the Lord is one" (Deut: 6:4), which Maimonides quotes as the source of the *mitzvah* to know His unity (*Hilkhot Yesodei ha-Torah* [Laws of the Foundations of the Torah] 1:7).

However, we have another text which fascinates us with its exalted message: "*U-bikkashtem mi-sham*, but from thence you will seek the Lord thy God and you shall find Him, if you search after Him with all your heart and with all your soul. In your distress, when all these things are come upon you in the end of the days, you will return to the Lord your God" (Deut. 4:29-30).

There is a separate commandment of "*u-bikkashtem mi-sham*," to search for God, to quest, yearn and crave for Him, to continue searching until one finds Him. The significance of the mitzvah I do not have to describe. Its fulfillment is the *conditio sine qua non* for the great historical messianic redemption. Apparently, questing for God is not just an "obsession" of a few

God-intoxicated people, but a real preoccupation of the *ish ha-Halakhah*, halakhic man, who is both realistic and intellectually minded. Since the Torah endorsed and recommended *bakkashat Elokim*, the search for God, we may say that it is not an esoteric art, for the Halakhah rejected esotericism. What is it? What does *bakkashat Elokim* signify? One can perform *mitzvot* and believe in God without searching for Him!

In my opinion, the Torah, in recommending to us the search for God, was concerned with total religious experience, with religious reason or, if I may say, religious sensibility or sensory experience. We are called upon not only to believe in Him, to have faith in Him, to comply with His law, but to find Him with our five senses, to perceive Him the way one perceives light, to feel His presence in our midst, to cleanse the doors of perception, as a mystic said once, in order to apprehend Him right here and now.

If the *Shekhinah* is here, if She is like a good loving mother who holds us in her embrace, cares for us, is concerned about us and never absents herself from us — then She expects reciprocity. A father wants to be respected and obeyed, a mother wants recognition and awareness of her presence. She is afraid to be ignored. As a father, God demands reverence and obedience. As a mother, *Shekhinah* wants only recognition, that the child be aware of the presence of the mother. Faith and belief satisfy the father. They do not make mother happy. She wants that her child be near, and that the child welcome her presence. The eye of the father is focused upon the objective expression of faith, the eye of the mother upon affection and love. The wish of Mother *Shekhinah* should not be ignored. One must quest for Her, search for Her. One will finally find Her if the questing is sincere and genuine, if it is done "with all your heart and with all your soul" (Deut. 4:29).

Index of Biblical and Rabbinic Sources

Note: In the case of large blocks of material, such as whole chapters, we have given the reference without an accompanying text.

BIBLE

Genesis 1:3 p. 99

ויאמר א-להים יהי אור ויהי אור.

Genesis 1:11 pp. 6, 96

ויאמר א-להים תדשא הארץ דשא עשב מזריע זרע עץ פרי עשה פרי למינו אשר זרעו בו
על הארץ ויהי כן.

Genesis 1:12 p. 6

ותוצא הארץ דשא עשב מזריע זרע למינהו ועץ עשה פרי אשר זרעו בו למינהו וירא
א-להים כי טוב.

Genesis 1:20-21 p. 6

ויאמר א-להים ישרצו המים שרץ נפש חיה ועוף יעופף על הארץ על פני רקיע השמים.
ויברא א-להים את התנינם הגדלים ואת כל נפש החיה הרמשת אשר שרצו המים למינהם
ואת כל עוף כנף למינהו וירא א-להים כי טוב.

Genesis 1:22 pp. 6, 96, 97, 98, 99

ויברך אותם א-להים לאמר פרו ורבו ומלאו את המים בימים והעוף ירב בארץ.

Genesis 1:23-26 p. 6

ויהי ערב ויהי בקר יום חמישי. ויאמר א-להים תוצא הארץ נפש חיה למינה בהמה ורמש
וחיתו ארץ למינה. ויהי כן. ויעש א-להים את חית הארץ למינה ואת הבהמה למינה ואת
כל רמש האדמה למינהו וירא א-להים כי טוב. ויאמר א-להים נעשה אדם בצלמנו כדמותנו
וירדו בדגת הים ובעוף השמים ובבהמה ובכל הארץ ובכל הרמש הרמש על הארץ.

Genesis 1:27 pp. 6, 33, 70, 95, 160

ויברא א-להים את האדם בצלמו בצלם א-להים ברא אתו זכר ונקבה ברא אתם.

Genesis 1:28 pp. 12, 32-33, 77, 95, 97, 98, 100

ויברך אתם א-להים ויאמר להם א-להים פרו ורבו ומלאו את הארץ וכבשה ורדו בדגת הים
ובעוף השמים ובכל חיה הרמשת על הארץ.

Genesis 2:7 p. 4

וייצר ה׳ א-להים את האדם עפר מן האדמה ויפח באפיו נשמת חיים ויהי האדם לנפש חיה.

Genesis 2:8-9 pp. 5, 10

ויטע ה׳ א-להים גן בעדן מקדם וישם שם את האדם אשר יצר. ויצמח ה׳ א-להים מן
האדמה כל עץ נחמד למראה וטוב למאכל ועץ החיים בתוך הגן ועץ הדעת טוב ורע.

Genesis 2:10-14 p. 5

ונהר יצא מעדן להשקות את הגן ומשם יפרד והיה לארבעה ראשים. שם האחד פישון הוא
הסבב את כל ארץ החוילה אשר שם הזהב. וזהב הארץ ההוא טוב שם הבדלח ואבן השהם.
ושם הנהר השני גיחון הוא הסובב את כל ארץ כוש. ושם הנהר השלישי חדקל הוא ההלך
קדמת אשור והנהר הרביעי הוא פרת.

Genesis 2:15 p. 5

ויקח ה׳ א-להים את האדם וינחהו בגן עדן לעבדה ולשמרה.

FAMILY REDEEMED

Genesis 2:16-17 pp. 5, 12, 14

ויצו ה׳ א־להים על האדם לאמר מכל עץ הגן אכל תאכל. ומעץ הדעת טוב ורע לא תאכל ממנו כי ביום אכלך ממנו מות תמות.

Genesis 2:18 pp. 5, 15, 16, 33, 69, 77, 135

ויאמר ה׳ א־להים לא טוב היות האדם לבדו אעשה לו עזר כנגדו.

Genesis 2:20 p. 18

ויקרא האדם שמות לכל הבהמה ולעוף השמים ולכל חית השדה ולאדם לא מצא עזר כנגדו.

Genesis 2:21 p. 5

ויפל ה׳ א־להים תרדמה על האדם ויישן ויקח אחת מצלעתיו ויסגר בשר תחתנה.

Genesis 2:23 p. 47

ויאמר האדם זאת הפעם עצם מעצמי ובשר מבשרי לזאת יקרא אשה כי מאיש לקחה זאת.

Genesis 2:24 pp. 29, 104, 165

על כן יעזב איש את אביו ואת אמו ודבק באשתו והיו לבשר אחד.

Genesis 2:25 pp. 5, 78

ויהיו שניהם ערומים האדם ואשתו ולא יתבששו.

Genesis 3:1-5 pp. 23, 101-2

והנחש היה ערום מכל חית השדה אשר עשה ה׳ א־להים ויאמר אל האשה אף כי אמר א־להים לא תאכלו מכל עץ הגן. ותאמר האשה אל הנחש מפרי עץ הגן נאכל. ומפרי העץ אשר בתוך הגן אמר א־להים לא תאכלו ממנו ולא תגעו בו פן תמתון. ויאמר הנחש אל האשה לא מות תמתון. כי ידע א־להים כי ביום אכלכם ממנו ונפקחו עיניכם והייתם כא־להים ידעי טוב ורע.

Genesis 3:6 pp. 23, 24, 115-16

ותרא האשה כי טוב העץ למאכל וכי תאוה הוא לעינים ונחמד העץ להשכיל ותקח מפריו ותאכל ותתן גם לאישה עמה ויאכל.

Genesis 3:7 p. 78

ותפקחנה עיני שניהם וידעו כי עירמם הם ויתפרו עלה תאנה ויעשו להם חגרת.

Genesis 3:16 p. 111

אל האשה אמר הרבה ארבה עצבונך והרנך בעצב תלדי בנים ואל אישך תשוקתך והוא ימשל בך.

Genesis 3:17-19 p. 25

ולאדם אמר כי שמעת לקול אשתך ותאכל מן העץ אשר צויתיך לאמר לא תאכל ממנו ארורה האדמה בעבורך בעצבון תאכלנה כל ימי חייך. וקוץ ודרדר תצמיח לך ואכלת את עשב השדה. בזעת אפיך תאכל לחם עד שובך אל האדמה כי ממנה לקחת כי עפר אתה ואל עפר תשוב.

Genesis 3:20 p. 105

ויקרא האדם שם אשתו חוה כי הוא היתה אם כל חי.

Genesis 4:1 p. 94

והאדם ידע את חוה אשתו ותהר ותלד את קין ותאמר קניתי איש את ה׳.

Genesis 4:25 p. 94

וידע אדם עוד את אשתו ותלד בן ותקרא את שמו שת כי שת לי א־להים זרע אחר תחת הבל כי הרגו קין.

— 182 —

Genesis 18:1 p. 119

וירא אליו ה׳ באלני ממרא והוא ישב פתח האהל כחם היום.

Genesis 18:9 p. 120

ויאמרו אליו איה שרה אשתך ויאמר הנה באהל.

Genesis 18:19 pp. 29, 123, 124

כי ידעתיו למען אשר יצוה את בניו ואת ביתו אחריו ושמרו דרך ה׳ לעשות צדקה ומשפט למען הביא ה׳ על אברהם את אשר דבר עליו.

Genesis 21:12 p. 118

ויאמר א־להים אל אברהם אל ירע בעיניך על הנער ועל אמתך כל אשר תאמר אליך שרה שמע בקלה כי ביצחק יקרא לך זרע.

Genesis 22 (entire chapter) p. 123

Genesis 27 (entire chapter) p. 118

Genesis 30:1 p. 112

ותרא רחל כי לא ילדה ליעקב ותקנא רחל באחתה ותאמר אל יעקב הבה לי בנים ואם אין מתה אנכי.

Genesis 32:24-33 pp. 26, 74

ויותר יעקב לבדו ויאבק איש עמו עד עלות השחר. וירא כי לא יכל לו ויגע בכף ירכו ותקע כף ירך יעקב בהאבקו עמו. ויאמר שלחני כי עלה השחר ויאמר לא אשלחך כי אם ברכתני. ויאמר אליו מה שמך ויאמר יעקב. ויאמר לא יעקב יאמר עוד שמך כי אם ישראל כי שרית עם א־להים ועם אנשים ותוכל. וישאל יעקב ויאמר הגידה נא שמך ויאמר למה זה תשאל לשמי ויברך אתו שם. ויקרא יעקב שם המקום פניאל כי ראיתי א־להים פנים אל פנים ותנצל נפשי. ויזרח לו השמש כאשר עבר את פנואל והוא צלע על ירכו. על כן לא יאכלו בני ישראל את גיד הנשה אשר על כף הירך עד היום הזה כי נגע בכף ירך יעקב בגיד הנשה.

Exodus 2:4,7,8 p. 118

ותתצב אחתו מרחק לדעה מה יעשה לו. ותאמר אחתו אל בת פרעה האלך וקראתי לך אשה מינקת מן העבריות ותינק לך את הילד. ותאמר לה בת פרעה לכי ותלך העלמה ותקרא את אם הילד.

Exodus 3: 14 p. 38

ויאמר א־להים אל משה א־היה אשר א־היה ויאמר כה תאמר לבני ישראל א־היה שלחני אליכם.

Exodus 6:7 p. 44

ולקחתי אתכם לי לעם והייתי לכם לא־להים וידעתם כי אני ה׳ א־להיכם המוציא אתכם מתחת סבלות מצרים.

Exodus 12:19 p. 156

שבעת ימים שאר לא ימצא בבתיכם כי כל אכל מחמצת ונכרתה הנפש ההוא מעדת ישראל בגר ובאזרח הארץ.

Exodus 20:12 pp. 126, 132, 158, 167

כבד את אביך ואת אמך למען יארכון ימיך על האדמה אשר ה׳ א־להיך נתן לך.

Exodus 21:10 p. 50

אם אחרת יקח לו שארה כסותה וענתה לא יגרע.

Exodus 22:24 p. 135

אם כסף תלוה את עמי את העני עמך לא תהיה לו כנשה לא תשימון עליו נשך.

FAMILY REDEEMED

Deuteronomy 15:7-11 p. 136

כי יהיה בך אביון מאחד אחיך באחד שעריך בארצך אשר ה׳ א־להיך נתן לך לא תאמץ את
לבבך ולא תקפץ את ידך מאחיך האביון. כי פתח תפתח את ידך לו והעבט תעביטנו די מחסרו
אשר יחסר לו. השמר לך פן יהיה דבר עם לבבך בליעל לאמר קרבה שנת השבע שנת השמטה
ורעה עינך באחיך האביון ולא תתן לו וקרא עליך אל ה׳ והיה בך חטא. נתן תתן לו ולא ירע
לבבך בתתך לו כי בגלל הדבר הזה יברכך ה׳ א־להיך בכל מעשך ובכל משלח ידך. כי לא יחדל
אביון מקרב הארץ על כן אנכי מצוך לאמר פתח תפתח את ידך לאחיך לעניך ולאבינך בארצך.

Deuteronomy 24:1 p. 65

כי יקח איש אשה ובעלה והיה אם לא תמצא חן בעיניו כי מצא בה ערות דבר וכתב לה ספר
כריתת ונתן בידה ושלחה מביתו.

Deuteronomy 26:15 p. 121

השקיפה ממעון קדשך מן השמים וברך את עמך את ישראל ואת האדמה אשר נתתה לנו
כאשר נשבעת לאבתינו ארץ זבת חלב ודבש.

Deuteronomy 33:4 p. 177

תורה צוה לנו משה מורשה קהלת יעקב.

Joshua 1:8 pp. 173, 175

לא ימוש ספר התורה הזה מפיך והגית בו יומם ולילה למען תשמר לעשות ככל הכתוב בו כי
אז תצליח את דרכך ואז תשכיל.

Judges chs. 4-5 (entire chapters) p. 119

I Samuel ch. 1 (entire chapter) p. 112

I Samuel 1:8 p. 52

ויאמר לה אלקנה אישה חנה למה תבכי ולמה לא תאכלי ולמה ירע לבבך הלוא אנכי טוב
לך מעשרה בנים.

I Samuel 1:11 p. 113

ותדר נדר ותאמר ה׳ צבאות אם ראה תראה בעני אמתך וזכרתני ולא תשכח את אמתך ונתתה
לאמתך זרע אנשים ונתתיו לה׳ כל ימי חייו ומורה לא יעלה על ראשו.

I Samuel 1:28 p. 114

וגם אנכי השאלתהו לה׳ כל הימים אשר היה הוא שאול לה׳ וישתחו שם לה׳.

I Samuel 20:34 p. 80

ויקם יהונתן מעם השלחן בחרי אף ולא אכל ביום החדש השני לחם כי נעצב אל דוד כי הכלמו
אביו.

I Samuel 25:10-11 pp. 52-53

ויען נבל את עבדי דוד ויאמר מי דוד ומי בן ישי היום רבו עבדים המתפרצים איש מפני אדניו.
ולקחתי את לחמי ואת מימי ואת טבחתי אשר טבחתי לגזזי ונתתי לאנשים אשר לא ידעתי
אי מזה המה.

I Kings 8:31-32 p. 67

את אשר יחטא איש לרעהו ונשא בו אלה להאלתו ובא אלה לפני מזבחך בבית הזה. ואתה
תשמע השמים ועשית ושפטת את עבדיך להרשיע רשע לתת דרכו בראשו ולהצדיק צדיק
לתת לו כצדקתו.

II Kings 2:3 p. 60

ויצאו בני הנביאים אשר בית אל אל אלישע ויאמרו אליו הידעת כי היום ה׳ לקח את אדניך
מעל ראשך ויאמר גם אני ידעתי החשו.

Isaiah 42:10 p. 168

שירו לה׳ שיר חדש תהלתו מקצה הארץ יורדי הים ומלאו איים וישביהם.

Isaiah 49:15 p. 107

התשכח אשה עולה מרחם בן בטנה גם אלה תשכחנה ואנכי לא אשכחך.

Isaiah 50:1 p. 63

כה אמר ה' אי זה ספר כריתות אמכם אשר שלחתיה או מי מנושי אשר מכרתי אתכם לו הן בעונתיהם נמכרתם ובפשעיכם שלחה אמכם.

Isaiah 66:13 p. 166

כאיש אשר אמו תנחמנו כן אנכי אנחמכם ובירושלם תנחמו.

Jeremiah 18:6 p. 170

הכיוצר הזה לא אוכל לעשות לכם בית ישראל נאם ה' הנה כחמר ביד היוצר כן אתם בידי בית ישראל.

Jeremiah 31:19 pp. 161, 164

הבן יקיר לי אפרים אם ילד שעשעים כי מדי דברי בו זכר אזכרנו עוד על כן המו מעי לו רחם ארחמנו נאם ה'.

Ezekiel 36:26 p. 170

ונתתי לכם לב חדש ורוח חדשה אתן בקרבכם והסרתי את לב האבן מבשרכם ונתתי לכם לב בשר.

Hosea 2:21-22 pp. 48-49

וארשתיך לי לעולם וארשתיך לי בצדק ובמשפט ובחסד וברחמים. וארשתיך לי באמונה וידעת את ה'.

Mikhah 4:6 p. 170

ביום ההוא נאם ה' אספה הצלעה והנדחה אקבצה ואשר הרעתי.

Malakhi 2:6-7 p. 59

תורת אמת היתה בפיהו ועולה לא נמצא בשפתיו בשלום ובמישור הלך אתי ורבים השיב מעון. כי שפתי כהן ישמרו דעת ותורה יבקשו מפיהו כי מלאך ה' צבאות הוא.

Malakhi 2:13-14 pp. 66, 67

וזאת שנית תעשו כסות דמעה את מזבח ה' בכי ואנקה מאין עוד פנות אל המנחה ולקחת רצון מידכם. ואמרתם על מה על כי ה' העיד בינך ובין אשת נעוריך אשר אתה בגדתה בה והיא חברתך ואשת בריתך.

Psalms 8:4-5 p. 9

כי אראה שמיך מעשה אצבעתיך ירח וכוכבים אשר כוננתה. מה אנוש כי תזכרנו ובן אדם כי תפקדנו.

Psalms 8:7 p. 98

תמשילהו במעשי ידיך כל שתה תחת רגליו.

Psalms 39:7 p. 81

אך בצלם יתהלך איש אך הבל יהמיון יצבר ולא ידע מי אספם.

Psalms 42:3 p. 153

צמאה נפשי לא-להים לא-ל חי מתי אבוא ואראה פני א-להים.

Psalms 89:3 p. 38

כי אמרתי עולם חסד יבנה שמים תכן אמונתך בהם.

Psalms 116:11 p. 21

אני אמרתי בחפזי כל האדם כזב.

Psalms 131:2-3 p. 166

אם לא שויתי ורוממתי נפשי כגמל עלי אמו כגמל עלי נפשי. יחל ישראל אל ה' מעתה ועד עולם.

TALMUD AND MIDRASH

Note: Only one reference is given for all texts,
although some appear more than once in the Talmud and Midrash.

אמר רבין בר רב אדא אמר רבי יצחק מנין שהקב"ה מצוי בבית הכנסת שנאמר א-להים נצב בעדת אל ומנין לעשרה שמתפללין ששכינה עמהם שנאמר א-להים נצב בעדת א-ל ומנין לשלשה שיושבין בדין ששכינה עמהם שנאמר בקרב א-להים ישפוט ומנין לשנים שיושבים ועוסקין בתורה ששכינה עמהם שנאמר אז נדברו יראי ה' איש אל רעהו ויקשב ה' וגו'.

Berakhot 28b p. 167

אמרו לו רבינו ברכנו אמר להם יהי רצון שתהא מורא שמים עליכם כמורא בשר ודם אמרו לו תלמידיו עד כאן אמר להם ולואי.

Berakhot 32a p. 170

אמר רבי חמא ברבי חנינא אלמלא שלש מקראות הללו נתמוטטו רגליהם של שונאי ישראל חד דכתיב ואשר הרעותי וחד דכתיב הנה כחומר ביד היוצר כן אתם בידי בית ישראל וחד דכתיב והסירותי את לב האבן מבשרכם ונתתי לכם לב בשר.
רש"י: אלמלא שלש מקראות הללו. שמעידין שיש ביד הקדוש ברוך הוא לתקן יצרנו ולהסיר יצר הרע ממנו.

Shabbat 31a p. 143

שוב מעשה בנכרי אחד שבא לפני שמאי א"ל גיירני ע"מ שתלמדני כל התורה כולה כשאני עומד על רגל אחת דחפו באמת הבנין שבידו בא לפני הלל גייריה אמר לו דעלך סני לחברך לא תעביד זו היא כל התורה כולה ואידך פירושה הוא זיל גמור.

Yoma 75a pp. 27-28

דאגה בלב איש ישחנה רבי אמי ורבי אסי חד אמר ישחנה מדעתו וחד אמר ישיחנה לאחרים.

Moed Katan 28b p. 137

תניא היה ר"מ אומר טוב ללכת אל בית אבל וגו' עד והחי יתן אל לבו דברים של מיתה דיספד יספדוניה דיקבר יקברוניה דיטען יטענוניה דידל ידלוניה.

Yevamot 117a p. 166

מתני': הכל נאמנין להעידה חוץ מחמותה ובת חמותה וצרתה ויבמתה ובת בעלה מה בין גט למיתה שהכתב מוכיח: גמ': ... והאנן תנן חוץ משבע נשים ההיא ר' יהודה היא דתנן רבי יהודה מוסיף אף אשת אב והכלה אמרו לו אשת אב הרי היא בכלל בת הבעל כלה הרי בכלל חמותה.

Gittin 9:10 at Gittin 90a p. 65

בית שמאי אומרים לא יגרש אדם את אשתו אלא אם כן מצא בה דבר ערוה שנאמר כי מצא בה ערות דבר ובית הלל אומרים אפילו הקריחה תבשילו שנאמר כי מצא בה ערות דבר ר' עקיבא אומר אפי' מצא אחרת נאה הימנה שנאמר והיה אם לא תמצא חן בעיניו.

Gittin 90b p. 66

דאמר רבי אלעזר כל המגרש אשתו ראשונה אפילו מזבח מוריד עליו דמעות שנאמר וזאת שנית תעשו כסות דמעה את מזבח ה' בכי ואנקה מאין עוד פנות אל המנחה ולקחת רצון מידכם. ואמרתם על מה כי ה' העיד בינך ובין אשת נעוריך אשר אתה בגדתה בה והיא חברתך ואשת בריתך.

Kiddushin 19b p. 49

והתניא האומר לאשה הרי את מקודשת לי ע"מ שאין לך עלי שאר כסות ועונה ה"ז מקודשת ותנאו בטל דברי ר"מ רבי יהודה אומר בדבר שבממון תנאו קיים.

Kiddushin 29a p. 162

תנינא להא דת"ר האב חייב בבנו למולו ולפדותו וללמדו תורה ולהשיאו אשה וללמדו אומנות וי"א אף להשיטו במים.

Kiddushin 30b p. 162

מאי כל מצות הבן על האב אילימא כל מצותא דמיחייב אבא למיעבד לבריה נשים חייבות והתניא האב חייב בבנו למולו ולפדותו אביו אין אמו לא אמר רב יהודה הכי קאמר כל מצות האב המוטלת על הבן לעשות לאביו אחד אנשים ואחד נשים חייבין.

Kiddushin 30b pp. 132, 167

ת״ר נאמר כבד את אביך ואת אמך ונאמר כבד את ה׳ מהונך השוה הכתוב כבוד אב ואם
לכבוד המקום נאמר איש אמו ואביו תיראו ונאמר את ה׳ אלהיך תירא ואותו תעבוד השוה
הכתוב מוראת אב ואם למוראת המקום.

Kiddushin 30b p. 142

ת״ר שלשה שותפין הן באדם הקב״ה ואביו ואמו בזמן שאדם מכבד את אביו ואת אמו אמר
הקב״ה מעלה אני עליכם כאילו דרתי ביניהם וכבדוני.

Kiddushin 30b-31a pp. 158-59

תניא רבי אומר גלוי וידוע לפני מי שאמר והיה העולם שבן מכבד את אמו יותר מאביו מפני
שמשדלתו בדברים לפיכך הקדים הקב״ה כיבוד אב לכיבוד אם וגלוי וידוע לפני מי שאמר
והיה העולם שהבן מתיירא מאביו יותר מאמו מפני שמלמדו תורה לפיכך הקדים הקב״ה מורא
האם למורא האב.

Kiddushin 31a p. 150

כי אתא רב דימי אמר פעם אחת היה לבוש סירקון של זהב והיה יושב בין גדולי רומי ובאתה
אמו וקרעתו ממנו וטפחה לו על ראשו וירקה לו בפניו ולא הכלימה.

Kiddushin 31b p. 168

רב יוסף כי הוה שמע קל כרעא דאמיה אמר איקום מקמי שכינה.

Kiddushin 31b p. 131

ת״ר איזהו מורא ואיזהו כיבוד מורא לא עומד במקומו ולא יושב במקומו ולא סותר את דבריו
ולא מכריעו כיבוד מאכיל ומשקה מלבים ומכסה מכניס ומוציא.

Kiddushin 32a p. 150

ת״ש שאלו את ר״א עד היכן כיבוד אב ואם אמר להם כדי שיטול ארנקי ויזרקנו לים בפניו
ואינו מכלימו.

Bava Metzi'a 62a p. 146

שנים שהיו מהלכין בדרך וביד אחד מהן קיתון של מים אם שותין שניהם מתים ואם שותה
אחד מהן מגיע לישוב דרש בן פטורא מוטב שישתו שניהם וימותו ואל יראה אחד מהם
במיתתו של חבירו עד שבא ר׳ עקיבא ולימד וחי אחיך עמך חייך קודמים לחיי חבירך.

Bava Batra 21a pp. 113-14

עד שבא יהושע בן גמלא ותיקן שיהיו מושיבין מלמדי תינוקות בכל מדינה ומדינה ובכל עיר
ועיר ומכניסין אותן כבן שש כבן שבע.

Sanhedrin 7a p. 174

דאמר רב המנונא אין תחילת דינו של אדם נידון אלא על דברי תורה שנאמר פוטר מים
ראשית מדון.

תוס׳ ד״ה אלא: והא דאמרינן בפרק במה מדליקין (שבת לא.) ששואלין לו נשאת ונתת באמונה
ואח״כ קבעת עתים לתורה התם באדם שעוסק בתורה מיירי אלא שלא קבע עתים והבא מיירי
כשלא עסק כלל.

Sanhedrin 19b p. 60

אמר רבי שמואל בר נחמני א״ר יונתן כל המלמד בן חבירו תורה מעלה עליו הכתוב כאילו
ילדו שנאמר ואלה תולדות אהרן ומשה וכתיב ואלה שמות בני אהרן לומר לך אהרן ילד ומשה
לימד לפיכך נקראו על שמו.

Avot 1:1 pp. 59, 176

משה קבל תורה מסיני ומסרה ליהושע ויהושע לזקנים וזקנים לנביאים ונביאים מסרוה לאנשי
כנסת הגדולה.

Avot 5:24 p. 79

הוא היה אומר: עז פנים לגיהנם, ובשת פנים לגן עדן. יהי רצון מלפניך ה' א-להינו וא-להי אבותינו שיבנה בית המקדש במהרה בימינו ותן חלקנו בתורתך.

Avot 5:26 p. 178

בן הא הא אומר לפום צערא אגרא.

Niddah 45b p. 117

א"ר חסדא מ"ט דרבי דכתיב ויבן ה' [אלהים] את הצלע מלמד שנתן הקב"ה בינה יתירה באשה יותר מבאיש.

Jerusalem Talmud, Bikkurim 1:4 (Venice edition, 64a)

תני בשם רבי יהודה גר עצמו מביא וקורא מה טעם כי אב המון גוים נתתיך. לשעבר היית אב לארם ועכשיו מכאן ואילך אתה אב לכל הגוים. רבי יהושע בן לוי אמר הלכה כרבי יהודה. אתא עובדא קומי דרבי אבהו והורי כרבי יהודה.

Genesis Rabbah 18:5 p. 67

אמר רבי חגי בשעה שעלו ישראל מן הגולה נתפחמו פני נשים מן השמש והניחו אותן והלכו להם ונשאו נשים עמוניות והיו מקיפות את המזבח ובוכות הוא שמלאכי אומר וזאת שנית תעשו שנייה לשטים כסות דמעה את מזבח ה' בכי ואנקה אמר הקב"ה מאן קביל מהם בכי ואנקה משגזלת וחמסת ונטלת יפיה ממנה אתה משלחה.

Exodus Rabbah 31:15 p. 135

ד"א לא תהיה לו כנושה הה"ד, טוב איש חונן ומלוה יכלכל דבריו במשפט. בא וראה כל בריותיו של הקב"ה לווין זה מזה. היום לוה מן הלילה והלילה מן היום ואינן דנין זה עם זה כבריות שנאמר, יום ליום יביע אומר. הלבנה לוה מן הכוכבים והכוכבים מן הלבנה וכשהקב"ה רוצה אינם יוצאים שנאמר, האומר לחרס ולא יזרח ובעד כוכבים יחתום. האור לוה מן השמש והשמש מן האור שנאמר, שמש ירח עמד זבולה. החכמה לוה מן הבינה והבינה מן החכמה שנאמר, אמור לחכמה אחותי את. השמים לוין מן הארץ והארץ מהשמים שנאמר , יפתח ה' לך את אוצרו הטוב את השמים. החסד לוה מן הצדקה והצדקה מן החסד שנאמר, רודף צדקה וחסד. התורה לוה מן המצות והמצות מן התורה שנאמר, שמור מצותי. בריותיו של הקב"ה לווין זה מזה ועושים שלום זה עם זה בלא דברים.

Song of Songs Rabbah 7:2 p. 45

ונחזה בך. אומות העולם אומרות לישראל עד מתי אתם מתים על א-להיכם ומשלמין לו הה"ד על כן עלמות אהבוך. ועד מתי אתם נהרגין עליו כדכתיב כי עליך הורגנו כל היום. ועד מתי אתם גומלים טובות עליו ולו לעצמו והוא גומל לכם רעות. באו לכם אצלנו ואנו ממנין אתכם דוכסין אפרכין ואיטרטלין. ונחזה בך. ואתון אינן מחזיתיה דעלמא הה"ד ואתה תחזה מכל העם. וישראל משיבין להם מה תחזו בשולמית כמחולת המחנים.

Pirkei de-Rabbi Eliezer 45 p. 119

דן אהרן דין בינו לבין עצמו אמר אם אני אומר להם תנו לי כסף וזהב מיד הם מביאים אלא הריני אומר להם תנו נזמי נשיכם בניכם ובנותיכם ומיד הדבר בטל שנאמר ויאמר אהרן פרקו שמעו הנשים ולא רצו ולא קבלו עליהן ליתן נזמיהן לבעליהם אלא אמרו להם לעשות עגל ותועבה שאין בו כח להציל לא נשמע לכם ונתן להם הקב"ה שכרן בעה"ז שהן משמרות ראשי חדשים יותר מן האנשים ונתן להם שכר לעולם הבא שהן עתידות להתחדש כמו ראשי חדשים שנאמר המשביע בטוב עדיך וגו'.

ZOHAR

Emor 91b p. 56

תא חזי בר נש דאתיליד לא אתמנא עליה חילא דלעילא עד דאתגזר. כיון דאתגזר אתער
עליה (רוחא) אתערותא דרוחא דלעילא. זכי לאתעסקא באוריתא אתער עליה אתערותא
יתיר. זכי ועביד פקודי אוריתא אתער עליה אתערותא יתיר. זכי ואתנסיב זכי ואוליד בנין
ואוליף לון ארחוי דמלכא קדישא הא כדין הוא אדם שלים שלים בכלא. אבל בהמה
דאתילידת בההיא שעתא דאתילידת ההוא חילא דאית לה בסופה אית לה בההיא שעתא
דאתיליד ואתמנא עליה.

Emor 104b, p. 81

ההוא צלם אוזמן לקבליה, עד דנפיק לעלמא. כד נפק, בההוא צלם אתרבי, בההוא צלם אזיל,
הה"ד אך בצלם יתהלך איש. והאי צלם איהו מלעילא.

BAHYA IBN PAKUDA

Hovot ha-Levavot, Sha'ar 3, introduction
(trans. Judah ibn Tibbon) p. 140

מפני שבארנו במה שעבר חיוב יחוד הא-להים בלב שלם ואופני בחינת טובותיו על האדם,
התחייבנו לזכור אחר כן מה שהאדם חייב לנהוג בו כשיתברר אצלו, והוא קבול עבודת
הא-להים כפי אשר יתחייבהו השכל למטיב על מי שהטיב לו. וראוי להקדים בפתיחת השער
הזה באור אופני הטובות וחיובי ההודאה עליהם מבני אדם קצתם לקצתם ונעלה מזה אל מה
שאנו חייבין בו לבורא יתברך מן השבח וההודאה על רוב חסדו וגודל טובו עלינו. ונאמר, כי
מן הידוע אצלנו, כי כל מטיב אלינו אנו חייבין להודות לו כפי כונתו להועיל לנו.

RAMBAM (MAIMONIDES)

COMMENTARY TO THE MISHNAH
(trans. Samuel ibn Tibbon)

Introduction to Helek, Sanhedrin, ch. 10 (Thirteen Principles of Faith) p. 171
Shemonah Perakim, ch. 8 (entire chapter) p. 171
Avot 1:6 p. 27

ואמר וקנה לך חבר זכר אותו בלשון קנייה ולא אמר עשה לך חבר או התחבר לאחרים הכונה
בזה שצריך לאדם שיקנה אוהב לעצמו שיתקנו בו מעשיו וכל עניניו כמו שאמרו או חברותא
או מיתותא ואם לא ימצאהו צריך להשתדל בו בכל לבו ואפילו אם יצטרך שימשכנו לאהבתו
עד שישוב אוהב ולא יסור מהמשך תמיד אחר רצונו עד שתתחזק אהבתו כמו שיאמרו בעלי
המוסר כשתאהב לא תאהב על מדותיך ואמנם תאהב על מדת אהוביך וכשיכוין כל אחד
משני האהובים אל זאת הצואה יהיה כונת כל אחד משניהם להפיק רצון חבירו ויהיה כונת
שניהם יחד דבר אחד בלא ספק. ומה טוב מאמר אריסטוטלוס האהוב אחד הוא והאוהבים
ג' מינים אוהב תועלת אוהב מנוחה ואוהב מעלה אמנם אוהב תועלת כאהבת שני השותפים
ואהבת המלך ומחנהו ואמנם אוהב מנוחה הוא ב' מינים אוהב הנאה ואוהב בטחון אמנם אוהב
הנאה כאהבת הזכרים לנקבות וכיוצא בהם. ואמנם אוהב בטחון הוא שיהיה לאדם אוהב
תבטח נפשו בו לא יישמר ממנו לא במעשה ולא בדבור ויודיעהו כל עניניו הטוב מהם והמגונה
מבלתי שירא ממנו שישיגהו בכל זה חסרון לא אצלו ולא זולתו כי כשיגיע לאדם בטחון באיש
זה השעור ימצא מנוחה גדולה בדבריו ובאהבתו הרבה. ואוהב מעלה הוא שיהיה תאות שניהם
וכונתם לדבר אחד והוא הטוב וירצה כל אחד להעזר בחבירו בהגיע הטוב ההוא לשניהם יחד
וזה האוהב אשר צוה לקנותו והוא כאהבת הרב לתלמיד והתלמיד לרב.

SEFER HA-MITZVOT (Book of Commandments)

(trans. Samuel ibn Tibbon)

Positive Comandment 4 p. 153

היא שצונו להאמין יראתו יתעלה ולהפחד ממנו, ולא נהיה ככופרים ההולכים בשרירות לבם ובקרי אבל נירא ביראת ענשו בכל עת וזהו אמרו את ה׳ א־להיך תירא.

MISHNEH TORAH

Yesodei ha-Torah 1:1 p. 179

יסוד היסודות ועמוד החכמות לידע שיש שם מצוי ראשון. והוא ממציא כל נמצא. וכל הנמצאים משמים וארץ ומה שביניהם לא נמצאו אלא מאמתת המצאו.

Yesodei ha-Torah 1:7 p. 179

לפיכך אי אפשר שיהיה אלא אחד. וידיעת דבר זה מצות עשה שנאמר ה׳ א־להינו ה׳ אחד.

Yesodei ha-Torah chs. 2-4 p. 168

Yesodei ha-Torah 2:2 p. 153

והיאך היא הדרך לאהבתו ויראתו. בשעה שיתבונן האדם במעשיו וברואיו הנפלאים הגדולים ויראה מהן חכמתו שאין לה ערך ולא קץ מיד הוא אוהב ומשבח ומפאר ומתאוה תאוה גדולה לידע השם הגדול. כמו שאמר דוד צמאה נפשי לאלהים לאל חי. וכשמחשב בדברים האלו עצמן מיד הוא נרתע לאחוריו ויפחד ויודע שהוא בריה קטנה שפלה אפלה עומדת בדעת קלה מעוטה לפני תמים דעות. כמו שאמר דוד כי אראה שמיך מעשה אצבעותיך מה אנוש כי תזכרנו. ולפי הדברים האלו אני מבאר כללים גדולים ממעשה רבון העולמים כדי שיהיו פתח למבין לאהוב את השם. כמו שאמרו חכמים בענין אהבה שמתוך כך אתה מכיר את מי שאמר והיה העולם.

Talmud Torah, headnote and 1:1-3 pp. 58, 60, 172

הלכות תלמוד תורה יש בכללן שתי מצות עשה. וזהו פרטן: א) ללמוד תורה ב) לכבד מלמדיה ויודעיה: וביאור שתי מצות אלו בפרקים אלו.

[א] נשים ועבדים וקטנים פטורים מתלמוד תורה. אבל קטן אביו חייב ללמדו תורה שנאמר ולמדתם אותם את בניכם לדבר בם. ואין האשה חייבת ללמד את בנה שכל החייב ללמוד חייב ללמד.

[ב] כשם שחייב אדם ללמד את בנו כך הוא חייב ללמד את בן בנו שנאמר והודעתם לבניך ולבני בניך. ולא בנו ובן בנו בלבד אלא מצוה על כל חכם וחכם מישראל ללמד את כל התלמידים אע״פ שאינן בניו. שנאמר ושננתם לבניך מפי השמועה למדו אלו תלמידיך שהתלמידים קרויין בנים שנאמר ויצאו בני הנביאים. אם כן למה נצטוה על בנו ועל בן בנו. להקדים בנו לבן בנו ובן בנו לבן חבירו.

[ג] וחייב לשכור מלמד לבנו ללמדו. ואינו חייב ללמד בן חבירו אלא בחנם. מי שלא למדו אביו חייב ללמד את עצמו כשיכיר שנאמר ולמדתם אותם ושמרתם לעשותם. וכן אתה מוצא בכל מקום שהתלמוד קודם למעשה מפני שהתלמוד מביא לידי מעשה ואין המעשה מביא לידי תלמוד.

Talmud Torah 1:4,5 p. 172

[ד] היה הוא רוצה ללמוד תורה ויש לו בן ללמוד תורה הוא קודם לבנו. ואם היה בנו נבון ומשכיל להבין מה שילמד יותר ממנו בנו קודם. ואע״פ שבנו קודם לא יבטל הוא. שכשם שמצוה עליו ללמד את בנו כך הוא מצווה ללמד עצמו.

[ה] לעולם ילמד אדם תורה ואחר כך ישא אשה שאם נשא אשה תחלה אין דעתו פנויה ללמוד. ואם היה יצרו מתגבר עליו עד שנמצא שאין לבו פנוי ישא ואחר כך ילמוד תורה.

Talmud Torah 1:8 pp. 172-73

כל איש מישראל חייב בתלמוד תורה בין עני בין עשיר בין שלם בגופו בין בעל יסורין בין
בחור בין שהיה זקן גדול שתשש כחו אפילו היה עני המתפרנס מן הצדקה ומחזר על הפתחים
ואפילו בעל אשה ובנים חייב לקבוע לו זמן לתלמוד תורה ביום ובלילה שנאמר והגית בו יומם
ולילה.

Teshuvah ch. 5 (entire chapter) p. 171

Keri'at Shema 1:2 pp. 57-58

ומה הוא קורא שלשה פרשיות אלו הן שמע והיה אם שמוע ויאמר. ומקדימין לקרות פרשת
שמע מפני שיש בה יחוד השם ואהבתו ותלמודו שהוא העיקר הגדול שהכל תלוי בו. ואחריה
והיה אם שמוע שיש בה צווי על (זכירת) שאר כל המצות. ואחר כך פרשת ציצית שגם היא
יש בה צווי זכירת כל המצות.

Isuhsl 41:1,2,5,7,8 pp. 15, 25

[א] עונה האמורה בתורה. לכל איש ואיש כפי בחו וכפי מלאכתו. כיצד בני אדם הבריאים
הרכים והענוגים שאין להם מלאכה שמכשלת כהן אלא אוכלין ושותין ויושבין בבתיהן עונתן
בכל לילה. הפועלין כגון החייטין והאורגין והבונים וכיוצא בהן. אם היתה מלאכתן בעיר עונתן
פעמים בשבת. ואם היתה מלאכתן בעיר אחרת עונתן פעם אחת בשבת. החמרים פעם אחת
בשבת. והגמלים אחת לשלשים יום. והמלחין אחת לששה חדשים. תלמידי חכמים עונתן פעם
אחת בשבת מפני שתלמוד תורה מתיש כהן ודרך תלמידי חכמים לשמש מטתן מלילי שבת
לילי שבת.

[ב] יש לאשה לעכב על בעלה שלא יצא לסחורה אלא למקום קרוב שלא ימנע מעונתה ולא
יצא אלא ברשותה. וכן יש לה למונעו לצאת ממלאכה שעונתה קרובה למלאכה שעונתה
רחוקה. כגון חמר שביקש להעשות גמל או גמל להעשות מלח. תלמידי חכמים יוצאין
לת"ת שלא ברשות נשותיהן שתים ושלש שנים. וכן רך וענוג שנעשה ת"ח אין אשתו יכולה
לעכב.

[ה] המדיר את אשתו שתאמר לאחרים מה שאמר לה או מה שאמרה לו מדברי שחוק וקלות
ראש שמדבר אדם עם אשתו על עסקי תשמיש הרי זה יוציא ויתן כתובה שאין זו יכולה להעיז
פניה ולומר לאחרים דברי קלון. וכן אם הדירה שתהיה פועלת בעת תשמיש שלא תתעבר.
או שהדירה שתעשה מעשה שוטים ודברים שאין בהן ממש אלא כשטות הרי זה יוציא ויתן
כתובה.

[ז] אסור לאדם למנוע אשתו מעונתה ואם מנע כדי לצערה עבר בלא תעשה שבתורה
שנאמר שארה כסותה ועונתה לא יגרע. ואם חלה או תש כחו ואינו יכול לבעול ימתין ששה
חדשים שמא יבריא שאין לך עונה גדולה מזו. ואח"כ או יטול ממנה רשות או יוציא ויתן
כתובה.

[ח] האשה שמנעה בעלה מתשמיש המטה היא הנקראת מורדת ושואלין אותה מפני מה
מרדה. אם אמרה מאסתיהו ואיני יכולה להבעל לו מדעתי כופין אותו לשעתו לגרשה לפי
שאינה כשבויה שתבעל לשנוא לה ותצא בלא כתובה כלל ותטול בלאותיה הקיימין בין
מנכסים שהכניסה לבעלה ונתחייב באחריותן בין מנכסי מלוג שלא נתחייב באחריותן. ואינה
נוטלת בשל בעל כלום ואפילו מנעל שברגליה ומטפחת שבראשה שלקחן לה פושטת ונותנת
לו וכל מה שנתן לה מתנה מחזרת אותו שלא נתן לה על מנת שתטול ותצא.

Bikkurim 4:3 p. 121

הגר מביא וקורא שנאמר לאברהם אב המון גוים נתתיך הרי הוא אב כל העולם כולו שנכנסין
תחת כנפי שכינה. ולאברהם היתה השבועה תחלה שיירשו בניו את הארץ. וכן כהנים ולוים
מביאין וקורין מפני שיש להן ערי מגרש.

Mamrim 6:3 p. 131

אי זהו מורא ואי זהו כבוד. מורא לא עומד במקומו. ולא יושב במקומו. ולא סותר את דבריו
ולא מכריע את דבריו. ולא יקרא לו בשמו לא בחייו ולא במותו. אלא אומר אבא מרי. היה
שם אביו או שם רבו כשם אחרים משנה את שמם. יראה לי שאין נזהר בכך אלא בשם שהוא
פלא שאין הכל רשין בו. אבל השמות שקוראים בהן את העם כגון אברהם יצחק ויעקב משה
וכיוצא בהן בכל לשון ובכל זמן קורא בהן לאחרים שלא בפניו ואין בכך כלום. אי זהו כבוד
מאכיל ומשקה מלביש ומכסה משל האב. ואם אין ממון לאב ויש ממון לבן כופין אותו וזן אביו
ואמו כפי מה שהוא יכול. ומוציא ומכניס ומשמשו בשאר הדברים שהשמשים משמשים בהן
את הרב. ועומד מפניו כדרך שהוא עומד מפני רבו.

Mamrim 6:7 p. 150

עד היכן הוא כיבוד אב ואם. אפילו נטלו כיס של זהובים שלו והשליכו בפניו לים לא יכלימם
ולא יצער בפניהם ולא יכעוס כנגדם אלא יקבל גזירת הכתוב וישתוק. ועד היכן מוראן אפילו
היה לובש בגדים חמודות ויושב בראש בפני הקהל ובא אביו ואמו וקרעו בגדיו והכוהו בראשו
וירקו בפניו לא יכלימם אלא ישתוק ויירא ויפחד ממלך מלכי המלכים שצוהו בכך. שאילו מלך
בשר ודם גזר עליו דבר שהוא מצער יתר מזה לא היה יכול לפרכס בדבר. קל וחומר למי
שאמר והיה העולם כרצונו.

Avel 14:1 p. 144

מצות עשה של דבריהם לבקר חולים. ולנחם אבלים. ולהוציא המת. ולהכניס הכלה. וללוות
האורחים. ולהתעסק בכל צרכי הקבורה. לשאת על הכתף. ולילך לפניו ולספוד ולחפור
ולקבור. וכן לשמח הכלה והחתן. ולסעדם בכל צרכיהם. ואלו הן גמילות חסדים שבגופו שאין
להם שיעור. אע"פ שכל מצות אלו מדבריהם הרי הן בכלל ואהבת לרעך כמוך. כל הדברים
שאתה רוצה שיעשו אותם לך אחרים. עשה אתה אותן לאחיך בתורה ובמצות.

MOREH NEVUKHIM (Guide of the Perplexed)
(trans. Samuel ibn Tibbon)
Part I, chapter 63 p. 38

ולמדהו השם אז מדע שיגיעהו אליהם יאמת אצלם מציאות השם, והוא א-היה אשר א-היה,
וזה השם נגזר מן היה והוא המציאות, כי היה מורה על ענין היה, ואין הפרש בין אמרך היה
או נמצא בלשון העברי, והסוד כלו הוא בשנותו המלה בעצמה המורה על המציאות בענין
התאר, כי מלת אשר אשר סובל זכרון התאר הנדבק בו, שהוא שם חסר, צריך אליו חבור, כי ענין
אלד"י ואלת"י בערבי, והושם השם הראשון, והוא המתואר א-היה והשם השני אשר תארו
בו א-היה, והוא הוא בעצמו, וכאלו הוא הראה שהמתואר הוא התאר בעצמו והיה זה באור
ענין שהוא נמצא נמצא לא במציאות, ובא באור הענין ההוא ופירושו כן הנמצא אשר הוא הנמצא
כלומר המחוייב המציאות, וזה אשר יביא אליו המופת בהכרח שיש דבר מחוייב המציאות
לא נעדר ולא יעדר כמו שאבאר מופתו.

Part I, chapter 72 (entire chapter) p. 168

Index of Topics and Names

A

Abraham
  Akedah, 123
  change of name and status,
    60, 123-24
  contrasted to Adam, 105-6
  as covenantal father, 121-25
  father of all nations, 105, 108
  father of redeemed communities,
    29–30, 60, 106, 107, 121,
    105-25 *passim*
  his fatherhood as commitment,
    108
  God's covenant with, 45, 121-23
  holiness through sacrifice, 74
  and Isaac, 117, 118, 122-23
  and Ishmael, 117-18
  as Knight of Faith, 45
  his loyalty and faith, 45
  See also Sarah

Adam
  aloneness and loneliness of, 5,
    15-18, 21-22, 33
  awareness of others, 101
  contrasted with Abraham, 105-6
  creation of, 5-6, 33, 77, 95, 160
  development from man-*natura*
    to man-*persona*, 10-24
  dominion over world and
    relation to the other, 100
  father of unredeemed (natural)
    community, 106, 107
  relation to nature, 18-21, 22, 25
  sin of, 22-23, 78
  See also Adam and Eve; Eve
  Consult also Index of Biblical
    and Rabbinic Sources on
    Genesis chs. 1-4

Adam and Eve
  as commanded beings, 11-15
  creation of, 4-8, 77
  as creators of metaphysical
    community, 17, 28
  ethical existence of, 11-15
  their *imitatio Dei,* 39
  meaning of *yado`a*, 94-95
  naturalness of, 7-8
  numinous and kerygmatic,
    62–63
  shame at their nakedness,
    78, 84, 93, 103
  sins of, 22-25, 78, 102, 115-16
  their urge to create, 39
  See also Adam; Eve
  Consult also Index of Biblical
    and Rabbinic Sources on
    Genesis chs. 1-4

adoption, 60-61, 109

adultery, 49-50, 65-66

Akedah (Binding of Isaac), 123

Rabbi Akiva, 65-66, 146

altar, symbolism of, 66-67

anamnesis (recollection), 59

animals
  blessing given to, 95-100
  comparison and contrast with
    humans, 7, 32, 35-36, 51, 56,
    77-78, 86-101 *passim*
  comparison and contrast with
    plants, 96-97
  creation of, 6
  have all powers at birth, 56
  naming of by Adam, 5, 18
  sex differentiation in, 67
  sexuality in, 34, 36, 51,
    86-101 *passim*

Aristotle
  eudaemonistic ethical theory, 134
  on friendship, 27
  on man as social animal, 15

Augustine, 7

B

Bahya ibn Pakuda, 140

Barak ben Avinoam, 119

Moses as leader, 118
Sarah as leader, 119-20
women as leaders, 115-19
loneliness
 of Adam, 21-22, 33
 vs. aloneness, 15-18
 and childless couple, 58
 as expressing antinomic character of being, 68-69
 and interdependence, 134-37,
  141-42
 and need for companionship,
  22, 33, 55, 84, 95, 134-35
 and reason for marriage,
  15-18, 33, 68, 95
 See also friendship
love
 divine and human desire to give,
  37-39
 in educational community, 39-41
 erotic, 47, 54, 94-95
 of God identified with love of
  parents, 132-33, 168
 God's, 39, 94, 113, 146, 166-71
 of Jewish people for God, 45-46,
  167
 and marriage, 36, 41, 48
 marriage not based on subjective love, 36, 41
 of neighbor, 40, 143-46
 of parents, 126–57 *passim*
 of parents as ontic oneness, 147
 as redeemer of loneliness, 41
 as response to divine summons,
  48
 reverential love of parents, 154
 as root of urge to create, 37-38, 39
 sexuality and, 37, 47, 86,
  104-5, *see also* sexuality

M

Maimonides, Moses
 on Abraham's fatherhood, 121
 on accepting yoke of Heaven, 57-58
 on cosmic dynamics, 168
 on fear of God, 153-54
 on filial obligation, 150-52
 on friendship, 27-29

on laws of marriage, 51, 52
on love of neighbor, 144-45
on teaching Torah to children
 58, 60
on Torah study, 172-76
Consult also the Index of
 Biblical and Rabbinic Sources
Malakhi, 59, 67
male and female. *See* Adam and
 Eve; fatherhood and motherhood; sexuality, human: sexual
 differentiation and bipersonalism; women
man (humanity)
 aspirations of, 10-11
 as autonomous, 20, 42, 53, 145
 cannot be known through
  objective observation, 20-22
 comparison and contrast with
  animals, 7, 32, 35-36, 51, 56,
  77-78, 86-101 *passim*
 comparison and contrast with
  plants, 32, 57
 differences between man and
  woman, *see* fatherhood and
  motherhood; sexuality:
  sexual differentiation and
  bipersonalism
 emotion and action, 39-41, 126-30
 as free and as dependent, 169-71
 Homo absconditus (hidden
  man), 21
 human sexuality, *see* sexuality,
  human
 interdependence of human
  community, 134-39
 levels of sexual life, 86-95
 as limited in his autonomy, 139
 loneliness and interdependence,
  134-37
 loneliness and need for companionship, 15-18, 22, 58, 68-69, 84,
  134-35
 man-*natura* vs. man-*persona*,
  4-26 *passim*, 87
 mastery over nature, 21, 25, 26,
  97-98
 motives for marrying, 31-48, 55